FEAR, ANGER AND FAILURE

FEAR, ANGER AND FAILURE

A CHRONICLE OF
THE BUSH ADMINISTRATION'S WAR
AGAINST TERROR
FROM
THE ATTACKS IN SEPTEMBER 2001
TO
DEFEAT IN BAGHDAD

William Pfaff

Algora Publishing
New York

Library of Congress Cataloging-in-Publication Data

Pfaff, William, 1928-
   Fear, anger and failure: A chronicle of the Bush administration's war against
terror / By William Pfaff.
      p. cm.
   ISBN 0-87586-254-3 (trade paper : alk. paper) — ISBN 0-87586-255-1 (hard
cover : alk. paper) — ISBN 0-87586-200-4 (e-book)
   1. War on Terrorism, 2001- 2. United States—Foreign relations—21st century. 3. United States—History, Military—21st century. 4. United States—Politics and government—2001- I. Title.

   HV6432.P49 2003
   973.931—dc22
                        2003027399

Front Cover: Women struggle to form a line at a gas distribution center in
Thawra, the Shia area of Baghdad formerly known as Saddam City.
                    — Photo by Thorne Anderson/Corbis Sygma

Printed in the United States

For David,
and for Juliet and James

ACKNOWLEDGMENTS

In the early 1980s, the expatriate, Paris-based American newspaper *The International Herald Tribune* was making itself into the first truly global newspaper, thanks to satellite publishing from multiple printing sites.

Between then and his retirement last year, Robert J. Donahue, its editorial pages editor, turned those pages into something unprecedented: the first truly global public policy forum.

What before had been a relatively parochial and innocuous sampling of American newspaper opinion and comment was turned into a space in which a continuing and increasingly important international dialogue and debate took form, engaging journalistic commentators, intellectuals, and public and political figures across the globe.

The *Herald Tribune's* editorial pages became immensely influential, read in every important foreign office, chancellery, and editorial room. It was where you could write with confidence that you would be read by virtually everyone in the international political and policy community.

I am grateful to Bob Donahue for having provided this space, in which I had the good fortune to spend a quarter century of my professional life.

During much the same period, Jesse E. Levine was constructing the Los Angeles Times Syndicate International (now become Tribune Media Services International), making it into the largest and most important international press syndicate in any language.

Thanks to him and his colleagues, in particular his splendid senior editor, Dinah McNichols, my articles were published in English or in translation in newspapers from Amsterdam to the Persian Gulf, and from Seoul to Buenos Aires, giving me, in combination with the *Herald Tribune's* audience, the privilege of addressing probably the largest international readership any American commentator has ever enjoyed.

I am grateful to them all, and thank them here.

Books by William Pfaff:

Fear, Anger and Failure

The Wrath of Nations

Barbarian Sentiments

Condemned to Freedom

Also, with Edmund Stillman:

Power and Impotence

The Politics of Hysteria

The New Politics

TABLE OF CONTENTS

INTRODUCTION

The defeat in Baghdad was given unspoken acknowledgement by President George W. Bush on Thursday, November 13, 2003, after consultation with his advisers and with Ambassador L. Paul Bremer, III, who had been abruptly summoned to Washington.

The President said that the United States had decided to adopt a new plan to "encourage more Iraqis to assume more responsibility" in the process by which American Occupation authorities in Iraq intended to hand power over to an Iraqi government.

This process would be speeded up, he said, so as to be completed in June 2004. He accompanied his description of the new plan with renewed assurances of American determination to persevere in the struggle for stability, security and democracy in Iraq for as long as it takes, and of his government's conviction of certain victory.

He nonetheless had revealed defeat. The capture of Saddam Hussein a few days later produced a bubble of optimism in Washington and at Coalition headquarters in Baghdad, but no change in the security situation. Saddam Hussein, it seemed, had ceased, even symbolically, to be a player in Iraq's conflict.

The Bush administration's original plan had envisaged the drafting of a new constitution by the U.S.-nominated Iraq Governing Council in collaboration with American authorities, with a referendum to follow. Then there would have been national elections for a new permanent government, and only after that, a formal hand-over of power. This methodical process was expected to take many months.

The Iraq government that would emerge from the election was expected to become a regional ally of the United States, invite the United States to build permanent military bases in its country, establish diplomatic relations with Israel, and privatize state-owned industry, including the energy sector.

The week before the policy reversal, Mr. Bush had told a National Endowment for Democracy dinner in Washington that "the establishment of a free Iraq at the heart of the Middle East will be a watershed event in the global democratic revolution." That had always been the ambition, or the illusion, that rationalized the intervention in Iraq.

The president and his advisors expected democratic transformation in Iraq to provoke quasi-revolutionary political change elsewhere in the Arab Moslem world, accelerating modernizing forces in Islamic society as a whole.

The president's new plan was to put Iraq behind him as an electoral issue. It was meant to allow the most rapid possible withdrawal of U.S troops from security duties in Iraq, replacing them with Iraqi security police, paramilitary forces, and private security contractors, in anticipation of the presidential election in November 2004.

However, it still assumed perpetuated American political and economic influence in Iraq. It assumed that a limited but accelerated transfer of power could end, or reduce, guerrilla resistance to the occupation, and attacks on coalition troops, international groups active in Iraq, and Iraqis working with the occupation authorities, all meant to undermine the American position in Iraq, demonstrate the American coalition's inability to establish security, and quite possibly to prepare for a future struggle among Iraqis to control the country, once the United States is gone.

The President's new plan changed nothing essential in the American position. No fundamental reconsideration had taken place. The administration remained in deep denial concerning the power of nationalism and sectarian interest in Iraq, and the irreconcilability of such forces with an unrenounced American ambition to make Iraq a permanent instrument of U.S. political, economic and security influence in the region.

There has been little or no discussion at the level of national politics and policy of the possibility that the U.S. might lose the Iraq war. There is an all but universal assumption that American power will in the end crush anything that resists it.

It is true that critics have warned of a "new Vietnam," but nearly always in terms that suggested only that the eventual victory might be more difficult and costly than the Bush government expected.

The Vietnam analogy is indeed mistaken in military terms. The insurgents in Iraq are not an organized and disciplined national movement, supported and supplied with arms and leadership from a sister-country across the border, itself within a nuclear sanctuary (as was the case with North Vietnam, allied with both the Soviet Union and China). The relevant analogy Vietnam offers, with respect to the present situation in Iraq, is a political one.

The Bush administration seems blind to the political lesson of Vietnam, which — translated into contemporary terms — is that no leader will be capable of rallying Iraq, or its major religious or ethic components (except the minority Kurds), whose program is not national sovereignty, an end to American occupation, and national renewal on Iraq's own terms — which means full control of its resources, its security, and its foreign policy. That is not what the Bush administration has envisaged.

The vital political forces in Iraq will inevitably develop in opposition to the American occupation, and in opposition to the United States itself so long as larger American policies in the Middle East, and elsewhere in the Moslem world, generate massive popular opposition. This is simply a fact of political life and historical process.

In Vietnam, frustrated by the inability of the Catholic mandarin and nationalist the U.S. had brought back from U.S. exile to install in power, Ngo Dinh Diem, to defeat Vietnam's Communist uprising, the Kennedy administration instigated a military coup to remove him, and acquiesced in his murder.

Yet Diem actually represented a real national force, the educated Catholic middle classes and political elites that had run the country when it was a French colony. However, they represented too small a segment of the population and were too politically compromised by colonialism to deal with the dynamic combination of peasant nationalism and Marxist utopianism that drove the Communist National Liberation Front.

Washington replaced Diem with a general, the first in a series. One after another, each in turn failed, essentially because each was seen as defending the interests and ideas of the United States against those of Vietnamese nationalism.

Eventually, the Nixon administration abandoned the last of these generals, Nguyen Van Thieu, and formally withdrew from the war, calling this "Vietnamization." When Saigon fell, two years later, President Nixon blamed the U.S. Congress and the liberal press.

In Iraq, the Bush administration is still in search of its Ngo Dinh Diem.

This book is a critical account, written as it occurred, of the war on terror. It is composed of newspaper columns dealing with that "war," and with the events and forces influencing it or provoked by it.

I begin with a column written the afternoon of September 11, 2001, and I end with those written in December 2003.

These articles deal with American policy and personalities, but also with the dramatic change the Bush administration's conduct produced in Washington's relations with its European allies (a development of which, writing from Paris, I was a privileged observer.) The Israeli-Palestinian struggle, crucial to American interests in the Middle East, was necessarily a major concern in what I wrote during these 27 months.

The articles were written principally for *The International Herald Tribune*, the 117-year-old American newspaper published in Paris and circulated throughout the world, and nearly all were published there. As distributed by Tribune Media Services International syndicate, the articles were published in other newspapers in Europe, the Middle East, Asia and Latin America, and, of course, in the United States.

The articles are published here as they were written on the dates appended to each. I have added explanations of occasional references to topical matters forgotten today, have clarified some language, removed repetitions and shortened some articles of digressions irrelevant to the war on terrorism. These cuts are ordinarily indicated by ellipsis marks. No political judgments or expressions of opinion have been changed, even when they have since proven to be wrong.

Male public figures, even villainous ones, ceased to be called "Mr." in my columns during 2003, when the *Herald Tribune* bowed to current journalistic convention and suppressed titles of respect, even for the president of the United States.

This is a biased book. The bias, however, is an old one, and has little specifically to do with George W. Bush. It is a bias that has been present in my political writing for the past 43 years (with negligible effect on American official thought), since my first book on American foreign relations, published in 1961.[1] That book said:

> Here is our flaw: a defective sense of history, a refusal to acknowledge our implication in time. For whatever we think, history is flawed and uncertain and incalculable. And if the American nation makes it its mission to solve history's riddle and bring time to a stop, it will wreck itself. That is what we are in danger of doing....[T]he American interest does not lie in clumsy para-empire or in the self-contradiction of ideologized democracy: the one is futile and the other a dangerous absurdity. We must remember that America is not exempted from the historical imperatives, the laws of life and decay. And the American destiny, whatever it may be, is certainly not to hold universal responsibility.

I regret to say that there is nothing to be added to that today, since the illusions of American government and policy community have changed little, or for the worse, from what they were in those relatively innocent times.

1.Edmund Stillman and William Pfaff, *The New Politics, America and the End of the Postwar World*, New York, Coward-McCann; and London, Secker & Warburg, 1961.

PART ONE

September to December 2001: From the Attacks on New York and Washington to Victory over the Taliban in Afghanistan

Paris, September 11, 2001 — The first thing that must be said about the attacks in New York and Washington is that they have demonstrated the vulnerability of the United States, as of any modern society, to an intelligently prepared and determined attack.

Military officials, and the uniformed and civilian analytic agencies attached to the U.S. defense establishment, have for decades formulated speculative scenarios of attack on the nation, but their work has been dominated by the high-technology mind-set of the Pentagon and by the engineering ethos of American society.

The planning has always suffered from the planners' assumption that an enemy would attack in a manner symmetrical to the defenses they already had in place, or that they planned to have.

Thus, they concentrated speculation and planning on the danger of attack by weapons of mass destruction, probably using more or less high-technology methods. The discussion almost entirely concerned missile attacks, rogue nuclear weapons, and chemical and biological agents.

The defense planners were not interested in rogue commercial aircraft.

The first real lesson — which was not learned — was provided nearly 60 years ago, shortly before the end of World War II, when a U.S. medium bomber, lost in the fog, crashed into the Empire State Building, then the country's highest skyscraper, in New York City.

The lesson: exotic methods and high technology are not necessary to produce devastating results. Today the lesson was validated. You merely need to crash three old-fashioned airliners into vulnerable targets in order to produce mass panic, shut down most of the government and force the evacuation of the centers of Washington, New York and other major cities.

A second lesson: the psychological and political consequences of such an event are not primarily measured on the scale of the casualties, but by the unexpectedness and drama of the attack. As long as the attack remains anonymous, fear and panic escalate.

The sought-after effect is to demonstrate the vulnerability of those targeted, and the continuing vulnerability of those who might be targeted the next time. And to show that high-tech defenses, of the kind in which the United States takes pride, can be circumvented using simple methods. It is to show that no real defense exists against an anonymous attack which makes uses of the ordinary functioning of civilian society.

Such an attack is possible so long as civil airplanes fly, trains run, power systems and public utilities function, people go to work, and business and markets continue. Each can be subverted, or intervened in, or exploited in ways that damage their users and the larger society.

Even a totalitarian security state cannot deal with this, not even if it were to suppress basic civil liberties. It is extremely important to understand this, since there will be two natural reactions to what has happened, both of them essentially futile.

First of all there will be continuing calls for revenge against those responsible, presuming that the authors are eventually identified or identify themselves.

The practical uselessness of revenge has been illustrated repeatedly and continues to be shown in the Middle East, since those who employ terrorism are not functioning on a pragmatic scale of reward and punishment. As the Israelis find, making martyrs of your enemies invites further martyrdoms.

The second reaction will be that the United States needs even more elaborate defenses than now exist. Yet the Pentagon, the CIA, the National Security Agency and the rest of the American apparatus of national security proved incapable of preventing today's attacks. They are incapable of preventing a repetition in some other version.

There are no technological defenses, as such, against this sort of thing. Surely, if nothing else comes out of these attacks, they ought to have demonstrated to Americans the irrelevance of national missile defense.

There are ordinary security measures that can be taken or improved, but the nature of attacks mounted from within the regular functions of society means that no comprehensive or conclusive defense exists. The history of terrorism in both the nineteenth and twentieth centuries has proved this.

The final and most profound lesson of these events is one that it will be hardest for government to accept, and this government in particular: the only real defense against external attack is a serious, continuing and courageous effort to find political solutions for national and ideological conflicts that involve the United States.

The immediate conclusion nearly everyone has drawn about the origin of these attacks is that they come out of the Israeli-Palestinian struggle. It is reasonable to think that this is so, although there is as yet no proof.

For more than 30 years the United States has refused to make a genuinely impartial effort to find a resolution to that conflict. It has involved itself in the Middle East in a thousand ways but has never accepted responsibility for dealing impartially with the two sides — locked in their shared agony and their mutual tragedy.

If current speculation about these bombings proves to be true, the United States has now been awarded its share in that Middle Eastern tragedy.

September 13, 2001 — The calls for war that have come from Washington since Tuesday's catastrophes — for "war" against terrorism, against evil, against enemies of civilization, open-ended declarations of war against whomever it may be that did this to us — these calls answer the psychological demands of the hour, the leaders' need to seem to lead, but they are wrong.

Without tangible content they fall short. They cannot satisfy. They echo the maddened King Lear:

> I shall have such revenges on you
> That all the world shall — I will do such things, —
> What they are yet I know not, — but they shall be
> The terrors of the earth!

9

They risk actions that make things worse, blows that hit only people that had nothing to do with these attacks, thus adding to the total of those hating the United States and willing to die to do it harm.

The riposte of a civilized nation, that believes in good in human society and does oppose evil, has to be narrowly focused and above all, intelligent.

Missiles are blunt weapons. Terrorists — these terrorists — are smart enough to make others bear the price for what they have done, and exploit the result.

Maddened American responses that hurt still others are what they want, to fuel the hatred that already fires their own self-righteousness about their criminal acts against the innocent.

What the United States needs is cold reconsideration of how it has arrived at this pass. It needs, even more, to foresee disasters that may lie in the future.

Osama bin Laden, peremptorily but plausibly accused of responsibility for the attacks, is in a position of power today because of past American policies focused on the short term, indifferent to the more distant future.

The United States does not need more of that.

Bin Laden is the product of revolutionary and anti-American forces in the Islamic world that today remain, for the most part, subterranean, but exist in his own country, Saudi Arabia.

They are the same forces that produced a revolutionary and anti-American upheaval in Iran 22 years ago.

The fact that the Saudi monarchy is the most important American ally in the Arab world has disguised from most Americans how fragile it is. Bin Laden belongs to a generation of well-educated (often American-educated) younger members of the Saudi ruling elite and its mercantile middle class who consider the monarchy's accommodation to the American alliance a great betrayal.

They are faithful to the source of Saudi identity, the eighteenth century Wahhabi Moslem reform movement, which holds that all changes or accretions to Islam since the third Islamic century (the ninth century A.D.) are illegitimate and must be expunged.

This doctrine, conceived among austere desert Arabs, is the official religion of an enormously rich state, in which many if not most of the ruling figures' private lives blatantly contradict the Wahhabi condemnation of luxury and ostentation.

The psychological as well as social tensions this has produced over the last 50 years, not only between the rich and poor of the country, but in the consciences and psychologies of the new generation — sons and grandsons of the desert Wahhabis — may easily be imagined.

The Saudi elite has appeased the alienated generation by subsidizing radical Wahhabi movements abroad. Saudi Arabia paid for the Mujahideen of the Afghan resistance. It subsidizes the Taliban. It paid for the Mujahideen who fought in Bosnia, and now it subsidizes Wahhabi movements in Central Asia and Africa.

Yet Saudi Arabia's own tortured compromise between alliance with the United States — capital of materialism, luxury and ostentation — and its professed Islamic fundamentalism, to which the Saudi masses are attached, must one day collapse: just as the Shah's regime in Iran collapsed.

The 44-year-old Osama bin Laden, by training and profession an engineer, is a committed Wahhabi Moslem whose first political engagement was at the side of the CIA in fighting the 1979 Soviet invasion of Afghanistan.

Like many of the Mujahideen, he refused demobilization when Russia abandoned the Afghan war. He had a new war to fight, to save his own country, and his religion, from the United States.

Osama bin Laden hates the United States because he believes that America is an enemy of Islam and has polluted the Islamic Holy Places. Washington took advantage of the Gulf War in 1991 to get Saudi acquiescence in permanent U.S. bases inside Saudi Arabia.

Bin Laden's cause is an Arabia free of foreign soldiers, purged of "infidel" influence, under fundamentalist Wahhabi rule.

He wants to "destroy" the United States because it is, to him, what it was to the Iranian revolutionaries, a source of literal evil in today's world.

Clearly the United States needs to deal with bin Laden's terrorist organization, but that is essentially a police and intelligence problem.

Long-term United States interests cannot afford a "war" that risks toppling Saudi Arabia and other conservative Islamic regimes into alliance with the radical movements already powerful in Iran, Sudan, Algeria, and influential in Egypt, Pakistan, the Balkans, the Caucasus, Central Asia, and sub-Saharan Africa. That, though, is the risk.

September 20, 2001 — President George W. Bush's impolitic call for a "crusade" by the civilized world against terrorism won more diverse support than he expected, but for reasons he did not expect.

The reason was that nearly everyone has their own "terrorism" problem, and each would like to invite the United States into their fight. They would at least like the U.S. to turn its official gaze away while they deal with their "terrorists" by using methods of which Washington in the past would not have approved.

Russia's Vladimir Putin endorsed Mr. Bush's call because he wants Washington's crusade to incorporate the brutal, but as yet unsuccessful, Russian attempt to crush the Chechen nationalists. Moscow has consistently identified the Chechen problem as a case of Islamic fundamentalist terrorism.

Ariel Sharon launched a battering of Palestine Authority sites during the hours that followed the attacks in New York and Washington, and described Yasser Arafat as a second Osama bin Laden, whom America and Israel should cooperate in crushing.

Washington rejected the comparison, knowing that if it wants Arab cooperation in dealing with Mr. bin Laden, Prime Minister Sharon has to be locked in a box.

Mr. Arafat had equal pressure put on him by Washington to become a blood donor, unconvincingly condemn terrorism, and to call off the Palestinians' gunmen, all of which he did.

China explained that its troublesome minorities and dissident provinces — such as Taiwan — are "terrorists and separatists." They should be condemned by the United States, China said, in exchange for China's support for Washington's anti-terrorism campaign.

India said that separatists in Kashmir are terrorists. Sri Lanka says the same thing about its Tamil insurrection. Turkey identifies Kurd national resistance as terrorism. Serbia says that Mr. bin Laden's organization has branches in Bosnia-Herzegovina, Kosovo and in Albania itself.

Even the Irish Republican Army, whose stalwarts were recently caught instructing Colombian rebels, and whose own record includes skyscraper bombings, saw that it was expedient to deplore the Trade Towers and Pentagon attacks.

The White House was eventually forced to clarify the matter. U.S. policy, it said, is to "eliminate" terrorism around the world, but only "when it threatens the United States."

Your nationalists are my terrorists. My freedom-fighters are your terrorists. This is not a cynical observation, nor the judgment of a political relativist; politically, it simply is the truth.

What in principle distinguishes terrorism is indiscriminate violence (in practice, modern violence is rarely discriminate). Civilians are considered legitimate targets in terrorist campaigns meant to achieve what otherwise might be defensible goals: democratic self-determination for Kashmir; an independent Kurdistan; Britain out of Northern Ireland; Israel out of the occupied territories.

The terrorist justifies terror as the only weapon available to the weak. He claims for himself (or herself; terrorism is an equal-opportunity enterprise) an expedient morality: that terror works — as frequently it does.

Mr. bin Laden, if indeed he is responsible for what happened on September 11, has well and truly succeeded in getting the attention of Americans. Vengeance is cried now. Who is to say that the World Trade Towers and Pentagon attacks may not, in the long run, turn out to have influenced the U.S. government to pull back from the Middle East?

It took a single act of terrorism in 1983 to get American troops out of Lebanon. President Ronald Reagan had sent them to sponsor order and democracy, but there were no complaints in Congress when he abruptly ordered home the survivors of the terrorists' bomb.

Rhetorical excess about crusades and "eliminating" terrorism-sponsoring nations is not only a political error, opening the situation to the exploitation and opportunism of others, but it confuses the issues for Americans themselves.

Susan Sontag suffered the usual criticism in conservative circles when, a few days ago, she called the New York and Washington attacks a monstrous "dose of reality" for America. She said that government and media descriptions of what happened were "infantilizing" the public, as if Americans were incapable of looking a fact in the face.

For the attacks were not, as Mr. Bush and his colleagues say, aimed "at western civilization" or "at those who cherish liberty." They were aimed specifically at the United States of America, for specific reasons.

They were meant to harm the United States and no one else. They were retaliation for specific things done by the United States, and for specific American policies carried out over the years.

Americans may think those policies and those acts were entirely right and justified, or they may not. But Americans have to take responsibility for them, and accept their consequences.

We Americans need to be lucid about what has happened. Logically, this terrible experience should lead us to a new and serious reflection on what we have done in the past, and should do now. But that will not happen until the dust has cleared, and vengeance has been had. The troubling thought is that it might not happen even then.

September 25, 2001 — The Bush administration still gives disturbing signs of unclear objectives in the war it has proclaimed against terrorism, and would seem about to launch in wretched Afghanistan — one of the poorest countries on earth, and possibly the saddest.

Its war is vast in ambition, global in scope, but unwinnable on the terms Washington has thus far stated.

On Monday the United States ordered banks to freeze the accounts of certain people and institutions with ties to Egypt, Libya, and Aden, as well as Pakistan and Afghanistan, supposed to be connected with the September 11 attacks.

Lists supplied unofficially to Washington journalists of alleged Islamic ter-rorist organizations include groups in Lebanon, Iraq, the Palestinian refugee camps, Egypt, Syria, Sudan, Yemen, Algeria, India, Pakistan, Austria, Britain, Israel, countries in Africa, and in the United States itself.

These are proclaimed enemies, but not the only ones. President George W. Bush told Congress last week that while America' war on terrorism begins with Osama bin Laden's al Qaeda group, "It will not end until every terrorist group of global reach has been found, stopped, and defeated."

A vast program. In the realm of practical policy, Mr. Bush appears to have opted for something more reasonable. He seems to have ruled in favor of Sec-retary of State Colin Powell and other supporters of limited and focused retali-ation for the Trade Center and Pentagon bombings.

Figures in the Defense Department, notably Deputy Secretary of Defense Paul Wolfowitz, some people in Vice President Dick Cheney's office, and main-stream neo-conservative commentators have argued that the United States should settle all of its problems at a single blow by attacking the Taliban regime in Afghanistan, Iraq ("the theater of decisive confrontation," as one writer says) and probably Iran, Libya and Syria.

The president seems to have decided otherwise. Reports of administration intentions say that bombing and ground action will initially be limited to targets in Afghanistan, with the intention of damaging, if not dislodging, the Taliban government and opening the way for special troops to seize Osama bin Laden before the deadly Afghan winter begins.

This alone seems to me an ambitious operation, with a large potential for going out of control because of reactions inside Pakistan and elsewhere. A French report claims that the U.S. has insisted on taking control of Pakistan's nuclear weapons, because of fear of popular unrest and rebellion in the army.

Unknown is whether Washington contemplates trying to replace the Taliban government. On Tuesday the White House said "no." But it is hard to see how it can do what it wants to do without that happening. The Taliban are in power today because after winning the war against Russia, the leaders of existing opposition factions, mostly ethnic, were unable to stop fighting over the spoils of war and cooperate in rebuilding the country.

Certainly the notion heard in some American circles that the U.S. should, or could, "go in and make that country a democracy," is the sheerest fantasy. Afghan specialists warn that a U.S. attack may actually lend to the Taliban a legitimacy, as defenders of national sovereignty, which they do not now possess.

As late as Monday, Defense Secretary Donald Rumsfeld was unable to give the press a specific statement of American goals, or a description of what would constitute "victory" in the war against terrorism.

Would Washington be satisfied by the capture or death of Osama bin Laden? Seemingly not. Or by ouster of the Taliban government? Under repeated questioning, Mr. Rumsfeld fell back on a statement that the United States government will consider that it has won when Americans and their children will again be able to "feel safe."

This is not serious. In the new conditions of international society, Americans of this generation may never again have reason to feel safe from the enmity of those who believe that the United States exploits them and corrupts their society.

Neither Israelis nor Palestinians have felt safe for years, and have little prospect of feeling safe in the future. The Afghans have lived with terror since 1979, and thanks to the new war about to be visited upon them will probably go on living with terror for months or years to come.

The Spanish, British and French have lived for decades with the reality or threat of terrorism by extremist Basque, Irish Nationalist, and Islamic fundamentalist groups. Individuals understand that the risk exists of being blown away tomorrow, but they get on with their lives. So will Americans, in the weeks to come, regardless of what happens to Osama bin Laden.

What else can people do? Governments do their best to protect them from terrorism, but there is a limit to what can be done.

15

The American response to the events of September 11 has so far insisted on denying that limit. This curiously contrasts with the Pentagon's "Weinberger Rules" for military engagement, proclaimed in the 1980s, and (then-General) Colin Powell's own doctrines on U.S. military interventions.

Both men demanded a clear statement of attainable political objectives in any use of American military force, and an equally clear statement of terms on which any intervention would be brought to an end. Today we have neither.

September 27, 2001 — The same Islamic fundamentalism that inspires Osama bin Laden is shared by the two Moslem states that are the United States' most important allies in its war against terrorism.

Saudi Arabia is an absolute monarchy ruled by the Wahhabi religious movement that is at the source of modern Islamic fundamentalism. The military government of Pakistan is heavily under the influence of the same fundamentalist convictions that animate the Talibans in Afghanistan.

Osama bin Laden, accused leader of the group responsible for the September 11 terrorist outrages in New York and Washington, is a Wahhabi — one who believes that his religion has been betrayed.

This Islamic reform movement originated in Arab resistance to Turkish rule in the eighteenth century. In the early twentieth century it overturned the orthodox Hashemite dynasty of Saudi Arabia, and took control of all the Arabian peninsula. Its leader then was Ibn Saud, and his puritanical and intolerant Wahhabi version of Islam became and remains the religion of Arabia.

It is officially intolerant of any other religion, enforcing a fanatically puritanical social order in which women are excluded from public life and primitive punishments are imposed for violations of traditional law.

Osama bin Laden's terrorist campaign is not primarily directed against the United States — which is expected eventually to collapse on its own, as a result of what the fundamentalists see as its decadence. His aim is to unseat the Saudi Arabian elite that has permitted an "infidel" United States to install itself in the nation of the Islamic Holy Places.

This is why the relationship between the United States and Saudi Arabia is so uncomfortable today. Washington is reluctant to talk about it because the U.S. is heavily dependent on Arabian oil, and the Saudi leadership is silent because it depends on American protection.

Washington has heavy political and military commitments to Saudi Arabia, while it has turned a half-blind eye to the Saudis' promotion of their radical and utopian version of Islam among the Taliban in Afghanistan, elsewhere in the Middle East, and in Central Asia and Africa.

The same discomfort exists in American relations with Pakistan, whose military government still (at this writing) has not fully agreed to Washington's demands for military bases and cooperation against a Taliban regime which the Pakistan intelligence services themselves installed in power in Afghanistan.

The source of radical Islam today is Saudi Arabia. So long as Saudi oil riches subsidize Wahhabi influence and expansion, fundamentalism with have a firm financial and political base.

Saudi Arabia is at the same time under attack from the radical and violent movement mobilized by the children of the Saudi elite — such as Osama bin Laden. He is joined by recruits from an alienated (and often well-educated) generation of young Moslems elsewhere, declared enemies both of the United States and of their own allegedly corrupted national leaders.

When one writes about the internal complexities in the war against terrorism, and the nature and origins of the terrorist movement, some readers say this amounts to giving aid and comfort to the enemy by offering an explanation for what they do. They are thereby humanized.

My own recent columns on the subject have provoked more hostile reception, mainly from readers in the United States, than I have experienced in the past when writing on any subject.

These readers seem not to want Islamic fundamentalist terrorism placed against an historical and cultural background, presumably because this constitutes an obstacle to seeing the enemy as simply a manifestation of evil.

A critic in Chicago asked, "are you trying to rationalize the murder of 6,000 innocent civilians?" There is a difference in the language between "explain" and "rationalize," which I would have thought my readers understood.

There has also been an angry reaction to my argument that Americans have to accept the consequences of the American policies that contributed to bringing us to this crisis.

Nations, like individuals, pay a price for what they have, or have not, done in the past. The terrorists are taking revenge, in their minds, for harm done to them and their society by the United States.

In the case of a puritanical and literally reactionary movement, such as the Wahhabis, the influence of the modern secular world is itself harmful. The role of the United States as a modernizing force in global society is, in this worldview, criminal in itself.

17

American critics of U.S. Middle Eastern policy often say that Washington is hated because it has supported dictatorial governments. These Middle Eastern critics hate the United States for the opposite reason, because it brings secular and liberal democratic ideas into the region.

America's support for Israel is not a primary issue for the bin Laden movement (even though American critics make much of it). It is a very important factor in opinion elsewhere in the Middle East, with particularly damaging effect among pro-democratic groups.

The fundamentalists are concerned with the condition of Islamic society itself — its integrity, its purity, its future. This is why their fanaticism is deaf both to America's threats and to reason.

Paris, October 2, 2001 — The Bush administration's diplomatic campaign against those believed responsible for the September 11 attacks on New York and Washington is thus far an imposing success — something Washington political circles and press don't seem yet to have grasped.

Immediately after the attacks, many expected President Bush to order the kind of missile and bombing attacks employed by previous administrations after terrorist outrages, even though in the past these usually proved futile or mischievous, accomplishing little and killing the innocent.

He continues to be criticized by some Republicans, and neo-conservative commentators, because (as of this writing) he hasn't bombed anyone. For them, acts of undeclared war are what win respect for the United States and demonstrate its "credibility."

Today, thanks to Mr. Bush's realism, and the massive diplomatic offensive his government has been conducting, American credibility is not only high, but may get a lot higher if its political measures combine with military threat to tighten the noose on Osama bin Laden.

The U.S. has persuaded both friendly and not-so-friendly governments to carry out police and intelligence investigations that have already produced many arrests and much evidence concerning the operations of the loose but extensive network making up what now must be called the New Terrorism, sharply different in methods, objectives, and agents from the state terrorism of the past.

Pakistan President Pervez Musharraf told the BBC on Monday that the Taliban government in Afghanistan already seems on its last legs. It is completely isolated from its former friends and sponsors in Pakistan and Saudi Arabia.

The Taliban authorities already have offered to share power in three provinces with traditional councils of elders, a significant concession.

The opposition Northern Alliance is getting new support, even though its ability to topple the Taliban is limited by its ethnic composition and its connections to Tajikistan, traditional rival of Pakistan for influence in Afghanistan.

According to reports, the United States is working to contact and mobilize Pashtun regional leaders in the south. That ethnic group dominates the area and is strong on both sides of the Pakistan-Afghanistan frontier.

That frontier was for years disputed with the former Afghan monarchy, which provides another reason why Pakistan is the critical actor in this affair and is under intense American pressure to cooperate in the political as well as possible military campaign against its former Taliban protégés.

Finally there is a plan, which seems to have originated within Afghan circles, which involves the former king, the 86-year-old Mohammad Zahir Shah, who lives in Rome (and avows that he has no ambition to recover his throne).

He has the right to call a grand council of tribal and religious elders, the 500 to 600-member "Loya Jirga," which traditionally possesses ultimate power in ordering Afghanistan's affairs and governance.

According to Rome reports, a "supreme council of national unity" will meet inside Afghanistan within two weeks to convoke the Loya Jirga, which in turn will call a constitutional convention — in which dissident Talibans will be welcome.

The king also has United Nations support because his government, forcibly ousted in 1973, remains in international law the legitimate government of the country, and holds Afghanistan's seat in the UN.

This plan to replace Taliban power, if agreed by the country's major factions and highest traditional tribal and religious authorities, could open the way to eventual seizure of Osama bin Laden and his network inside Afghanistan.

It is undoubtedly the only way this could be peacefully accomplished, and is probably the only way it can be accomplished at all, since all seem agreed that Mr. bin Laden is not going to be taken unless the populace wants him taken, and hands him over to what is seen as legitimate Afghan authority.

If the population sees him as the victim of foreign intruders, and collaborates in resisting that intrusion, western soldiers are unlikely to track him down. He probably could hold out indefinitely, and perhaps eventually disappear.

The Bush administration has in three weeks put together a formidable political offensive, which if it succeeds can not only solve the problem of Mr. bin

Laden and his Qaeda network, but the humanitarian and political tragedy of Afghanistan. Success could also have a very positive effect in Pakistan, and possibly even in the Kashmir conflict.

It would give the Bush administration an international triumph. It might even embolden it to take on the bloody Israeli/Palestinian stalemate.

The project may also fall apart. It is likely to require discriminating application of military power to contribute to unseating the Taliban.

But if that power were exercised at the request of the legitimate government of Afghanistan, and with the agreement of the United Nations, the U.S. would have made a major contribution to international order. Its credibility would be great indeed.

Washington, October 16, 2001 — Eight years ago, Samuel Huntington of Harvard said that the idea of "clash between civilizations" provided a valid model for thinking about the future. It was a "simplified picture of reality" which officials could use to orient their thought and planning around a seemingly plausible, if not necessarily correct, picture of the future. This has proved a terrible suggestion.

The theory followed on earlier policy models, or paradigms. The most important was that of cold war confrontation between equally powerful superpowers, each threatening the other's survival. That model was wrong, since the Soviet Union was not really a superpower at all, and eventually collapsed of its own internal failures.

Another was the Asian Communism paradigm. From the 1950s to the end of the Vietnam war, it portrayed China as capable of organizing the "rural world" to defeat the United States, capital of the "urban world," by means of Communist-led revolts progressing from one country to another by domino effect.

This too proved false, although the United States fought a war because of it. The Vietnamese Communists defeated the United States, but nothing else followed. There was no domino effect.

All policy paradigms amount to simple projections of certain perceived current trends. The clash of civilizations model came out of the Islamic fundamentalist revolution in Iran, hostile to the United States. This should not have been unexpected, but was. The utopian idea of returning to an idealized past is a recurrent phenomenon. In Islam, it first appeared in this century with the Moslem Brotherhood, founded in Egypt in 1928.

Another influence was the idea, much discussed in the 1980s, that "Asian values" exist, superior to western values, which are responsible for the rapid economic growth of Japan, South Korea, Singapore, and Taiwan. There since has been Asian economic crisis and stagnation.

However September 11 suddenly made a great many people in the United States and Europe think that the clash of civilizations had arrived. A great many more, inside the Islamic world, have wanted to believe that this is true.

They saw the spectacular attacks carried out against American cities, presumably organized by Osama bin Laden and his network, as justified retaliation for the harm they think has been done to Moslems by America and by the West.

They specifically hold the U.S. responsible for forcing its military bases into their countries, for what they see as the dispossession and oppression of the Palestinian people, and for the sanctions that have punished the Iraqi people since the Gulf war. They blame the West generally for the backwardness of Moslem society since the rise of modern science and liberal western governments.

Yet Osama bin Laden, the Taliban movement, Saudi Arabian official fundamentalism, Pakistani popular fundamentalism, and Palestinian terrorists do not make up Islamic civilization. They are merely individual phenomena inside Islamic society.

The fundamentalists do not even represent mainstream orthodoxy in Islam. They are driven by a fanatical and ideological version of religion, resembling nationalism. They are themselves often western-educated, ignorant of much of the content and culture of Islam, radicalized by a personal quest for meaning in a society affected by modernization.

There are somewhat more than 100 million Moslems in the Arab world, and another 140 million in Pakistan and Afghanistan. These communities are involved in today's conflict with the West.

There also are 174 million Moslems in Indonesia, 100 million in India, 103 million in Bangladesh, and some 160 million in sub-Saharan Africa — plus six million in the United States. Still more Moslems live in Turkey, Western Europe, North Africa, the Caucasus, and Central Asia.

These people may feel sympathy for their fellow-Moslems in Palestine, Iraq, Afghanistan and Pakistan, but they are not part of the bin Laden jihad. The danger is that they might become convinced that the United States is at war with Islam.

21

The United States and the West are not at war with Islam as either religion or civilization. They are at war with individual terrorists or terrorist organizations. For them, the issue of conflict is political, not cultural or religious.

President Bush and Secretary of State Colin Powell have repeatedly been saying this. So have Western Europe's leaders. Individual western groups, such as the Sant'Egidio community in Rome, have been organizing dialogues with Moslem leaders to stop this conflict from assuming a religious character.

The idea of war between civilizations substitutes a cultural entity, the civilization, which has no responsible political existence or center of authority, for the responsible decisions and actions of governments. It says that the West and Islam must go to war because of cultural predestination.

This idea is identical to that which a century ago saw race war as the world's future. That forecast convinced Hitler. We do not want to see that repeated. War between civilizations is a pernicious idea — and only an idea, not a reality. It must be resisted.

Washington, October 18, 2001 — [The bombing campaign in Afghanistan has begun.] America's frustrations in its war on terrorism are likely to deepen, as the international political structure upon which the war rests weakens.

The latest blow to that structure came Wednesday, with the assassination by Palestinians of a departing Israeli cabinet minister committed to the expulsion of Palestinians from all of the territories.

A ferocious Israeli retaliation will undoubtedly follow. The notion that the United States could put the Palestinian conflict on ice while pursuing its own war is wholly unrealistic.

American war tactics and strategy increasingly are criticized. Even conservative and pro-American newspapers, such as London's popular daily, *The Daily Mail*, are asking what is accomplished by once again bombing "a backward and ignorant people" whose actual responsibility for what happened on September 11 is slight.

The pro-American *Süddeutsche Zeitung* in Germany asks, "where is the political offensive?" *La Repubblica* in Italy accuses the United States of searching for political solutions in force and technology, and believing that it "can eradicate terrorism and fanaticism by inflicting fire and bloodshed on a distant country."

So long as the military campaign is conducted only from the air, such criticisms will increase. People are very uneasy about "asymmetric war" against an already ruined and impoverished state.

Yet the American strategy is clear. What is lacking is an articulated and achievable long-term political objective. The aim in Afghanistan is to unseat the Taliban and replace them with a grand coalition of all Afghanistan's major forces, including the ethic Pashtuns of the south, perhaps former Talibans among them, and the ethnically diverse members of the Northern Alliance.

None of these show much current interest in collaboration. It's nonetheless hoped that with the support of Mohammed Zahir Shah, the exiled king, and the help of the United Nations, such a successor government can be put together.

However the Talibans have to be ousted first, and there is as yet no evidence that bombing is going to make them collapse, or make them produce Osama bin Laden. He and his international brigades are thought more concentrated and powerful now than the Taliban authorities themselves.

The ominous trend Washington faces is that the fragile structure upon which the Afghanistan intervention relies is getting weaker. Pakistani President Pervez Musharraf's position is fragile. His army is itself divided on the issue of supporting the United States against an Afghan Taliban government that the Pakistani services themselves created.

India is taking advantage of the situation by pressing its conflict with Pakistan over Kashmir. Secretary of State Colin Powell tried to defuse this situation during his visit last week, but in current conditions it cannot be defused. It is as difficult a problem as Palestine, and with India and Pakistan both nuclear powers it may be even more dangerous.

The other weakened component of the American coalition is Saudi Arabia, which, as everyone by now knows, is where Osama bin Laden's terrorist network began. Many of his followers are Saudi Arabians, recruited because they believe that the military bases and troop contingents the United States insists on maintaining in that country desecrate its holy sites.

The risks are first, that events in Israel and Palestine destroy what's left (if anything indeed is left) of the Middle Eastern truce — at a moment when the Egyptian public is restless about Egypt's pro-American position.

There is danger that popular unrest deepens in Pakistan, or even that a military coup might be attempted. The Saudi monarchy's position could come under even more pressure than now is the case. Anti-American protests in Indonesia are widening. All of this jeopardizes the anti-terrorism alliance.

This is why time and results are important in Afghanistan. Mr. Bush's warning last Wednesday that the war against terrorism could go on for "years" in "a variety of theaters" is having a bad effect on the alliance.

The crucial question is what America really wants. Would Washington be content with a new and moderate Afghan government, and Mr. bin Laden's head presented on a platter?

President George Bush has repeatedly talked about the war in language that says it is not simply against identifiable terrorists but against "evil" and disorder.

There is a notorious debate going on between the State Department, skeptical about wars, and some leaders in the Defense department and the neo-conservative intellectual community who want to attack Saddam Hussein in Iraq, and possibly other rogue states.

Last week, in a meeting here, I heard an otherwise thoughtful member of the university policy community explain that a new era has begun, in which the United States and its allies will need to go on from Afghanistan to dismantle the other rogue states, giving them new governments, and then take over the "failed" and failing states, where poverty and disorder creates fanaticism and anti-Americanism.

A new world order indeed! More realistically, what he was talking about was a new cold war — one that the United States could never win, and would abdicate its own values in trying to win.

Paris, October 23, 2001 — Behind the false idea that Osama bin Laden's attacks on the United States launched a modern war between civilizations is the historical reality of a real war between empires and nations that began with the Moslem conquest of Roman Jerusalem in 638. The Arab empire went on winning that war until the late middle ages, and then it began to lose.

Europe's Crusaders took Jerusalem away from the Moslems in 1099, but a century later it was retaken by Saladin, and from then on remained part of a vital and expanding Moslem empire that had marched on western Europe and very nearly conquered it. The Crusades were not a one-way street.

Arab Moslem power was imposed in Egypt and North Africa, onward to Spain and southern France, and through the Balkans to Vienna. Moslem civilization was at that time the equal or superior of western Europe's by virtually every standard of military, political, economic, and aesthetic accomplishment.

Had the Venetians and Spaniards lost the battle of Lepanto, the French under Charles Martel failed at Poitiers in 732, or the Austrians and Poles lost at Vienna in 1683, we might all be speaking Arabic today. Gibbon, the historian of the decline and fall of Rome, has a famous passage in which he reflects on the prospect of Koranic teaching in the schools of Oxford, had Charles Martel lost.

Even though the Arabs were eventually forced out of Spain, and parts of their North African empire became autonomous, they ruled the Balkans, or most of it, until 1914.

It was only after the Ottoman Empire was defeated in the first world war that the Arabs found themselves dominated by Europeans in a series of new states, set up under League of Nations mandates, in the former Ottoman territories.

The independent Arab and Egyptian governments that emerged after the second world war proved another defeat. The supposed reformers of the Ba'ath movement in the eastern Mediterranean turned Iraq and Syria into hereditary dictatorships. Egypt became that anomalous modern phenomenon, the quasi-democracy, or consultative dictatorship.

Islamic society failed to take off economically, falling under the commercial control of western oil companies, banks and businesses. It remains technologically backward, under the intellectual domination of western ideas and western science on the one hand, challenged by a reactionary and utopian religious fundamentalism on the other.

What went wrong?

Islamic society, the West's equal at the time of the European Renaissance, failed to make the transition to a modern society. In matters of material power, the Europeans passed from crafts and artisanal technology to empirical science, and eventually to industrial technology. They explored the world, establishing global systems of trade, commerce and intellectual exchange.

They experienced political evolution — sometimes violent — that limited monarchical power, empowered the middle and professional classes, and eventually produced modern liberal democracy. They developed institutions of law, adjudication, and contract.

The sophistication of Arab mathematics, astronomy, governmental administration and military organization was very great at the end of the Middle Ages. There had been a remarkable philosophical flowering, and advanced theoretical science.

The Arabs had preserved Greek philosophy, transmitting it to western thinkers. They failed to make use of it themselves, as the westerners did, to reform their institutions and to reestablish the basis of their political and social thought.

Islam proved incapable of formulating a modern conception of politics and government, able to cope with a non-Islamic world much more powerful in material means, organization and science.

There seem to be two fundamental reasons for this, both of them religious in origin.

The first was that religious and state authority were separated from the start in the Christian West. In Islamic society they have never been fully separated. Efforts to establish an intellectually legitimate non-theological basis for independent state authority have failed. This means that an independent civil society has never emerged.

The West had a biblical basis for independent secular political authority in the distinction made by Jesus between the things that belong to Caesar and those that belong to God. Caesar was acknowledged the ruler of an autonomous political and social order. In 800 Charlemagne was crowned emperor of the Holy Roman Empire by the Pope himself.

The second basic reason the West could create modern society was that from the Middle Ages forward, philosophy was distinguished from theology.

Adopting Aristotle's philosophy of natural reason, Thomas Aquinas argued that reason is a source of truth independent of theological reasoning, and authentic in its own terms. He said that reason and religious faith are two harmonious but distinct intellectual realms. This was the historical basis for the independent speculative life of the West, which gave us the modern world.

Islam since 1914 has failed to make a serious intellectual response to the modern West. Culture and intelligence, not power, decide the quality of societies. This is the failure that has produced Osama bin Laden and his al Qaeda, and it is a failure more dangerous to Islam than it can ever be to the West.

October 25, 2001 — The Pentagon's admission that Taliban forces in Afghanistan are not folding under the weight of the American bombardment, and that the Northern Alliance has not begun to march towards Kabul, casts doubt on the tactics being employed by the Pentagon to run this war.

Its tactical model is familiar by now: airpower applied from a safe height, with collaborating ground action by allied or proxy forces. In Kosovo, the

Kosovo Liberation Army assumed the ground role. In Bosnia, it was the European force already there.

Difficulties in Afghanistan also raise questions about the political assumptions and expectations that govern the campaign. American policy has assumed that the Northern Alliance, and possible Taliban defectors or dissident tribal groups elsewhere in the country, would do the ground fighting to overturn Afghanistan's present government, once airpower had broken its resistance.

This so far is not happening. One reason is that Taliban military structures are rarely elaborate enough to be broken. The Pentagon announces that it has destroyed "command and control" centers at Afghan airfields, but correspondents who know the country say that a command and control facility is likely to consist of a wooden hut with a telephone that doesn't always work....

The Pentagon's reluctance to do more on the ground results not only from its allergy to casualties but from the common-sense observation that ground warfare in Afghanistan, as winter approaches, would likely give the Taliban, not a hypermodern American army, most of the advantages of "asymmetric warfare."

Anyway, the U.S. is supposed to be conducting a war on terror, not a war on Afghanistan. Before September 11, Washington had for years demonstrated little or no interest in what was going on in Afghanistan.

Since then, Washington's difficulty in finding and capturing Osama bin Laden has seen it substitute the goal of overturning the Taliban government, an undertaking with which it can come to grips. If the Taliban are out of the way, the terrorist leader can be found — or so it is assumed.

Merely setting up a new government to replace the Taliban would allow Washington to claim a victory, even if it is not the victory it set out to have.

In the meantime, of course, Osama bin Laden may have decided that it would be wise to ride a mule out of the country, shave his beard, and using his wealth and one of the various passports undoubtedly available to him, check in at the St. Regis in New York or the Ritz in Paris.

If that seems exaggerated, it nonetheless is true that he and his organization can go to ground, and "exterminating" terrorism would become a more formidable job than it already is.

This is in the mind of those in Washington who want to go on from Afghanistan to Iraq, to get rid of Saddam Hussein. That would be another substitute goal, offering a tangible victory at whatever cost, even if it did nothing to eliminate Osama bin Laden's Qaeda organization....

That is why difficulties in Afghanistan are likely to promote the ideas of those who want to raise the stakes, and take the war to Iraq. That offers another substitute for the promised, but impossible, victory over terrorism. However Americans have heard for many years the slogan that in war, there is no substitute for victory.

October 30, 2001 — What set out to be a war on terrorism has become a war against Afghanistan, under its present government.

The reason for this transformation is that war against Afghanistan is easily within the power of the United States, while war against terrorism is war against something which at best is ill-defined and in some respects undefinable, since the attempt at definition leads into the moral entanglements of who does what to whom, with what motivations.

Narrowly considered, the primary enemy is the clandestine organization or association of like-minded Muslim enemies of the United States which we are calling al Qaeda, taken to be inspired and controlled by Osama bin Laden.

I qualify the language because it remains unclear how closely organized and disciplined the group really is. There is some reason to think that it could be a fairly loose association of self-motivated and even self-financing activists, as some nihilist or anarchist terrorist groups were in the nineteenth and early twentieth centuries.

However war against Osama bin Laden is hard because the United States can't find him. (War against al Qaeda is easier because it is a matter of police and intelligence work, and remarkable progress has been made during the last four weeks, thanks to unprecedented international cooperation.)

Since Osama bin Laden is in Afghanistan (or has been there), it is logical to demand that the Taliban government hand him over. The government's refusal is what put us where we are today.

But where are we?...The original plan depended less on bombing than on organization of the existing military and political opposition; cutting off the support Pakistan was giving to the regime; and enlistment of the country's other neighbors, including Iran, all with ethnic or religious clients inside Afghanistan. The authority of the former king and the United Nations was to underwrite a new coalition government.

This plan has suffered a series of setbacks, and official Washington is rapidly losing interest in political solutions. There is an increasing disposition toward brute force, and the use of whatever allies are at hand, even if that threatens to leave Afghanistan in chaos, and the war on terrorism stranded. We could see unqualified backing for the Northern Alliance, and introduction of the B-52s....

Washington might take the time to reflect on its responsibility, which is to deal intelligently with the terrorist threat to the United States. Bin Laden and his group are merely instances of that threat. If he is killed, he will be replaced. The causes of terrorism will remain, and they are political.

Afghanistan and its people are no threat to the United States, but they are the ones taking the full weight of America's indignation. The administration's priorities are upside-down.

Paris, November 1, 2001 — There is an obvious if controversial connection between the West's war against terrorism and the war between the Palestinians and the Israelis.

So long as nothing is done about the latter, America's position is undermined in the Islamic world and in its current alliances with Pakistan, Saudi Arabia, Egypt, and the Gulf states.

This is so even though Osama bin Laden's organization looks on the Palestinian cause as a secondary matter. It is driven by Saudi Arabia's puritanical version of Islamic orthodoxy, and by the conviction that the U.S. "pollutes" the holiest sanctuaries of Islam by its military and political presence in Saudi Arabia.

Palestinian militancy has mainly been secular, even though the status of Jerusalem and the fate of Moslem holy places there and in the occupied territories have been basic issues in the struggle.

Christians from the former Palestine and from Lebanon have been prominent figures in the conflict with Israel that has been going on since the partition of Palestine was voted by the UN in 1948, and was violently rejected by the Arab governments of the time.

For the masses of Moslem Arabs, Egyptians and Iranians, the Israel-Palestine conflict remains a permanent provocation. It is their main motive for detesting the United States, Israel's defender.

This, of course, is why the Bush administration reacted so harshly to the Sharon government's recent invasions of territories supposed to be under permanent Palestinian control.

Now something new has been introduced into the situation. Shlomo Ben-Ami, foreign minister until February in Israel's Barak government, is appealing for international intervention to replace failed and discredited direct negotiations between Israel and the Palestinian authority.

"It should be clear by now that an agreement freely reached between the parties themselves is simply not possible," he wrote on Monday in London's *Financial Times*. The Mitchell plan for ceasefire and interim agreements is useless. "The assumption that this is a conflict of land for peace, a mundane bargaining over real estate, has been destroyed."

"Yasser Arafat," he writes, "has made clear that that even if all the occupied territories are returned to the Palestinians, Israel will not attain peace."

The ex-minister could have added that the Sharon government is incapable of returning all the occupied territories, even in exchange for peace. Colonization of the Palestinian territories has continued ever since the Oslo agreements, and goes on today. The intifada is mainly, although certainly not exclusively, about Israel's continuing expansion into the territories.

Ben-Ami writes that no trust remains on either side. An international solution has to be imposed "or there will be no solution at all." As a major figure on the Israeli scene, with unique experience of the negotiations sponsored by the Clinton administration that seemed on the edge of success last December, his proposal deserves attention, and is getting it....

If the effort failed, he would lose. It's a gamble, but one of greater historical importance than the war against terrorism — which may not be winnable without a Palestine settlement. The electoral danger to the administration from not acting may be as large as the risk posed by following Mr. Ben-Ami's advice.

A George Bush who made peace in the Middle East, after more than 50 years of war, would be a bigger man than a president who merely caught (or lost) Osama bin Laden. Mr. Bush should think about it.

November 6, 2001 — Demonstrations demanding liberalization of Iran's Islamic fundamentalist government spontaneously erupted at recent World Cup football [soccer] qualification matches in that country. They add to the evidence that the power of fundamentalism in Iran is fading.

This happens at the moment when Saudi Arabian fundamentalists, and the militants under their sway, have taken their war against the United States to a new intensity of terrorism, while the American riposte is an attack on the fundamentalist Taliban regime in Afghanistan.

Football match disorders, and demonstrations producing pro-American slogans and protests against Iran's religious oligarchy, remain for the moment an inchoate youth reaction against the intellectual stultification of Iranian society. The ruling clerics have thus far been successful in resisting efforts at democratization and reform.

It is interesting, however, that one influence on what is happening in Iran are the satellite television broadcasts of the former Shah of Iran's 42-year-old son, Reza Pahlavi. His message is non-violent resistance and secular democracy, and he holds out the prospect of Iran's becoming a European-style society.

The vast majority of his listeners have no real notion of what that means, nor any direct experience or memory of the realities of his father's government — which fell because it pushed breakneck westernization, and neglected Iran's Islamic legacy.

The late Shah preferred a romanticized or mythologized version of his country's Persian imperial past, identifying himself with Cyrus the Great. He organized an immense celebration of the 2,500th anniversary of Cyrus's rule, at Persepolis in 1971 — an act of personal hubris that contributed to provoking the 1979 Iranian revolution.

That revolution's leader, Ayatollah Ruhollah Khomeini, had the same ambition that Osama bin Laden's al Qaeda organization proclaims today: to achieve the utopian goal of a society with perfect justice, based on the Koran and traditional Islamic law.

However, as a French specialist on Islam, Olivier Roy, has recently remarked, there was a sophistication in what was being attempted two decades ago that is lacking today. The young intellectuals around the Ayatollah Khomeini were trying to conceptualize how to adapt strict Islam to the modern world: "what the place of women should be, what should characterize an Islamic state." They worried about technology and finance.

"For the generation around bin Laden," Olivier Roy says, "it's all summed up in two lines: the Sharia, all of the Sharia, and nothing but the Sharia — plus death to the West and its values."

The emotional force behind fundamentalism has always been a form of nationalism, as well as religion. The Iranian revolution was inspired by Iran's domination from the 1950s through the 1970s by the United States, and before that by more than a century of British and Russian rivalry over control of the country.

Al Qaeda is also a nationalist movement, in that it wants to expel foreigners and foreign ideas from the Islamic world. The Taliban movement itself was

31

forged in Afghanistan's struggle against Russian invasion and a Russian-controlled Afghan Communist party.

Now the Pashtuns of the quasi-autonomous tribal areas of Afghanistan's neighboring Pakistan are joining the Pashtun Taliban to fight the United States and its allies.

However, dramatic as all this seems at the moment, Iran is not the only place where there is evidence that the fundamentalist movement is losing influence. It's true in Algeria, Egypt, elsewhere in the Middle East, and even in Europe's Moslem ghettos. The Taliban themselves were beginning to lose part of their original support. Their control remained strong in the cities, but not in the countryside, as travelers in the country last spring discovered.

This was foreseeable and indeed predicted. The events of September 11 and after have quite possibly done net damage to the movement, because they have brought out the essential nihilism of what fundamentalism has become. They demonstrate its futility.

The actual attempts to create a utopian religious society in Iran and Afghanistan, and the terrible violence between fundamentalists and army that has torn Algeria apart in recent years, have alienated ordinary people.

The movement's original appeal was to elites, resisting the cultural challenges of westernization. Today, the leading members of the bin Laden organization have proven to be relatively well-educated, semi-westernized young men, caught between the crisis of their own civilization and a western society whose integration they resist.

Fundamentalist activists in Europe have nearly all been second-generation members of Europe's immigrant ghettos, often unemployed and poorly integrated. They went back to their parents' countries of origin — or to war in Bosnia or Afghanistan — in order to establish identities of their own.

They resemble those partly-integrated children of earlier western ethnic immigrations to the U.S. or the advanced West European countries who proved vulnerable to the revolutionary appeal of Stalinism and Trotskyism.

In the countries where fundamentalism has been tried, it has proven to have no real solutions to Islamic society's problems. This is why its days are numbered in Iran and even Afghanistan. It survives in Saudi Arabia, and in those other countries where it is still only a dream.

November 8, 2001 — ...In Washington on Tuesday, in his joint press conference with French President Jacques Chirac, President George W. Bush warned that good intentions are not enough for members of the anti-terrorism coalition. He said that it is important "for nations to know that they will be held accountable for inactivity. You are either with us or you are against us in the fight against terror."

Mr. Chirac then intervened, saying that he wanted to remind the press that it was a resolution of the Security Council of the United Nations that obliged "all nations to join the fight against terrorism...according to their capabilities." He added that it was also the Security Council that had conferred international "legitimacy" on the U.S. response to the September 11 attacks.

He was trying to make the point that the world does not automatically endorse the U.S.'s unilaterally giving the orders on war and peace. But that, of course, is what's happening. Europe once again finds itself trying to accommodate a situation where the United State is doing things that make some Europeans uncomfortable, even though they endorse Washington's overall aims.

The New York financier Felix Rohatyn, America's former ambassador to France, gave a talk a few days ago to a Paris audience that cast light on the underlying transatlantic problem, in which France is the critical actor.

He said he felt that the Soviet threat has increasingly been replaced since 1989, in the view of many French political and intellectual leaders, "by the menace of American hegemony or of an American-inspired globalization."

He noted that the events of September 11 had provoked an explosion of French sympathy and generosity towards the United States, but that nonetheless, as he left his Paris post earlier this year, he had felt a certain discouragement at the state of French-American relations.

He thought that the two countries' paths were diverging, and that in favoring a multipolar world, France actually wanted "to make the new united Europe not a partner of America but an alternative to it."

He described this parting of the ways with regret rather than anger, saying that France has nothing to fear from globalization or American hegemony. He implicitly ascribed France's actions to "nostalgia for past grandeur."

This is a common American diagnosis, or mis-diagnosis, of France — a more superficial one than might have been expected from Mr. Rohatyn. He also seemed to be warning France, saying (as the president did), that "the vision Americans now have of other countries" is defined by where they stand with respect to the war on terrorism.

France's relationship to the U.S. is not at all like that of most other Europeans. Yet President Chirac's remark at Tuesday's press conference, identifying the Security Council, not the U.S. government, as the legitimate source of authority in the anti-terrorist coalition, would undoubtedly be seconded by the other European Union governments.

All of them, including France, are quite aware of the fact that the United States is running the war, and intends to remain in control of it. However they understand, as Washington may not, that this point about Security Council authority is one that could make serious trouble in the future. The U.S. needs the coalition, but the coalition depends on the Security Council.

Moreover, all of the Europeans really do see the European Union as an alternative to the United States, contrary to what Felix Rohatyn and other Americans think. They see it as offering ways of life different from the American way, for nations with distinct histories, and cultures different from those of the U.S., running market economies with different standards, social emphases, and social protections than in the U.S.

They don't see why this kind of Europe can't be a partner at the same time that it is an alternative. The French, being pessimists, are skeptical as to whether the U.S. really wants partners. They conclude that it's necessary to struggle to defend the European vision of society and international order. That is the difference between them and the other Europeans.

November 15, 2001 — It was a famous victory, even if was not the victory wanted, Osama bin Laden being still at large.

Victory over the Taliban nonetheless will do. It has made wonderfully evident that the Islamic fundamentalism that has so obsessed Washington, and had so pernicious an influence on people and governments in the Moslem world, is a phantom. It was blown away by the first serious attack made upon it.

Its reality proved, in Afghanistan, to be a mask for the power conflict among tribal and ethnic interests, manipulated by the Pakistan military intelligence service in order to advance the Kashmir struggle and provide Pakistan with what was expected to be a secure frontier. Theirs was a reckless plan, which now has recoiled on Pakistan's fundamentalists.

Assuming that fugitive Taliban power in the south of the country continues to disintegrate, as tribes rally to causes with a more promising future than Osama bin Laden, and assuming that international efforts to establish and supervise a workable coalition of forces to govern in Kabul are successful, the affair can finish with large and positive consequences. It could begin the end of the Islamic fundamentalist threat to international stability.

It could replace Washington's Manichean formulation of war against evil, which by definition can never be won, with real victories: restored Afghan state and society, and new practical defenses against residual terrorist gestures by what remains of the al Qaeda organization and those who would emulate it....

Popular repudiation of the Taliban government demonstrates that Islamic fundamentalism is fragile because it lacks intellectual and political substance. It is incapable of providing constructive answers to the demands of society (as Iran has also been painfully discovering).

This lesson inevitably will cool the attractions of fundamentalism elsewhere in the Moslem world. The Taliban government was supposed to express the deepest beliefs and ambitions of the Afghan people. The people, with rejoicing and relief, repudiated it once its military bluff was called.

The Mullah Omar's tribal allies melted away, and he was left with little more than the Arab and Pakistani recruits to the Talibans' messianic message.

Similarly, the reputation of Osama bin Laden as evil mastermind of a global network of agents challenging and humiliating the United States, has come tumbling down.

Now he can be seen as a megalomaniac fugitive, leader of a utopian sect, abandoned by the Pashtun tribes who had given him refuge, and had used him as he had used them.

It must be said that his reputation was greatest in the United States, promoted by both Clinton and Bush administrations, as if evil geniuses were as essential to the intellectual formulation of American foreign policy as they are to the scenarios of James Bond movies.

The gross exaggerations of the American government, in attributing to him global subversive powers, explains in part why the Trade Towers and Pentagon attacks were such traumatic events for Americans: they were taken as demonstrations that it was all true!

Administration officials and the policy community nonetheless relentlessly went on, speculating on where al Qaeda would strike next, repeatedly issuing and debating warnings against unspecified and unspecifiable new terrors. Now Osama bin Laden, the re-imagined Dr. No, the reanimated Dr. Fu Manchu, the new Yellow Peril, is seen shaking his fists and promising the destruction of the United States itself — while fleeing for his life.

What has happened greatly clears the air. Or it should. Fundamentalism is a delusion, which solves none of the real problems of the Islamic world. Nothing but good can come from the sight of the people of Kabul welcoming Americans as liberators.

The risk, for the United States, is that the victory may be thrown away. It must be understood in Washington that victory lies in the fact that the Afghans see themselves as liberated.

It was not a victory for bombing. Bombing discredited the Taliban military challenge, but the fundamental reason victory was possible was that the Taliban themselves had squandered the position they once held as nationalists, defenders of peace and integrity in Afghanistan.

They turned themselves into oppressors. They invited into the country the al Qaeda Arabs and the Pakistani agents who exploited the Afghan people. By doing so they prepared the victory that has been collected by the coalition Washington formed. It remains a fragile victory.

November 20, 2001 — It is possible to be optimistic, if prudently so, about the damaging consequences the Talibans' humiliating defeat will have for the reputation and influence of the Islamic fundamentalist movement elsewhere in the Moslem world.

Osama bin Laden's followers succeeded in bringing down the World Trade towers in New York and attacking the Pentagon, but in Afghanistan, where it counts, the rout of the Talibans, their allies and protectors, was greeted with popular rejoicing. Not even the Talibans' Pashtun constituency would fight for them, or for him.

Looking to the future, the important question is what this victory will do to the United States, which, unlike Islamic fundamentalists of any stripe, has global power and conceives itself as possessing a global destiny.

It is an important question because, even before September 11, an important American debate was under way between those who believe that the United States, at the peak of its power, should impose what they expect to become a Pax Americana, and other Americans who believe that such an undertaking would prove a rash and dangerous over-reaching.

The latter are often attacked as liberals, afraid to use power, but actually are deeply conservative. There is a crucial difference between the American so-called neo-conservatives, ascendant in this administration, and dictionary conservatives, disposed "to preserve what is established; opposed to change... adhering to sound principles...."

36

The latter by definition are skeptical about foreign policies intended to engineer vast changes in international society. They regard a radical program for overthrowing named regimes in the Islamic world, and installing American client-governments, as an invitation to very large troubles.

The neo-conservatives have a program for what they describe as "Phase Two" of the war against terrorism. Their national candidates for overthrow are the present governments of Iran, Iraq, Saudi Arabia, Somalia, Libya and Sudan.

Some neo-conservatives even imply that the U.S. government is disseminating "disinformation" when the FBI profiles the sender of the anthrax letters as more likely an American crank murderer rather than an al Qaeda terrorist working under Iraq's influence. They say this steers U.S. public opinion away from making new attacks on guilty Moslem states.

The Bush Administration actually has been remarkably restrained, given the pressure it is under from such individuals within its own ranks, as well as from what must be called the War Party in press and the Congress.

In part this follows from the lack of realism in such recommendations. Secondary administration figures, such as Douglas J. Feith, the undersecretary of defense for policy, recommend that the United States fight terrorism "at the wholesale level," "compelling" those who don't voluntarily comply with American demands concerning terrorist complicities. More sensible figures ask what actually would come from politico-military interventions in still other Moslem countries.

The problems of succession for such regimes are insoluble by foreigners, as Afghanistan at the present moment vividly demonstrates (and as George Bush's father grasped at the time of the Gulf War).

The warlords who before the Talibans took power had given Afghanistan 20 years of death and chaos now are telling the UN, foreign troops, foreign journalists, and the international aid agencies to get out of their country. They are unwanted.

If the warlords have their way, it is quite possible that the Taliban will soon be back. The last condition of that country could yet prove worse than its first. And all we need is Iraq, Saudi Arabia, Iran, Somalia, Libya and Sudan in similar condition.

America's success in Afghanistan feeds the ambition to escalate, nourishing the illusion that there is a final defeat to be inflicted on evil, with a happy ever-after. De-escalation is what rather is needed.

It is needed for another realistic reason: to preserve the domestic health of American society. The war against evil has, since September 11, given the United States effective elimination of habeas corpus for foreigners illegally in the country. It seems about to give it military courts of exception, by which the United States unilaterally assumes a right to seize any non-U.S. person anywhere, try him or her before U.S. military judges, and if so-judged, execute the prisoner.

The war against terrorism has produced all but unprecedented governmental censorship — with equally unprecedented, and virtually unquestioning, acquiescence on the part of journalists and news organizations formerly jealous of their constitutionally-guaranteed position as the nation's Fourth Estate.

Notwithstanding this, there is not going to be a Pax Americana. The reason is that the American people are not imperialists, do not imagine themselves imperialists, and lack the ruthlessness to impose and maintain an empire.

If they don't themselves realize that now, or their representatives in Washington fail to do so, they will all, as in Vietnam, discover the truth the hard way.

Paris, December 11, 2001 — The response and long-term remedy for Islamic fundamentalism proposed by nearly every Western commentator and official is a big and cathartic dose of modernization: globalization, democratization, women's liberation, secular education, rural electrification, lots of computers and a market economy — and all that only for starters.

Yet the leading figures in the terrorist movement that brought down the New York Trade Towers and attacked the Pentagon, overturning the complacency by which Americans lived before September 11, were, for the most part, from the most modernized strata of the two most modern countries in the Middle East.

The extended bin Laden family is one of the best-educated, richest, most widely traveled and best-connected families in Saudi Arabia. It is in business with the Bush family in Washington. Its members are investors in the Carlyle Group, which is, politically, the most powerful operation in Washington, nearly every one of its members a former Republican administration official.

Osama bin Laden's al Qaeda lieutenants have included Egyptian professional men and Arab intellectuals. The men who carried out the attacks in the United States were westernized mid-level technical people. If modernization is the answer, why did all they commit the acts that launched the war against terrorism?

Today's Islamic radicalism began as an eighteenth century modernizing movement. It is an important force today because, as Ira M. Lapidus, an American historian of Islam, has written (in a 1983 University of California policy paper, "Contemporary Islamic Movements in Historical Perspective"), its leaders "mobilize the religious yearning for salvation and project it into modern politics. The revival embodies a totalistic and utopian dream of a perfected human condition — not only in private morals, but in political life, not in the next world, but in this one."

Until the 1940s, Islam was deeply conservative in social and political views, accepting the world as it was, without deep questioning of the material and political circumstances in which Moslems lived.

"While traditional religious beliefs were grounded in the hope of salvation in the world to come, the revival forms of political Islam demand fulfillment in the here and now." The revival started when the Saudi tribal family allied itself with the reformist movement we know today as the Wahhabi, which eventually took over most of Arabia, including the holy cities of Mecca and Medina.

The Saudi patrician and would-be world revolutionary, Osama bin Laden, came out of a radical tradition that began as a religious movement nearly three centuries ago but became politicized by European imperialism.

The foreigners were proselytizing Christians and condemned certain Moslem practices as immoral. Fundamentalist violence against British imperialism first broke out in what then were the Indian Northwest Frontier Provinces — today the frontier provinces and tribal areas of Pakistan, bordering Afghanistan. The Pashtun people were involved, who make up the vast majority of today's Taliban.

Islamic radicalism is dangerous to the Islamic people themselves because it is going nowhere. It is incapable of reforms that would allow the Moslem people to cope with the political and economic pressures of modern international society. That was the Taliban's failure.

It is dangerous to the West because it gives an apocalyptic religious interpretation to what fundamentally is political conflict.

That is why recent developments in the Palestinian-Israeli conflict are alarming. The collapse of the Taliban in Afghanistan and the popular joy that greeted their defeat were dramatic demonstrations to the rest of the Islamic world of how insubstantial — and in power, how unpopular — the radical movement really is.

It was a moment of great importance for modernizing reformers in the Moslem world who aim at a discriminating assimilation and adaptation of the good things modern technology and modern political culture can offer to Islamic civilization today.

At exactly this moment, the United States seems to have endorsed Israel in what appears to be an attempt to destroy the Palestine Liberation Authority, leaving Hamas — the radical Islamic terrorist movement that wants to destroy Israel — as the only surviving force for Palestinian liberation.

The Palestinian Authority is a hapless and indeed hopeless force today, with an incompetent leader. However, since the Oslo talks more than a decade ago, it has been the only Palestinian group willing to negotiate with Israel to find a way by which the two peoples can share historic Palestine and Jerusalem, and coexist.

It represents rational, secular Arab nationalism, with Christian as well as Islamic origins, with which the West not only can deal but has been dealing, from Oslo until last winter's collapse of the Camp David negotiations.

If it is destroyed, the message to the Islamic world will be that the United States prefers terrorist Moslem enemies to rational Arab reformers. It is a message that validates what the Islamic radicals have said since the beginning.

December 20, 2001 — The problem in looking for decisive solutions to political problems — even when the ambition is less apocalyptic than President George W. Bush's ambition to conquer evil — is that the effort invariably opens up new, usually more complex and possibly more frightening possibilities.

That is not a counsel for passivity. Action is necessary to solve problems. Slavery was solved by a war. It is arguable that the American South would have abandoned slavery of its white population's own consciousness of slavery's evil before, or soon after, the twentieth century began. But war settled the matter (while opening up Jim Crow's style of oppression, lasting until the 1960s, or beyond).

The issue of Hitler was solved by a war. Had it been different, and he had won the second world war, it nonetheless is arguable that Nazi Germany would have ended the way the Soviet Union ended, well short of the thousand-year Third Reich Hitler had promised.

We are talking about balancing evils, which unfortunately is what you do in political decisions, commonly presented in the United States in terms of virtue confronting iniquity.

40

It is obvious that Washington's Afghanistan victory is as yet unsatis-factory, in that Osama bin Laden and the other principal leaders of al Qaeda have not been brought to justice.

The oppressive and reactionary Taliban government has been shattered, but that was incidental to what Mr. Bush set out to do, serving as the focus for what he otherwise was not in a position to do. The war on Afghanistan was a means to an end — a desirable end, even though thousands of Afghanis who believed in the Taliban's version of Islamic religion have died under the American bombardments.

But few would contest that Afghanistan has been defeated at a heavily destabilizing cost to it and to Pakistan. The latter's army, the most important institution in the state, was deeply involved with both the Taliban and with those other activists — "terrorists" — who are struggling to make Muslim Kashmir, governed by Hindu India since Indian independence, into either an independent nation or a part of Pakistan....

India was long ostracized by Washington because of the irksome moralism of its Cold War neutrality but, since September 11, has been warmly courted by the United States and is itself pleased to identify the violence in Kashmir as still another manifestation of the terrorism the Bush administration promises to stamp out.

Israel is taking advantage of the post-September 11 atmosphere to try to force a final settlement, or surrender, onto the Palestinians, again with destabi-lizing effect internationally, including, in a very serious way, reducing European public support for the United States.

Ariel Sharon is a great promoter of violence as the solution to problems, with, however, a discouraging record of actual success in problem-solving. There are close observers of the situation in Israel who believe that Mr. Sharon will be gone long before Yasser Arafat loses his grip on Palestinian power.

The United States is challenging in very dramatic and decisive ways those around the world that hate or fear it and want it harmed. It is doing this in the proclaimed interest of international order and stability. Mr. Bush wants to establish that new world order which his father announced but failed to deliver.

What does not seem adequately understood in Washington is that a foreign policy of active military interventionism destabilizes; it does not sta-bilize. Pakistan was as stable as it has ever been when all of this erupted. The India-China-Pakistan relationship was fairly stable.

Now the stability is gone, and rumors abound of U.S. interventions in the Horn of Africa, Sudan, in Asia. The big current debate in Washington is whether (or how) the United States should have another go at toppling Saddam Hussein.

Administration policy might be characterized as intent on surgically removing the cancers of violence and radicalism that destabilize international relations today. Unfortunately, the cancer metastasized some time ago. Some say in the Garden of Eden. There is not much the United States can do about that.

PART TWO

December 2001 to March 2002: From Ambiguous Victory in Afghanistan to the Campaign Promoting an Attack on Iraq

Paris, December 27, 2001 — The world is about to begin the second year of the new century in a situation without precedent in history. One country enjoys a position of military and economic power without rival.

Even without its nuclear power — itself effectively invulnerable, deployed under and above the oceans, in hardened missile bases inside the United States, soon, if Washington's ambitions are gratified, to be actively defended by anti-missile systems — the United States is in a position to inflict anything from disarming violence on any other nation on earth, to damage that would cause an enemy's complete social and economic breakdown.

No nation has ever before possessed such power. Universal empire has always been an impulse in western civilization, formed in the belief in the universal imperium of God.

This was not true for most other societies. China and Japan, for example, held themselves to be exclusive and superior, surrounded by lesser peoples, incapable of either challenging or emulating them.

The West took for granted that it provided the universal norm, and that the rest of the world had to eventually conform to western standards and beliefs.

This western conviction of superiority began in religion, in which both Jews and Christians claimed exclusive truth, and then was taken over by the Enlightenment West, which considered its ideas of human rights, individual freedom, and (in the American formulation) the individual pursuit of happiness, the true human values, which all the rest would sooner or later accept.

The Francis Fukuyama argument about history was a naïve expression of this: history had come to an end, he said, because the last rival to American liberal values, the Soviet Union, had collapsed, and the time had arrived when American values would inevitably be accepted universally.

The widespread popularity of American popular entertainment, mass culture, and lifestyle fashions and fads seemed to lend weight to this idea. The Americanization of global popular culture seemed to presage a coming Americanization of political and economic values all over the world.

Americans themselves have always believed in the universality of American values and ideas. They have also believed that American society represents what is best and most advanced in the world. Hence the common, but complacent and profoundly mistaken notion many people have that the reason others "hate America" is simply that they envy the U.S.

However MacDonalds and popular movies do not add up to a civilization. The American political system has been fundamentally altered in recent years by the Supreme Court holding more than a decade ago that ruled that spending money to elect candidates and to promote private and commercial interests is a form of constitutionally protected free speech.

This ruling changed the United States from a democracy of individuals, in principle politically equal to one another, into a plutocracy in which elections and the decisions of government tend to be determined by money. This is a change that seems, as a matter of practical politics, all but irreversible.

It bears on the fundamental issue of the next two to three decades (or more): how will the United States employ the amazing power domination it now exercises over the rest of the world?

The "universal empires" of the past were all trivial in scale by comparison. The Greek empire was Mediterranean, and the Roman the Mediterranean world plus Germany, France and Britain.

Spain and Portugal divided up the non-western world in the fifteenth century, and in the "Golden" sixteenth century Spain became the first empire on which "the sun never set." Britain's later empire was greater, but France's was not.

However they all shaped the history not only of their time but of times up to our own day by their cultural power. Latin America, North America, the Philippines, India, Pakistan, Indochina, Burma, Persia, Egypt, much of the rest of the Middle East as well as of the Maghreb and sub-Saharan Africa, are what they are today because of the cultural influence of the western colonizers — even in the places where the colonizers were violently expelled: nearly always because of westernized ideas of human rights and national independence).

Paris, January 3, 2002 — Two developments of the past few weeks, and indeed the past few days, are certain to be crucial to the evolution of international balance in the twenty-first century.

First was the spectacular military performance in Afghanistan of U.S. high-technology air attacks, directed by special forces on the ground, supporting local forces prepared to act as American auxiliaries. The U.S. air and ground components of this combination will always be available. The willing auxiliaries will not, which is the flaw in the combination.

Second was the overwhelming success of the launch of Europe's new currency, the euro. Its introduction evoked enthusiasm even from the Germans, supposed still to begrudge their loss of the deutsche mark. The currency markets immediately marked it up against the dollar and yen.

The importance of the euro, however, lies less in the caprices of the markets than in what the currency's initial success implies about the future and the nature of Europe's further unification. Once again, "Europe" has demonstrated that it progresses through economic change, rather than political initiative.

The specific quality of European development is that economic decisions and actions have always been indispensable to the producing of political progress. They even have substituted for it, which is likely to prove the case with the euro, since during the same weeks that led up to the currency change-over, the European Union nations were again demonstrating the EU's inconsequence in world political and military affairs.

The consensus among EU governments and European public opinion today is more hostile than it has ever been to Israeli and U.S. policies toward the Palestinians.

The European Union nonetheless is incapable of expressing a serious protest against what has amounted to the termination of a political process that, since Norway's courageous convocation of secret Israeli-PLO talks a decade ago, has promised eventual Palestinian autonomy.

Europe's embarrassing demand for a military role in the U.S. intervention in Afghanistan proved unwanted by Washington, all but useless in the event and largely ignored. The affair was entirely dominated by Washington's decisions and American military force.

British Prime Minister Tony Blair, acting independently, did his best to inject a European influence into Washington's decisions by means of tireless promotion and travel to boost support for President George Bush. His efforts were politically welcome, but his hope to influence Washington was wasted effort....

A precarious new world balance is emerging. The United States is preoccupied with military power, political leadership and domination of world financial markets.

It had all three even before September 11, but the political class and the public were divided on whether such assets should be exploited to make the United States into an informal empire or globally hegemonic political power, with all of the ostensible rewards, but also the griefs, which history provides to those with such ambitions. September 11 made the choice — or so it now seems.

The Europeans have always had political ambitions for their union, mostly expressed in terms of federation, an imprecise term whose actual definition most European officials avoided.

A foreign-affairs chief and a high representative were named to conduct a European foreign policy that never emerged, and which will certainly not be possible on matters other than elementary self-defense in a Europe expanded beyond 15 members.

But economic Europe, trading Europe, single-market Europe, single-currency Europe, industrially cooperating Europe, protectionist and subsidizing Europe, cultural exception Europe, social-protections Europe, health-care Europe, anti-trust Europe, anti-"dumping" Europe — and, to a certain measure, anti-globalization and anti-American Europe, all have emerged and are doing very nicely.

Where will this put us as the century advances? The only rival the United States has is Europe, and Europe is not, and will not become, a political or military power. Pressed, it could form a defensive coalition of sorts, and of course, there is latent military power in Europe's economic strength, in aggregate greater than that of the United States. The question, for which we have no answer, is how much military power will really count in the years to come.

January 8, 2002 — The war against terrorism needs to be freed of the hypocrisy, cynicism and partisan exploitation that surround it.

It began as a war against evil but turned into a war against the Taliban government in Afghanistan. You can go to war with a government, but the Pentagon cannot attack evil.

The Afghanistan war has been won, but terrorism is still at large, and not only in the persons and entourages of Osama bin Laden and the Mullah Mohammed Omar (assuming that either is still alive).

Politicians and governments worldwide have expanded the war by re-designating their own enemies as terrorists. This has been easy because Washington's definition is elastic and arbitrary. Terrorism is what bad people do.

The war now is against terrorism itself, if Washington is to be taken at its word; and this objective (ostensibly) is to be pursued in disregard of the terrorists' political causes.

Terrorism thus is identified with Kashmir's separatist guerrillas, and the Pakistani activists and government agents who have supported them. The fact that India has for a half-century occupied Muslim parts of Kashmir, where people would prefer either independence or attachment to Pakistan, is treated as if it were an irrelevance.

India is pleased to discover that the logic of Washington seems to have put the United States on India's side in this venerable politico-religious conflict. It was never there before.

Vladimir Putin has been delighted to reinterpret the Chechen war as still another front in the war against terrorism.

Ariel Sharon is an enthusiastic ally of a Bush administration that apparently has changed America's previous policy of serious support for Palestinian autonomy.

Washington is now judging the Palestinians on whether they confine themselves to nonviolence in resisting the Israeli settlers' occupation of those territories, taken in the 1967 war, which they (and international law) consider Palestinian.

Terrorism is a form of politico-military combat that deliberately attacks civilians, because the terrorists can't get at the political and military figures they really want to kill.

The Chechen nationalists fighting for separation from Russia would happily blow up President Vladimir Putin and his entourage. They have a problem with the security that surrounds him.

47

Hamas and Islamic Jihad would not kill Israeli civilians if instead they could kill Ariel Sharon and his cabinet. The Israeli government reacted with far greater ferocity to the killing last month of an Israeli cabinet minister than to any of the Palestinian extremists' recent civilian atrocities.

Another reason terrorists kill civilians is that it shocks and frightens populations and disposes them to make compromises or offer concessions to the terrorist cause. Israel finally withdrew from that part of Lebanon which it had occupied since its first invasion of that country in 1978 because, after more than two decades, the Israeli public grew weary of Hezbollah rockets from Lebanon falling on Israeli towns. They were tired of having young conscript soldiers killed in ambushes in what was supposed to be the country's security zone in Lebanon.

It is a fact of history that terrorism is the weapon oppressed populations have always employed against those they consider their oppressors, usually because it is the only weapon available.

Ask the Irish what liberated Ireland, or the Serbs what liberated Serbia from the Turks in the nineteenth century, or the Vietnamese what freed them from French colonialism.

As for war against civilians, a few decades ago you could have asked an older generation of Georgians and South Carolinians about how William Tecumseh Sherman broke the Confederacy.

In the second world war, Britain was not the first to bomb cities. But after the Blitz had been defeated, Britain made terror bombing its principal weapon against Nazi Germany from 1941 forward.

Bombing was the only way it could strike at Germany, and the heavy bombers of the period were incapable of the accuracy that would allow discrimination between industrial and civilian targets. A deliberate decision followed: to bomb civilians to destroy Germany's will to war.

The effort culminated in the great 1944-45 firestorm raids on German cities, replicated in Japan by the United States. More Japanese civilians were killed by fire-bombing Japanese cities during the summer of 1945 than were to die at Hiroshima and Nagasaki.

The second world war was a war of annihilation — the first, in Europe at least, in a thousand years, as the British military historian Michael Howard has said. "All belligerents now regarded civilians as legitimate targets." This assumption was, and continues even today, to be implicit in nuclear deterrence.

Thus we should perhaps be grateful that we today have only civilian terrorists killing other civilians, rather than the professional military of the great industrial states doing it to one another.

January 15, 2002 — The curious personal response of President George W. Bush to Vladimir Putin at their first meeting — that he felt he could see into Mr. Putin's soul and know that he was good — was followed after September 11 by a political alliance in the war against terrorism.

I say "curious" because a year ago, the expressed opinion of Condoleezza Rice, Mr. Bush's national security advisor, was that Russia continued to represent a threat to the West and, she added, particularly for the European allies of the United States.

Now Russia has become one of the European allies of the United States, at least so far as terrorism is concerned. Since Chechnya is a terrorist problem, according to Mr. Putin (he was, after all, elected president two years ago on the assurance that he was the man who would settle the problem of Chechen separatism), one can ask if the United States now is implicitly allied with Russia on Chechnya.

As reports of death squads, torture, intimidation and exemplary reprisals against noncombatants continue to arrive from Chechnya by way of Russian human rights groups, the implications of Russia's way of waging war against terrorism merit more concern in Washington than they now receive.

The Russian journal *Kommersant* quotes a military spokesman who justifies "frequent attacks on innocents" by the necessity of making "inhabitants understand that they suffer because of the activity of bandits, and [that] if they were to help us, this would stop."

The Chechen issue has also inspired Mr. Putin to quash critical reporting on the war. The independent news operations of two private Russian television stations, NTV and now TV6 (both owned by "oligarchs" at odds with the Russian president), have provoked officially inspired civil lawsuits that closed down NTV and seem about to do the same to TV6.

The space for independent or critical comment on the war now is down to a single radio station and several limited-circulation publications. Mr. Putin meanwhile uses state television to solidify his image as a strong leader and to consolidate his power. He seems to be distancing himself from associates of Boris Yeltsin, the man who plucked Mr. Putin from obscurity and sponsored his ascension to the country's highest office.

The prospect this presents — of a reconstructed authoritarian Russia with a politically subservient press and broadcast media — is not only a plausible outcome of events since the collapse of the Soviet Union, but a logical one, since the version of democracy introduced into the country after 1989 bestowed economic ruin and a criminal economy on the country, and authoritarian reform under a young and dynamic leader has obvious appeal.

If that leader sees his own interests served by collaboration with the United States in its war against Islamic terrorism, in exchange for U.S. acquiescence in his own program to restore Russian control or influence in the Caucasus, Ukraine and elsewhere in what formerly was the Soviet Union, the Bush administration may consider the trade-offs worthwhile.

That would be a mistake. Washington always tends to discount long-term interests, which in this case concern much more than human rights. The challenge posed by the current U.S. bid for power in resource-rich Central Asia, among states formerly part of the Soviet Union, makes the Putin-Bush alliance a convergence of short-term interests only. The context is long-term rivalry.

In any case, a good many democratic scruples are being pushed aside these days, in the interest of the war on terrorism. These are scruples about with whom Washington allies itself, but also scruples about the standards the United States itself has traditionally respected.

Much has already been written about the effective suspension of habeas corpus in cases concerning noncitizens of the U.S., and about the kinds of trials and punishments the administration proposes to apply to persons seized abroad by the United States or handed over to American authorities. Torture is a subject of debate.

There is also censorship. The degree of censorship applied to the war in Afghanistan is without precedent in U.S. history. No journalists were allowed to accompany operations, no officers have been allowed to offer independent accounts or background briefings even to specialized journalists, and any officer giving other than the sanitized and euphemized account of what has been going on faces severe punishment.

Secretary Donald Rumsfeld tells the press the official line with wit and intelligence, and the press writes it down. The spokesmen for the services provide a story-board account of today's war, constructed for the evening television news, preferably with a heart-warming sidebar or two, but otherwise they "don't know," "have not been informed on that," "will have to check into this" and, fundamentally, have nothing to say.

50

I am not talking about a search for scandal, failures, or military bungling. I mean simply that the public has been given no way of independently ascertaining what really has gone on. If it demands to know, it is told that it is playing the enemy's game. This may work in Russia, but surely it can't go on working in the United States.

January 24, 2002 — Denials aside, real disagreement exists between Saudi Arabia and the United States over use of the big American Air Force installation in that country and over the continuing U.S. military presence.

Some in Congress and the Pentagon are indignant that the Saudi government should have barred the United States from raiding Afghanistan from the expensive air operations center recently built at the Prince Sultan Air Base near Riyadh.

The head of the Senate Armed Services Committee, Sen. Carl Levin, a Michigan Democrat, has said that the Saudi Arabians "act as though somehow or other they're doing us a favor." He and others talk as if U.S. withdrawal would punish Saudi Arabia.

He doesn't understand that the Saudi leadership does not consider itself doing a favor, but as having been forced to accept the U.S. presence, against important political interests of its own.

The Washington view is that the United States fought the Gulf War to defend Saudi Arabia; is defending it again in the war against terrorism (even if leading terrorists are Saudi dissidents); and deserves thanks and cooperation.

The widely held Saudi view is that the United States fought the Gulf War to defend its own oil interests, put Saudi Arabia in an uncomfortable position by the way it did it, and refused to go home when the war was over.

The Saudis' awkward guests insisted on enlarging their presence (from a rotating detachment just after the Gulf War to a force of some 6,000 last year, before September 11). They are seen as interfering, directly or indirectly, in Saudi affairs, and their presence offends Muslim religious sensibilities.

The tale is a cautionary one of self-inflicted damage, the result of Pentagon expansionism, military ambition and the steadily increased power of neo-conservative hawks in a Washington now convinced that global extension of American power and control is our new Manifest Destiny. U.S. security and leadership is held to depend on worldwide military deployment.

Political and cultural factors are largely ignored but were behind the fanaticism that inspired the World Trade Center and Pentagon attacks (specifically identified as revenge for the "blasphemous" American presence near the Islamic Holy Places).

There is no value in a military deployment, meant to stabilize a region and support conservative governments, that actually destabilizes or subverts them, or which strengthens Islamic fundamentalism and wins it recruits.

This will be a recurring issue as the war against terrorism goes on. There already is trouble in the Philippines, caused by the arrival of U.S. Army Special Forces to advise the Philippine army's campaign against a Muslim separatist movement in Mindanao and neighboring islands. This group until now has mostly been in the kidnapping and ransom business, but is believed to have links to al Qaeda.

It now numbers in the hundreds, but separatist sentiment is a latent force of considerable strength throughout the Muslim region in the southern Philippines. In the country as a whole, there has been popular hostility to American military presence since the U.S. first took over the Philippines in 1898, and fought an insurrection claiming national independence that lasted two years and was bloodier and more costly than the Spanish-American war had been.

American bases were not withdrawn until nearly a century later, in the 1990s, after the Philippine constitution was amended to bar any foreign troop presence not authorized by the nation's Senate. The current U.S. deployment enjoys no such authorization.

President Gloria Macapagal approves of the American presence. Secretary of Defense Donald Rumsfeld says that the Philippine separatists are part of "a global problem we are addressing globally, not just in Afghanistan."

The United States displayed efficiency and dispatch in overturning the Taliban government in Afghanistan and breaking up the al Qaeda organization there. The efficiency resulted in part from the same unilateralism and the same indifference to the opinion of others that the Bush administration practiced pre-September 11, with respect to global warming, the United Nations, war crimes tribunals, land-mine bans and trade conflicts.

The evident assumption of Mr. Bush and Mr. Rumsfeld is that while it is agreeable to be admired and respected abroad, it is better to be feared and obeyed. There is something to be said for that opinion, but practice of such advice can end in maximized negatives rather than positives. The latest example is the treatment of the Taliban prisoners at Guantanamo.

The United States has the power to get practically anything it wants from other governments, but it paid a price for pressing Saudi Arabia to accept a permanent U.S. deployment. The deployment itself may now be forced out, or be pulled out because of Saudi restrictions on its use.

The defeat of Islamic radicalism in Afghanistan, and the popular rejoicing that followed, dealt a real blow to the notion that fundamentalism is a powerful movement with a great destiny. It would be a mistake for Washington to underestimate that victory, or permit overconfidence or arrogance to undermine it.

New York, January 29, 2002 — In New York, September 11 is still called the day that changed the world, but it's not true. The events of last September 11 changed the United States, not the world — and go on doing so.

They changed America's modern history, and the American consciousness. The rest of the world has had to live with terrorism, accommodating its shocks and demands. No other country has ever believed itself invulnerable. Among nations, only the United States possessed a conviction of invulnerability — which it lost on September 11. At the same time, an American sense of impunity was reinforced, which lies behind its unilateralist policies today.

The international controversy over the status and treatment of the prisoners at Guantanamo Bay has posed important legal and human rights issues, but it also is contributing to the definition — or redefinition — of the moral identity of America, not only in the eyes of the world, but for Americans themselves.

Common sense would say that if there is indeed a war against terrorism, as Washington has declared, then the prisoners are prisoners of that war, unless Washington is prepared to assert that its war against terrorism is in some way not a war.

The position the administration has taken is that the combatants of al Qaeda are outside the law because they carry out, or defend, terrorism. However, the combatant who places himself outside the law, as these people have done, nonetheless falls under the jurisdiction of law when he is captured and held by a nation of law.

This would seem to be true, even if the prisoners fall into one (or both) of the categories of combatants excluded from the protection of the Geneva conventions: forces that do not themselves observe the laws of war (terrorists, death squads, ethnic militias, etc.); and civilians who engage in hostilities.

The United States has claimed that because its prisoners were not uniformed members of the forces of a generally recognized government, they have no rights in international law; and as they are not American citizens and are not on American territory, they have no rights in American law, and cannot claim due process. (That an American military base on indefinite lease to the United States is not American territory, for purposes relevant to the prisoners' case, is disputable.)

The Geneva Conventions provide that if "any doubt" exists as to status of prisoners, they must be treated as prisoners of war until a "competent tribunal" decides the matter. A similar requirement is in U.S. Army regulations. Secretary of State Colin Powell and the State Department want the United States to observe the Geneva conventions.

President George W. Bush has said that his government will never "call them prisoners of war," but that he will "listen to all the legalisms."

Law, however is one thing. Something else is involved here. Vice President Richard Cheney said last Sunday that these prisoners deserve extraordinary treatment because "these are the worst of a very bad lot. They are devoted to killing millions of Americans — innocent Americans."

The President said Monday that the prisoners "are killers, these are terrorists, they know no countries. The only thing they know about country is when they find a country that's been weakened and they want to occupy it like a parasite."

From the beginning, the rhetoric of this administration has identified the enemy in terms of absolute evil, the war as expression of a metaphysical combat between good and evil, and the al Qaeda fighters and their Taliban allies as people not to be defeated, but destroyed.

During the early stages of the Afghanistan fighting, Secretary of Defense Rumsfeld indicated in so many words that he wanted no prisoners taken. (He later backed off, as such a recommendation is illegal in international law. The Allies hanged Japanese officers in 1945 for not taking prisoners.)

The shackled, hooded, kneeling prisoners photographed at Guantanamo Bay seemed a fulfillment of this rhetoric of dehumanization and demonization. That is why the photo was such a shock to international opinion. It seemed a photo from a penal colony.

The administration's unwillingness to concede the prisoners a legitimate status in international law has reinforced the notion that the United States considers them less than human.

Dehumanization of the enemy nearly always occurs in war and is responsible for its worst atrocities. The Nazis identified Jews as an enemy to be exterminated, and told their soldiers that Poles and Russians were subhuman peoples

54

to be treated as slaves. That lay behind the terrible crimes committed during the war on the Eastern Front.

Dehumanization is the force that drives ethnic killing. During the war in Bosnia, Radovan Karadjic never tired of telling his visitors that Bosnian Muslims were no better than animals.

In democratic countries it is the responsibility of leaders to govern their language. National policy must respect the humane values defended in their constitutions, and treat even enemies with the dispassion required in a nation that has willingly submitted itself to the regime of law. Otherwise the democracy betrays itself.

New York, January 31, 2002 — If President George W. Bush's State of the Union assurances concerning the war on terrorism are to be believed, the United States has its work cut out for it.

Iran, Iraq and North Korea, the "axis of evil," are either to have their governments replaced or be deprived of their ability to construct weapons of mass destruction. (White House officials add that there are no immediate plans for military action.)

The surviving al Qaeda camps "in at least a dozen countries" are to be destroyed, and "tens of thousands" of potential terrorists neutralized. By implication, other Islamic fundamentalist groups that have been in contact with al Qaeda, including elements of the secessionist movement active in the southern Philippines are to be suppressed.

American Special Forces soldiers have already joined the Philippine army forces engaged in the latter effort, as Americans did early in the twentieth century, when the "Moros" ("Moors," as the Spaniards had called them) were already fighting for separation from what had become the American Philippines.

The war on terror has only started, according to Mr. Bush. The peril it confronts "draws closer and closer." "The world's most dangerous regimes" will not be allowed "to threaten us with the world's most destructive weapons," according to the president. He repeats that permanent mobilization of the American nation is required, as well as greatly increased military spending.

The alarmist language of the State of the Union address and its identification of the enemy in metaphysical, rather than political, terms (the enemy is "evil," not a band of terrorists, or several foreign governments) were consistent with all that the White House already has said about the terrorist threat.

Once again, though, the old "rogue nations" issue aside, the president has persisted in giving to the Islamists what they presumably most want: admission of American vulnerability, and recognition of themselves as America's greatest challenge.

He did so despite the fact that the al Qaeda movement is much less well financed and organizationally powerful than, say, organized crime or international drug cartels. It is a movement of self-sustaining and, it seems, largely self-financed individuals, motivated by religious conviction and by hatred of the United States as the embodiment of what they see as contagious moral and political corruption.

It has many sympathizers in the Islamic world. But the United States is the most powerful nation in history, and as Paul W. Schroeder, a University of Illinois historian, writes in the current issue of the conservative Washington quarterly, *The National Interest*, "by endlessly rehearsing the magnitude of the [September 11] loss, labeling it a national tragedy, disaster and even catastrophe, by hyperventilating in denouncing the action and demanding vengeance, and by panicking at the fear of still more attacks, [Americans] have encouraged the terrorists to believe that the United States really can be badly hurt by actions like these."

And this, of course, is not in the least true. The September 11 attacks took many lives but did no serious objective damage to the United States, as a nation. The attacks challenged American self-esteem, but the damage thereby done to the country was self-inflicted. Americans in another time were supposed to be a people that made cool, laconic and collected responses to crises — as New York firemen still do.

The al Qaeda group, moreover, what remains of it, is surely shaken and dispersed by the American raids and bombing attacks on its leadership in Afghanistan, the Taliban defeat and by the mobilization of police and intelligence services nearly everywhere to penetrate and neutralize its networks and arrest its members.

The American public nonetheless seems to accept the White House assessment of terrorist power and the rogue-nation threat. A Wall Street Journal/NBC News poll released just before the State of the Union address indicated that 64 percent of the public thinks that most of the military action in the war against terrorism is yet to come.

Thus, Mr. Bush's call for sustained mobilization and his administration's demand for new military spending finds a receptive audience. Yet there was never this level of anxiety in the United States about future events, or fear of enemy attack, during the Cold War, or during the Korean or Vietnam wars, and certainly not during World War II. Seventy percent favor military intervention in Somalia and the Philippines, half favor military action against Iraq, and 80 percent think another "major" terrorist attack on the United States is likely.

There is something fake, or faintly Orwellian, in Washington's insistence that the threat is immense, mobilization must be permanent, the military budget vastly increased, civil liberties restricted and critics attacked as unpatriotic. All this is provoked by concern about a few thousand politico-religious fanatics clever enough to realize that airliners are also flying bombs.

There is something wrong here. The threat and the reaction don't match. The greed and corruption that went into the Enron affair is a bigger threat to the United States than Osama bin Laden will ever be, and I would think most Americans, in their hearts, know it.

Paris, February 7, 2002 — The Year of Sharon has been the most violent year in two decades for Israel, and the most futile year in the whole of its history.

Moral recoil from Ariel Sharon's policies has cracked the edifice of Israeli public solidarity. Until this week, this recoil seemed still a marginal phenomenon, but Prime Minister Sharon's popular support now, for the first time, has fallen below 50 percent. His first year in office has failed to provide either the peace or the restored security he promised.

There has been a revolt by a number of army reservists, mostly from elite combat units, who have announced their refusal to return to occupation duties in the Palestinian territories seized in the 1967 war. They characterize these duties as "ruling, expelling, starving and humiliating an entire people."

A commission of Israel's national bar association has condemned the government's policy of "eliminating" Palestinian leaders held to be implicated in terrorism. The commission described this as illegal imposition, without trial, of the death penalty. It warned the officials and soldiers involved that they risked prosecution outside Israel for war crimes.

The legal counselor of the Ministry of Foreign Affairs acknowledges that he has advised military and internal security officers of their risk of arrest in certain European countries, as happened to General Augusto Pinochet, Chile's former dictator, seized in Britain in 1998 after Spanish prosecutors requested his trial on charges of crimes against humanity.

These signs of public unease recall the moral crisis within the Israeli Defense Forces that contributed to Israel's retreat from the occupation of Lebanon, following its 1982 invasion of that country. That invasion was also intended by Ariel Sharon to destroy the Palestinian liberation movement.

The Israeli public, traumatized by the suicide bomb attacks of Hamas and Islamic Jihad, nonetheless has difficulty seeing a convincing alternative to the Sharon government's policy of assassinations, home destructions, and attacks on Palestinian security forces, meant to destroy PLO authority.

The Palestine movement itself is splitting, with violent clashes between factions maneuvering to succeed Yasser Arafat, if he is killed or driven away, and between the PLO and the extremist groups determined to go on with the suicide bombing campaign.

The latter are Mr. Sharon's political, as well as moral, counterparts, determined to destroy compromise between the sides, fanatically pursuing the unrealizable goal of expelling Israel from its U.N.-recognized 1949 borders.

The prime minister's reciprocal ambition, acknowledged to the Israeli press (although not often to the international press), is to gain the rest of the Palestinian territories for Israel — or as much of them as possible. His current policy is meant to destroy any possibility of a viable independent Palestinian state.

He believes that the Palestinians, under this pressure, will eventually abandon the PLO and resign themselves to existence under Israeli domination, and to a steady expansion of Israeli settlements.

He would prefer that the Palestinians found life in these circumstances so miserable and hopeless that they would choose on their own initiative to leave — for Jordan, or another Arab state, where, of course, they are unwanted.

The United States now is irrelevant, so far as any solution is concerned. Israeli policy is Bush administration policy. Mr. Sharon has successfully exploited the September 11 terrorist attacks to de-legitimize Yasser Arafat, in Bush administration eyes, and indeed to de-legitimate the Palestinian struggle itself, as if it were simply a terrorist affair rather than a national independence movement.

Initiatives inside Israel and from Israel's friends abroad to restore some movement to the blocked peace negotiations have included proposals for imposed solutions, working through the U.N. Security Council.

The United Nations recognized the state of Israel in its 1949 borders but has never legally relinquished its territorial authority over the rest of what previously had been the British Mandate of Palestine. But this and other possible outside initiatives will be thwarted so long as the United States gives unqualified support to Mr. Sharon, as now is the case.

Some Israelis want unilateral withdrawal from some Palestinian territories and from Gaza, and separation of the two communities by physical barriers. However it is objected that this might merely displace the violence, not end it. It would also contradict the Sharon government's essentially expansionist policy.

The most poignant proposal has come in an open letter in the mainstream newspaper *Ha'aretz*, addressed to Foreign Minister Shimon Peres by one of his former associates in government, Gideon Levy, now a leading journalist.

Mr. Levy accuses Mr. Peres of dissociating himself from the Sharon government in private while serving it in public. He insists that Mr. Peres is not, as he claims, playing a moderating role by staying in Mr. Sharon's cabinet, but has rather made himself accomplice in what Mr. Levy calls "a government of crime."

He appeals to Mr. Peres, now the most eminent survivor in Israeli public life of the leaders who founded and shaped the nation, to resign from the Sharon government (before he is forced out). He asks him to "tell the world what is (perhaps) in your heart." Despair is written into that sentence, in the parenthesis.

February 14, 2002 — America's celebrity intellectuals are now signing manifestos endorsing the war on terrorism. We already have committees to name and shame university teachers critical of American policy.

Yet there actually has not been that much dissent. There are those opposed to the virtual abandonment of the Palestinians to the mercies of Ariel Sharon, but that debate preceded September 11.

There are honorable pacifist critics of any military action, and others who say that Islamic militancy comes out of poverty and American-tolerated misgovernment in the Islamic world. The latter include figures from the established left and also from the RAND Corporation, which recommends striking "at the social, economic and political roots of terrorism."

But it would be hard to collect many names of influential people who are against a war on terrorism, even if they are critical of how this one has been conducted.

In their case, the questions are practical ones: How? Where? With what methods? What about the feasibility of what you specifically intend to do? What is the situation you think you are going to have when you are finished?

These are basic questions to answer before going to any war. But then war ordinarily is a simple (or not-so-simple) affair of defeating the military forces of an identified enemy government.

That is why the war against terror (or as President George W. Bush prefers to call it, the war against evil) quickly turned into a war against the Taliban government of Afghanistan. That made it a tangible assignment the United States Army, Air Force, Navy and Marine Corps could carry out — with a little help from the CIA.

No one yet is asking very loudly where are the defeated terrorists. Some may be in cages at Guantanamo Bay, but Osama bin Laden and major identified leaders of the al Qaeda organization are either in mass graves in Afghanistan or still alive, presumably looking for trouble.

According to some officials in Washington, thousands of terrorists still roam the world, and the United States is in greater danger than it ever was before, even during the cold war. If that is so, where is our victory? Liberating the Afghans from their government was a happy result of the war against terrorism, but that certainly was not America's policy before September 11.

Once again, it is to simplify matters that the war against terrorism now is apparently turning into a war against Iraq (and Iran), whose actual connection with anti-U.S. terrorism in recent years has been pretty remote: money for Hamas and Islamic Jihad, no doubt, but theirs are not the people flying airplanes into New York skyscrapers.

The United States could certainly attack and defeat the armed forces of either, or both, rout their governments, install successors, et cetera. How easily it could do it can be discussed, and who will be doing the real fighting (the Kurds, London or Paris-based exile groups, the U.S. Army itself?), but that is part of the feasibility problem, not the policy problem.

Finally, what do you have when you are finished? The Project on Defense Alternatives in Cambridge, Massachusetts, which is advised by a number of responsible figures from such impeccably patriotic organizations as RAND, the Massachusetts Institute of Technology and the Brookings Institution, has just issued a "critical appraisal" of the Afghanistan operation and what it accomplished.

It finds that most al Qaeda facilities and forces in Afghanistan had to do with the civil war there, while most of its terrorist capabilities were and remain elsewhere. While the war drove the Taliban from power and uprooted the al Qaeda organization there, "substantial humanitarian costs were associated with these outcomes." "Stability costs" must be added to those, since the outcome has led to "warlordism, banditry, and (revived) opium production," and power fragmentation along ethnic and tribal lines.

"In some areas virtual anarchy prevails.... In sum: the new Afghanistan is more chaotic and less stable than the old. The task of stabilization has barely begun and remains contingent on substantial, long-term support from the outside."

The United States has no intention of leaving a long-term stabilization force in the country, and the provisional government has opposed deployment of the other foreign troops in the country beyond Kabul and its airports. President Bush's father left Saddam Hussein in power in Iraq after the Gulf War because his administration anticipated exactly these kinds of problems in a defeated Iraq. Does a U.S. military intervention leave the United States, and the world, better off than before?

The elder Bush asked the question. Many in Washington today say that doesn't matter, that what is important is to act, and the result can be forced to conform to what the U.S. wants.

The younger President Bush seems to have decided. A Defense Department circular reportedly puts a stop, as of late this month, to all regular Army and active reserve separations from service, in a long list of sensitive military specialties. Washington gossip has it that Iraq really is next, perhaps by summer.

Paris, March 5, 2002 — The Saudi Arabian Crown Prince Abdullah's peace proposal is the only positive development in the Middle Eastern tragedy in more than a year, but its prospect of success is slight, unless the Bush administration throws America's weight behind it, and that is unlikely.

To do so would reverse present U.S. policy and take President Bush into dangerous domestic political waters. However not to do so would undermine the administration's ambition to unseat Saddam Hussein, and would provocatively worsen already tense relations between the United States and Saudi Arabia.

There are powerful forces in and outside the U.S. blocking any serious new move to find a settlement, including elements in the Arab camp. The fixed policy of the Sharon government in Israel is to control and expand settlement of the territories under military occupation, the issue that has motivated the two intifadas. That it would accept withdrawal from the occupied territories is hardly imaginable.

61

The Saudi proposal is rightly criticized as offering nothing new. It proposes full recognition of Israel by all of the Arab governments, with normal political and trade relations, provided that Israel returns to its pre-1967 borders.

It is important because the Saudi Arabians have a reasonable chance of bringing the other Arabs along, provided that the United States supports their proposal.

It requires Israel to yield the territories on the West Bank and in Gaza which the country holds by virtue of military conquest in the 1967 war, and has subsequently settled, but which the international community, the United States included, has never recognized as legitimately part of Israel.

Under the proposal, Arab East Jerusalem would also have to be evacuated by Israel, unless some compromise were reached, such as condominium or joint sovereignty, or international sovereignty, all rejected by Israel in the past.

The "right of return" of Palestinian refugees whose homes were in what now is Israel would also have to be compromised, as everyone understands. The usual formula is a symbolic return of a limited number of hard cases, and compensation and resettlement elsewhere for all the rest.

Syria has already indicated its disagreement with the Abdullah proposal, and some Palestinians have always insisted that they will settle for no less than Israel's destruction. It is perfectly possible that even if the Abdullah proposal were accepted, some Palestinians would go on setting bombs.

However the political climate would be vastly changed by an agreement, and the overwhelming majority of Palestinians and Arabs elsewhere would have been given a basic interest in making the agreement work.

Today the Palestinians, even those most devoted to a peaceful settlement, automatically have an interest in violence because, historically, only violence has moved the Israelis toward compromise.

Both sides have always used violence to get what they wanted. That is why the violence will certainly continue, and undoubtedly worsen, if compromise is again rejected.

The Palestinians won't stop now; they are winning their second intifada. Their capacity to endure suffering and strike back is proving greater than the Israeli public's willingness to accept suffering and inflict punishment.

The power of the weak lies in inviting the powerful to do their worst, and to take it, drawing the powerful onto ground where they either hesitate and break, or commit moral suicide.

A year ago, disillusioned with Yasser Arafat, convinced that they had offered the Palestinians as much as they could afford to offer — possibly even more than then-Prime Minister Ehud Barak could have delivered — the Israelis were ready to listen to Ariel Sharon's promise that he could end the violence through repression.

They believed him, but he has failed, and much of the public and press have turned against him. The peace movement is again active. The army, composed of citizen-soldiers, is now experiencing a crisis, with more than 500 reserve and noncommissioned officers refusing duty in what they consider an immoral war.

The prime minister has led the country to a chaotic stalemate. His policy offers only two possible further steps, one of them materially impractical and the other something that would extinguish Israel morally.

The first is radical separation — barriers, fences, pits, perhaps even mine-fields. Some of this has begun but a total separation is neither materially nor economically feasible, certainly not for the more isolated settlements.

The other is to drive the Palestinians out of Palestine by force, otherwise known as ethnic cleansing. Some Jewish extremists want this. It is now an issue in the public debate, included as a choice in public opinion polls — as observers have noted, a first for Israeli democracy: crime against humanity as a policy option.

Nothing can be excluded. This is a war that Israel cannot win, and which divides and demoralizes the country. A forceful American intervention backing the Abdullah proposal might be the only thing that can save not only the Palestinians but Israel.

March 12, 2002 — President George W. Bush's speech on Monday, recalling the World Trade Towers and Pentagon attacks, provided a more coherent statement than we have yet had on the policy he is following.

The policy's objective and limits nonetheless remain unclear, which adds to the impression that Washington's new working assumption is the reverse of the Orwellian postulate that "war is peace," which is to say that for the United States now, or at least for the Bush administration, peace is war.

The president again raised the stakes by insisting upon the danger of "terror on a catastrophic scale" if America's enemies are not defeated, whoever and wherever they are.

He declared that the rout of al Qaeda and Taliban forces means little without a new and "sustained campaign to deny sanctuary to terrorists" in the

Philippines, Yemen, the Republic of Georgia (adjoining Chechnya), Indonesia, Somalia (of unpleasant Pentagon memory) — and unspecified "elsewheres."

Elsewhere obviously starts in Iraq, which has no established connection with al Qaeda, but whose president, Saddam Hussein, has given two Bush administrations ample motive for hatred and revenge.

However there, as with Somalia, where the U.S. army has accounts to settle, the means to be employed remain a problem, even if the United States were prepared to commit mass ground forces of its own, as in the Desert Storm campaign of 1991.

Saudi Arabia is no longer ready to accommodate an American ground build-up, and the Arab world generally is hostile to the United States' responsibility in Israel's war to crush not only Palestinian terrorism, but Palestinian national aspiration.

In justification of the largest American military budget since the Reagan administration, Mr. Bush warned of new, unprecedented and seemingly everlasting risks, although he cited only the familiar threat of "rogue nation" attack, which has been political currency in Washington for years.

Yet nothing that has happened during the past six months in Iraq or North Korea makes either more dangerous to the United States than it was before, which is to say not very dangerous. The scenario that explains what interest North Korea has in lobbing a primitive nuclear weapon, contained in a primitive missile, into Alaska (or by missing it, into the Canadian arctic) has yet to be written.

During the past six months, investigations in the United States, and the detention of thousands of foreigners illegally in the country, have not, so far as is known, produced a single "sleeper" cell or agent of al Qaeda.

The two principal suspects held in the U.S. are Richard Reid, the Briton with the shoe-bomb, and a Frenchman of Maghrebian origin thought to have been one of the original group responsible for the September 11 attacks.

Investigations by European authorities, where Islamic extremist terrorism has been a police preoccupation for a number of years, have been more successful. Connections have been discovered between individuals in Spain, Belgium, Italy, Germany and France, and organizations or individuals believed close to Osama bin Laden.

However, bin Laden himself has disappeared, possibly killed in Afghanistan, his followers there defeated and dispersed. Those of his people now held in cages at Guantanamo Bay do not seem to have yielded exploitable intelligence about the international ramifications of what Washington insists is a "catastrophic" threat.

To meet this threat, the United States government has nonetheless proposed a $48 billion increase in defense expenditures, largely in strategic weapons systems (including missile defense and three advanced fighter aircraft systems). A new series of nuclear weapons for contingency first-strike use against identified non-nuclear states is sought.

Washington proposes to lower its nuclear-use threshold, and to warehouse rather than destroy existing nuclear weapons removed from inventory, thereby jeopardizing arms reduction agreements with Russia and alarming China (and Washington's allies).

The United States has also effectively suspended habeas corpus for non-U.S. citizens in that country, and for the prisoners it is holding in Cuba and Afghanistan, for whom it also denies prisoner-of-war status.

It claims the right to seize persons of whatever nationality outside the U.S., hold them indefinitely or have them transferred, sometimes in defiance of local law or court rulings, to third countries whose intelligence services, linked to the CIA, function outside American legal constraints. That is to say, they can torture them.

None of this really fits together. The action-reaction proportions are all wrong.

This administration is making use of the September 11 tragedy to do what the neo-conservative right has wanted for a long time, which is to renounce inconvenient treaties, junk arms control, build and test nuclear weapons, attack Saddam Hussein, and abandon multilateralism, cooperation with international organizations and compromise with allies, all in order to aggrandize American international power and deal expediently with those who challenge it.

The bin Laden threat has been grossly exaggerated to justify extravagant military spending and suppress the inconveniences caused to national leadership by the rule of law and international convention and treaty.

It undoubtedly sounds cynical to say this. That is nothing by comparison with this administration's cynicism in actually doing it.

March 19, 2002 — Margaret Thatcher has a new book that will come out in April, attacking the European Union as a utopian project, a product of "the vanity of intellectuals," which inevitably will fail. She wants Britain to enter into a closer economic and political relationship with the United States.

This is no surprise; the former British prime minister has said this for years. The book, titled *Statecraft*, is more forthright than ever about Europe, from which, she says, "most of the problems the world has faced [in my lifetime] have come, in one fashion or another."

The solutions to those problems, she goes on, have come from outside Europe, from the English-speaking nations — Britain, the United States, and what used to be called Britain's "white dominions."

There is something to be said for this argument. Any American or European who survived the second world war is likely to have a positive response to the proposition that the English-speaking "Anglo-Saxon" countries saved Western civilization, even if they needed Russia to absorb, engulf and eventually pulverize Germany's eastern front armies.

There was a serious argument to be made after the second world war for English-speaking union. This was the underlying message of the four-volume *History of the English-speaking Peoples* which the half-American Winston Churchill published in the 1950s.

The barrier to this project was that the United States did not want a union on any terms that would have been acceptable to Britain.

It went out of its way to cut Britain down. The latest volume of Robert Skidelsky's biography of the economic statesman John Maynard Keynes makes painful reading for an American, as Skidelsky recounts how ruthlessly the United States stripped Britain of its remaining postwar assets, as payment for wartime U.S. assistance. The spirit was that of the isolationist senator Hiram Johnson, on the question of forgiving allied war debts after the first world war. He said: "They hired the money, didn't they?"

Then there was Suez in 1956, when the United States forced a run on sterling to compel Britain to halt its invasion of Egypt, meant to recover the Suez canal, nationalized by Egypt's president Gamal Abdal Nasser. Britain, broken, has never since done anything that might offend the United States.

The superpower wants acolytes, assistants to do the dirty work in Afghanistan and the Balkans, choristers of praise, legitimators, but it doesn't really want or need allies. Allies expect to have a say; that is bothersome, and may even become seriously annoying.

President George Bush last fall recruited a wide coalition of what he called allies to support his war against terrorism, but they already are shuffling their feet, looking elsewhere, complaining about what's being done to the Palestinians and refusing to be counted on for an attack on Iraq.

NATO, the very model of a successful modern alliance, has begun to come apart ever since it was called on actually to do military things in the Balkans. For practical military purposes, the United States has now withdrawn from NATO. Like Sheriff Gary Cooper, the U.S. walks alone.

Washington guards its influence in Brussels in order to have NATO's endorsement for its own initiatives, such as the war on terrorism, and to make sure that the European allies don't do anything that would make difficulties for the United States, such as starting a European army.

The organization has found a new political function by taking in the ex-Communist states, providing them a sense of security, and through its institutions of support and military reorganization buttressing their democratic structures. But there are other organizations to do that.

Owen Harries, the wise and, regrettably, just-retired editor of the Washington quarterly, *The National Interest*, recently said that the superpower is the one actually in danger when it spurns allies. He quoted Edmund Burke, when that eminent political thinker was warning the eighteenth-century British parliament about the risks of supreme power:

"I must fairly say, I dread our *own* ambition; I dread our being too much dreaded.... We may say that we shall not abuse this astonishing and hitherto unheard of power. But every other nation will think we shall abuse it. It is impossible but that, sooner or later, this state of things must produce a combination against us which may end in our ruin."

Such words are not much heard in the Washington of George W. Bush and his warrior administration, and I doubt that Mrs. Thatcher, a warrior woman if one there ever was, would be saying quite that to the president, if Britain acquired a new political link to the United States (to create what some elderly and nostalgic, or young and romantic, Britons would call the "Anglosphere").

Owen Harries quotes another wise man, this one Israeli (Israel once had wise men, although there seem few left), Abba Eban, the former foreign minister. His advice might be weighed in Britain's choice concerning the current imbalance between Europe and America. Eban said, "The alternative to a balance of power is an imbalance of power, which has usually provoked wars, and has never consolidated peace."

March 21, 2002 — The frustrations and backlashes to a global war against evil are beginning to be felt in Washington.

The war against terrorism was originally conceived as a series of decisive military and intelligence-service blows against the al Qaeda network and other terrorist groups.

Yet "terrorism" was the enemy, which is merely an unscrupulous method of war that is employed by people lacking the arsenal that would allow them to attack armies, or defend against armies. Osama bin Laden has no bombers, so his people use box-cutters and hijacked airliners. The Palestinians use human bombs because they don't have tanks.

The distinguishing mark of terrorism is that it deliberately strikes civilians, either significant or symbolic individuals, or enemy civilians en masse.

A war against terrorism, in principle, would have engaged the United States to fight the revived Italian Red Brigade, which cold-bloodedly murdered a noted economic advisor to the Italian Ministry of Labor last week. It would demand tracking down those people in Chicago who are mailing death threats to certain Serbian liberals in Sarajevo who defended liberal democracy and opposed ethnic cleansing in Bosnia during the 1991-95 war.

Those threats, incidentally, have been signed "The Association Gavrilo Princip" (he is the man who assassinated the Hapsburg Crown Prince in 1914, touching off the first world war), just to remind us that terrorism was not invented last year.

Osama bin Laden is not an original. He merely made himself known in an original way last September. He thereby gave the United States and the Bush administration an urgent global mission, previously lacking.... However, it has not produced the decisive blow against terrorism that Washington wants. The Afghanistan intervention destroyed the Taliban government, an obscurantist religious sect defended by peasant soldiers, hardly that "determined group of killers ... who would rather die than surrender" that the president talks about.

His description does fit the "Arab" militants of al Qaeda, but their leader, Osama bin Laden, and his principal associates have vanished. The renewed battles in Afghanistan have failed to locate them, while the ordinary militants slip away.

The United States wants to move on — above all to Iraq — but is stuck in Afghanistan, which has fallen into pieces, with quarreling warlords and rampant banditry, in need of the "nation-building" the Bush administration has forsworn....The United States is eager to attack Iraq, but Vice President Dick Cheney found last week that America's Arab interlocutors are unanimous in saying that Iraq must not be invaded until the Palestinian conflict stops.

The administration still refuses to recognize that violence in Palestine and Israel concerns fundamental national aspirations on both sides. It is useless to call for Middle East cease-fires and still more talks. The two sides have talked since the first Oslo meetings a decade ago, and have arrived at today's quasi-war.

For the Palestinians to call off their uprising against Israel would be to abandon their national cause. They are unwilling to do so because they have nothing else. This Israeli government cannot halt the violence because it will not yield on the issues of the colonies and Jerusalem....

When the American public endorsed Mr. Bush's declaration of war on terrorism, it was not asked for a declaration of war on Iraq, nor was it voting for the occupation of Afghanistan and indefinite new troop deployments in Southeast Asia, the Caucasus and Palestine.

It didn't quite know what this "war" meant. Things were, as they remain, abstract. President Bush prefers to give a metaphysical designation to the war against terrorism. He calls it the war against evil and consistently has returned to that formulation, despite the uneasiness the expression has inspired in secular quarters.

Some observers have suggested that the president, who describes himself as a born-again Protestant Christian, means this expression literally, and sees the war in the context of ideas held in some Protestant fundamentalist circles in the United States: that the September 11 attacks, together with the accomplished return of the Jews to Jerusalem, are signs of those Last Days described in the Book of Revelations and in certain books of the Hebrew scriptures. This is a matter, I think, which the president should clarify.

PART THREE

FROM APRIL TO AUGUST 2002: THE DECISION TO TRANSFORM THE MIDDLE EAST THROUGH WAR

Paris, April 4, 2002 — Ever since Communism collapsed, the notion has been put about in Washington that the United States should exercise its unrivaled power to form an empire.

This is held to be the way to bring stability to international society and solve the problems of terrorism, rogue nations, weapons of mass destruction and so forth.

We are told (by a writer in Washington's *Weekly Standard*), that troubled lands "cry out for enlightened foreign administration." It seems that, to some in Washington, empire seems a career opportunity. To the ordinary American, I suspect, it simply looks like trouble....

Advocates of American empire are usually seduced by the notion that Washington's imperial authority would be accepted as positive, and that the empire would therefore be consensual.

This idea rests on the uninformed assumption that the United States is generally seen abroad as a benevolent or "righteous" nation, offering others readily recognized benefits of democracy, globalized trade and industry, and human rights — that, as Mr. Bush put it, they know out there "how good we are."

Mr. Powell should explain to the president, and to others in Washington who share that view, that even in allied Europe, disposed for more than 50 years to think well of the United States, Washington's exercise of power is now seen as a serious international problem.

American unilateralism, which mostly used to be a containable matter of Congressional egos and petulance, has now been turned into a foreign policy by the Bush administration.

This undermines the fragile structure of international law and convention built up during the last three centuries, to which the United States made important contributions in the past.

International law, since the seventeenth century, has rested on two principles: national sovereignty and the legal equality of nations, both of which Washington ignores whenever convenient.

American political, economic and cultural influence is not generally stabilizing. It uproots stable structures, for good or for ill. It means to do so. The Bush administration is a crusading government. The purpose of American economic policy and trade pressure is to destroy national regulation and make radical changes in how other economies function.

There seem to be many in the Bush administration who are convinced that military force used with sufficient ruthlessness can impose desirable political solutions. They think that Israeli Prime Minister Ariel Sharon has been doing a good job.

Brute force can solve political problems, but it usually creates others. A solution for Israel's problem would be to drive all of the Palestinians out of Gaza and the Palestinian territories into neighboring countries. One nonetheless doubts that is the road to lasting peace in the Middle East.

The statesman Edmund Burke once remarked that no greater calamity can befall a nation than to break with its past. The American past has been the rule of law, constitutional order, a free press, suspicion of power politics, avoidance of foreign entanglements and even, hard as it may be to believe today, hostility to standing armies.

The country's one serious adventure into imperialism, in 1898, proved not very satisfactory, and 18 years after fighting a war to acquire the Philippines, Congress promised the islands independence.

The Cold War broke American from that past. For a long time, one could think that when the Cold War ended the United States would return to its better past. It hasn't happened.

The proposals for empire offered today are not intellectually serious, but they are significant. The American political class and bureaucracy have become addicted to international power. They want more. The question is whether the people will follow.

Ditchley Park, England, April 16, 2002 — For many years, the conferences held in the great house here, near Oxford, have been dedicated to Anglo-American understanding.

The focus has widened in recent years, with enlarged participation from all parts of the world, including old enemies. But the central concern has remained international cooperation in the tradition of the alliance formed in and after the second world war to secure international peace and freedom.

The latest conference here, last weekend, was therefore noteworthy because the issue that forced itself upon all the participants was mounting division between the United States and its allies.

The war against terrorism has opened this breach. None of America's friends and allies is against a war against terrorism, but the United States has failed to provide an explanation of how this war is to be conducted and won that convinces or reassures them that Washington understands the risks of what it is doing.

George W. Bush has said that this is a war against evil, which makes Europeans and others uncomfortable: By definition, a war against evil is unlimited and interminable. There is no exit strategy there.

One European participant observed that even if the definition of the enemy is narrowed down from "evil" to the political and military phenomenon of terrorism — violence against innocent persons to extort political concessions — such a war is not one where a zero-sum, win-loss strategy is possible. Terrorism can only be contained, since it is something any number of different people and movements can use in any number of political causes.

However, this kind of argument makes many Americans think Europe today just doesn't get it. To quote an American who was *not* at the conference, the political writer Walter Russell Mead, in *The Atlantic Monthly*, "Americans just don't trust Europe's political judgment.

"Appeasement," he continued, "is [Europe's] second nature. Europeans have never met [a dictator, from Hitler to Saddam Hussein] they didn't think could be softened up by concessions."

Those Americans at Ditchley who are close to the Bush administration insisted that the next step in the war against terrorism must be an attack on Iraq.

They argued that the United States must unseat Saddam Hussein because only then will the other states of the Middle East (and troublesome states elsewhere) understand that Washington means to destroy its enemies wherever they are, and will do so whether the Europeans, or "the international community," like it or not.

Victory over Saddam, Mr. Bush's supporters say, will unlock everything. Other Arabs will see that nothing can be gained from supporting terrorism. They will turn against al Qaeda, and will tell the Palestinians to put away the bombs, arrest the bombers and take whatever settlement Israel offers.

A new pro-American government in Iraq will demonstrate the virtues of democracy and the advantages of cooperation with the United States. People elsewhere in the Arab world will demand democratic, free-market, pro-American governments. When they get them, the misery, injustices and resentment that nourish extremism and terrorism will dry up.

On the evidence of what the Bush administration's supporters say, such is the structure of the wishful thinking, not to say fantasy, which underpins the tough-talking and supposedly tough-minded policy of the Pentagon and White House hawks who are running the war on terrorism.

Allies who can't believe their story, and oppose an attack on Iraq, were twice reminded by Americans at the conference that the United States does not need allies. They suggested that if NATO fails to support the United States on Iraq it might find itself out of business.

A European participant noted that Russia has already said to some Europeans that America, Russia and Israel make up a new anti-terrorism alliance. Each is really fighting terrorists — al Qaeda, the Chechen separatists, the Palestinian bombers.

The Europeans are outsiders, making ineffectual objections, proposing political negotiation to deal with "the roots of the problem."

Whatever Washington may think about this new, if putative, alliance with Russia and Israel, the old allies don't like it. The split at Ditchley was not just U.S.-European. A Canadian bluntly addressed the following message to the Americans in the room: The United States has no international mandate to make war on Iraq, he said. If it does so, it will have no allies.

To the Bush administration's defenders, that warning seemed to present no problem. It was possible to think that it even offered them a welcome release from onerous constraints.

What was plain was that the United States and its old Cold War allies no longer have a shared view of the world and its dangers.

The Europeans have been dealing with home-grown and international terrorism for years, and they don't think the threat today is new in anything but scale. They think that launching a new war against Iraq will make things worse, not better.

The Bush administration obviously disagrees. The disagreement is the most important that has existed between the allies since NATO began. It could destroy NATO. Worse than that, it could set the former allies against one another.

Paris, May 2, 2002 — The agreement reached between Saudi Arabian Crown Prince Abdullah bin Abdulaziz and President George Bush at their Texas meeting is described by Bush administration figures as setting "a division of labor" by the two governments in making Middle Eastern peace.

A division of labor, however, is meaningless without agreement on the objective. The White House says Prince Abdullah's recent peace proposal is "the only positive development that's taken place in the last year, and something that the president is moving quickly to take advantage of." Acceptance of the Abdullah plan therefore seems to be what the two men are after.

The Abdullah proposal offers Arab recognition and full normalization with Israel in exchange for full Israeli withdrawal from the illegally occupied Palestinian territories and East Jerusalem, and recognition of a sovereign Palestinian state.

Support for this offer makes quite a change from what the White House was saying two weeks ago. President Bush then was congratulating Prime Minister Ariel Sharon on his "war against terrorism" — despite Mr. Sharon's defiance of the president's demands that Israel withdraw from Palestinian territory. The president was refusing to deal with Yasser Arafat.

Now, according to explanations given the press, the United States has committed itself to convincing Mr. Sharon that "the psychology of violence" has to be broken.

Mr. Bush has his work cut out for him. Mr. Sharon's policy in Lebanon and the Palestinian territories has always been based upon manipulation of the psychology of violence, in the interest of Israel's perceived national interests.

Mr. Sharon was an original sponsor of colonization of the Palestinian territories seized in the 1967 war. He makes no secret of his belief that Israel should further expand, and has, in the last few days, once again stated his determination never to yield a single Israeli settlement to the Palestinians.

Prince Abdullah has an equivalent problem. He will travel to the Arab capitals to organize a meeting of Arab leaders with Yasser Arafat, meant to convince the latter that a negotiated peace even now is possible, and that more terrorist violence serves no purpose. Yet the Abdullah plan, at least in its original form, requires Israel to give up all of the illegal settlements.

So what does the prince and the president's "division of labor" actually mean? No Sharon government is going to give up the colonies. No Arab government is going to accept the Abdullah plan unless some Israeli government — Mr. Sharon's, or a successor's — does give them up.

Where does George W. Bush now stand? According to *The New York Times*, Mr. Bush's father, Vice President Richard Cheney and other figures from the first Bush administration with interests in Saudi oil and Arab arms purchases, have told the younger Mr. Bush where American business and political interests really lie.

Has the president been convinced? Mr. Sharon certainly doesn't think so. He obviously believes the Texas agreement was the start of just another interminable series of talks he can stall and afford to ignore.

He has electoral reasons for thinking that President Bush is unlikely to change his policy. The president's father made trouble for Israel when it was disclosed that American money was being spent on colonies constructed on what legally is Palestinian land, and his father was not re-elected.

Colony construction continues even now, despite the Oslo, Camp David and Wye Plantation agreements, all of which postulated eventual Israeli withdrawal from all or most of the disputed territories.

Those agreements neglected to specifically forbid new seizures of Palestinian land and colony construction. Successive Israeli governments therefore went on doing what they had been doing, with the intention of creating "irreversible facts" on the ground.

There now are more than 400,000 Israelis living in fortified towns and settlements built in defiance of international law governing territories under military occupation.

Finally, what does Crown Prince Abdullah think about what really will result from the Texas meeting? He cannot go to other Arab capitals only to be made to appear a fool. The United States cannot really afford that, either.

76

The younger President Bush's recent and all but unconditional support for Ariel Sharon has rested in part on political calculation. And there is a new source of popular support for Israel: A large fraction of the Protestant fundamentalist electorate in the U.S. now supports Israel for religious reasons.

The Old Testament records God's promise that the Jewish people will return to Jerusalem. In the Protestant fundamentalist reading, Israel's existence today is fulfillment of that promise, so that American support for the Jewish state is a divine obligation.

However, an irony exists in this, which seems unrecognized in an era of considerable religious ignorance among Israelis, as well as among many American Jewish supporters of Israel.

The American Protestant fundamentalist interpretation of the Scriptures sees the Jewish return to Jerusalem as initiating those Last Days foreseen in the Christian New Testament, which will culminate in the return, as the true Messiah, of the Christians' Jesus of Nazareth.

May 9, 2002 — American policy spokesmen (such as Under Secretary of State Marc Grossman, at The Hague in April) insist that NATO is "the key to the security policy of the United States" and must be expanded, "open to all of the democracies from the Baltic to the Black Sea."

At the same time, the Bush administration displays indifference to the transatlantic alliance and hostility toward the European allies, whom it sees as reluctant combatants in "the war on terrorism."

NATO and Russia are reportedly on the verge of an agreement, to be signed at the end of this month, that would give Moscow a substantial voice in alliance policy, as well as what the Russians see as reestablished influence in global affairs.

The former members of the Warsaw Pact who are new candidates for NATO membership see in this a limit on who else will get into the alliance, and as weakening the security they have expected from NATO membership.

Some are now asking if the European Union might offer a better security guarantee than NATO, since Washington and Moscow have become allies in the war on terrorism. Until now, NATO membership was what they wanted most.

The transatlantic relationship is on the brink of a big change. Today the most powerful policymakers in the White House and at the Pentagon have lost interest in NATO. NATO is history (subject only to artificial respiration should an Article 5 vote be needed).

NATO's utility to Washington ended in the difficulties the allies made during the Kosovo bombing campaign — chiefly, but not only, the French. An obituary for the alliance has not been published because some things don't have to be published. Unnecessary embarrassment is thereby avoided. West Europeans (France the exception, and Britain occasionally so) have spent more than 50 years as contented followers of the United States. That now is ending. The Bush administration, without intending it, is forcing Europe to consider its alternatives.

Recent initiatives to give the European Union the means for independent security and foreign policies have until now been treated without urgency, and without serious funding.

As a Belgian diplomat recently remarked, Europe's internal discussions of a potential role as a serious world power have "been meant to keep the French quiet, while never, for one instant, seriously examining the question."

The Bush administration is forcing the Europeans to be serious. The strangest part of this is that the ones doing it are the same people whose practical interest is to keep the West Europeans as docile allies, content with a Europe that remains an economic giant and political dwarf. These are the Americans who are angering, and even frightening, the Europeans.

Britain's Chris Patten, who is the European Union's commissioner for external relations, said it all in *The Washington Post* other day, when he declared that he now finds in Washington a view of the Europeans (in this case, on the Mideast issue) that amounts to "a mad and grotesque assault on reasoned debate."

Philippe Grasset, a French analyst and longtime critic of the U.S., argues that a dozen (or even more) allied European countries have for 54 years been content with a de facto abandonment of national sovereignty in security matters. This became taken for granted in West European political culture.

These countries had a notion of a post-Cold War European future as eventually something like a big Switzerland, cooperating with the United States in the United Nations and other multilateral international institutions, building a new world order of international law and cooperation.

The people now in power in the Bush administration have forced them to see that this is not likely to be what Europe's future is going to be about. Characterized, Grasset says, "by irresponsibility and arrogance, ready to sacrifice everything to a vanity which amounts to an astonishing political phenomenon," these Bush administration leaders have succeeded in undermining America's best friends in Europe. Atlanticism in the Dutch or Norwegian style now is discredited: There is no one listening at the other end.

By repudiating arms control treaties and international law conventions it signed in the past, by its conduct in the Middle East, by resuming the nuclear first-use option — the list of unilateralist policy choices is familiar by now — Washington has brutally recalled to Europeans that the world is run by force and intimidation, and that those who want to survive had better have political and military power equivalent to Europe's economic weight.

It is a paradox that this administration would so casually undermine the advantages and influence in transatlantic relations the Cold War has given the United States. Instead, it is radicalizing Europe.

It is alienating those who have been America's closest friends, making them once again think about the world responsibilities Europe's economic power imposes upon European society. It is not a welcome meditation; but Grasset says, it is "a duty to history."

May 14, 2002 — The murder of the Dutch politician Pim Fortuyn has provoked unexpected candor and seriousness in the international debate on immigration and Islam, until now locked into the pieties of postmodernist value relativism and multiculturalism.

The flamboyantly homosexual Fortuyn's frank and intelligent talk about immigration ("the Netherlands are full") suddenly and unexpectedly made him an important national figure. At this writing, polls suggest that despite his murder, his party may do extremely well in the Dutch national elections that take place May 15.

He attacked the multicultural social model, which dominates politics in northern Europe and is extremely influential elsewhere, including in the United States (where the idea originated in the 1960s, as an indirect outcome of Vietnam war guilt).

That model proposes that no culture is better than any other, values are relative and that to ask immigrants to conform to the social norms and accept the values of their host society is "right-wing extremism" and an act of aggression against them and against their native culture and values.

It is largely useless to talk in generalities about the superiority or inferiority of civilizations and cultures without specifying the criteria by which the judgment is to be made.

On the other hand, it is possible, and indeed indispensable, for a community to assert the values by which it wishes to live. That is what constitutions are about, and such affirmations of rights as the American Declaration of Independence and Bill of Rights, and the French Declaration of the Rights of Man and Citizen.

In terms of the political system a given community has adopted for itself, and the human values to which it is committed, it has every right to set terms on which it is prepared to welcome and harbor immigrants.

Whatever the merits of other cultures, a nation has the right to give priority to its own historical culture and to its established values and practices. One can even argue that it has a duty to do this, since if it does not it may experience not only the violently obscurantist reaction against immigrants and "others" mobilized in France by Jean-Marie Le Pen and by the far right in other democracies, but it risks undermining its own values.

This risk should not be underestimated. International attention is focused on Europe at the moment, but Americans should not forget that the United States was a "bi-cultural" society for many years — of free men alongside chattel slaves.

Even in the twentieth century, it enforced or tolerated atrociously discriminatory practices against an "immigrant" population brought to America in chains. I grew up in that society, in the state of Georgia in the 1940s and 1950s. Those practices began seriously to change only when President Harry Truman ended racial discrimination in the military services in 1948.

The United States was not a fully democratic society until the civil rights legislation of the 1960s. Its black population still is not fully integrated socially. Its white immigrants have been a great deal more fortunate. While the founding majority was Caucasian and predominately Protestant, it was itself from "elsewhere," and for more than three centuries, the main immigrant groups that entered the United States were close enough to the existing majority to be culturally assimilable.

The new nation believed in itself with a firmness that made assimilation imperative from the viewpoint of those already installed, and desirable and advantageous for the immigrants themselves.

The same thing was true in France, the only West European country with a history of successful assimilation of large numbers of immigrants: Italians, and Russian and East European Jews, in the nineteenth century, and Poles, Spaniards, Portuguese and Asians in the twentieth.

The problem today, at least in Europe, is that immigration is mostly coming from non-Western societies, is usually racially identifiable and very often is Muslim, which, in its currently most influential versions, offers few compromises to other religions or other values.

On that, Pim Fortuyn said what no one else in the Netherlands had said: Host-country values must prevail. If Muslims wish to live in Europe, they must accept the imperatives of assimilation: secular education in state schools for their children and the interdiction of such practices as polygamy, arranged marriages and female circumcision, which contradict the values of the host country.

The only solution is that the host government disperse Islamic ghettos, do its utmost to get young immigrant men and women into meaningful work, promote higher education and professionalization among the immigrants to encourage the emergence of an assimilated Islamic middle class, and support the development of a Muslim religious leadership educated in the West.

All very simple to say, of course. But if it is not said, and done, particularly in the poisonous international climate that prevails today, of "war" on Islamic terrorism and a hate-filled war between Palestinians and Israelis, Europe's immigrant populations are going to confront governments with increasingly divisive and explosive situations.

May 16, 2002 — Vladimir Putin has played a weak hand very well. With the NATO-Russia Council agreement, announced in Reykjavik last Wednesday, he has reestablished the image, if far from the reality, of the superpower duopoly of the Cold War.

Thanks to his endorsement of Washington's war on terrorism, Putin has been made a major participant in NATO decision-making. He has converted the American perception of his war against Chechen separatism into the equivalent of Washington's war against Al Qaeda and Israel's war against Palestinian terrorists.

He pays a price that might eventually make domestic difficulties, since he has allowed the United States into the Caucasus — with U.S. troops now in Georgia — and former Soviet Central Asia, where new U.S. bases (or basing arrangements) have been agreed. Many in Russia, and in the Russian army, do not like this.

He has weakened NATO by contributing to the existing confusion over what NATO now is all about. Before, a quasi-moribund NATO, deprived of its military importance by the end of the Cold War and lacking a real justification for its continued existence, had compensated by developing some useful new political functions.

It consolidated and formalized the political transformation of the former Warsaw Pact countries. Admission of three new NATO members from Central Europe, and the grant of membership in the Partnership for Peace (leading toward full membership) to two-score others, created a climate of security in the region and provided education in democratic methods and ethics.

The prospect of NATO membership relegated certain ancient grievances of the region to the background, offering rewards for good behavior and penalties for bad behavior. European institutions and a number of nongovernmental organizations were doing the same thing in Central and Eastern Europe, also to good effect.

The Reykjavik agreement between NATO and Russia has conferred equal standing to Russia in some limited but important matters, and is seen in Washington and Moscow as completing the dismantlement of the Cold War.

To others, it is a disturbing development, suggesting to East Europeans that alliance with the West is no longer a guarantee of security. The Baltic states, Romania and Bulgaria want to join NATO because they want a NATO fence between them and Russia. Now the United States has taken down the fence.

To some in Western Europe, another old anxiety has been reawakened: that of Moscow and Washington settling big issues over the heads of everyone else. This is a baroque anxiety today, since the biggest issues are economic and nobody can leave the Europeans out of that. But it is true that to Washington, consultation with the allies has come to mean ringing them up to tell them what the U.S. has decided.

It has been made plain to the allies that membership in NATO means integration into, and contribution of resources, to an American foreign policy determined in Washington.

There is nothing wrong with that, if the allied government sees American policies as sound, and as serving its own interests, as well as those of the U.S. However it means a cession of sovereignty to the U.S.

The technology of modern war makes this clear. Lord Robertson, NATO's secretary general, like many others in Europe and in Washington, repeatedly warns that unless the Europeans "modernize" their military forces, they will become marginalized.

He is talking about the fact that American weapons increasingly function as components in highly developed and integrated electronic systems of intelligence acquisition, command and control — usually directed from a headquarters far from the battlefield. The war in Afghanistan, for example, was conducted from Florida.

Lord Robertson is saying that the Europeans should buy equipment that will integrate them into American combat systems. Britain and the Netherlands have agreed, and joined the American Joint Strike Fighter (F-35) program (although the just-elected Netherlands parliament will have to ratify the Dutch decision).

The JSF is the ultimate link in a system that connects to the U.S F-22 air-control fighters, to NATO or U.S. AWACS electronic surveillance aircraft, and ultimately to a combat control center. It is not much use outside the system.

However, as the Reykjavik agreement shows, NATO no longer has a high-technology war to fight. Thus some other European countries are angry with the Dutch for not buying European-made aircraft usable outside NATO.

When the Europeans decided to establish a common foreign and security policy they expected to cede a serious measure of sovereignty in those matters to Brussels, in the interest of greater European autonomy (vis-à-vis Russia, for example).

The United States, through NATO, is today making a separate and competitive claim on their defense and security resources, which would have the effect of reducing European autonomy.

That is the issue of the unspoken debate between the Europeans and Americans at NATO, and between Europeans and other Europeans.

May 24, 2002 — President George W. Bush is now in a Western Europe that is not really hostile toward the United States, but puzzled and a little fearful. Polls say Mr. Bush is negatively viewed by the popular majority in Germany and France — but this is transient sentiment.

Transatlantic foreign policy differences are significant, but individually they are no worse than on occasions in the past. Think of the Vietnam War, for example.

The European reaction to what it sees in the United States today is puzzlement that a nation that has a larger armed force than most of the rest of the world combined should express such insistent fear of the threat of Osama bin Laden and "rogue states." It's this fear, combined with Bush administration unilateralism, that scares them.

The warning by Vice President Dick Cheney that new attacks are "almost a certainty," Secretary of Defense Donald Rumsfeld's expressed "certainty" that terrorists will use nuclear, biological or chemical weapons against the United States and — at the Reichstag on Thursday — the president's own comparisons of the threat with Pearl Harbor, the Berlin Blockade and Hitlerism — all these sound more like avowals of fear and vulnerability than the expressions of competence and confidence formerly expected from the United States.

Italy, Germany, France, Britain and Spain have all been through this problem. Spain continues to experience assassinations and terrorist attacks by ETA, the Basque separatist organization.

The ETA has plotted to kill King Carlos and is a constant threat inside Spain, but the king does not move about the country surrounded by what, in Mr. Bush's case, seems a light-armored brigade.

The British never considered locking down government and society out of fear of the Provisional IRA during the 1970s and 1980s. After all, the IRA did its best to blow up a financial district skyscraper in London and bring it crashing down, regularly bombed other British mainland targets and murdered British officials.

Washington does not seem to understand the message it really is sending to its allies.

The transatlantic policy differences listed by Bush advisor Richard Perle in recent interviews with the European and American press begin with the disagreement over Iraq and Iran.

The Europeans think that Iraq's Saddam Hussein is a containable menace even to regional order, not to speak of the world order. They say he is like a dozen other Middle Eastern despots who have come, seen their day and gone. Between American satellite and other technical intelligence on Iraq, and the UN and other international presences in his country, not much important goes on that is not known.

In any case, the Iraq threat scenarios are un-serious. Attacks of mass destruction on the United States or Israel? What is Saddam Hussein to gain from strategically irrational attacks on these countries? He certainly shows no suicidal tendencies (quite the contrary), and neither do the military and secret police entourages that surround him.

Iran seems to most West Europeans a state on its way back toward occupying a normal place in international society. The internal struggle between Islamic rigorists and reformers goes on, but the worst weight of intolerance has lifted. Iran finances Islamic groups conducting anti-Israeli terrorism, but so does Washington's ally, Saudi Arabia. Neither Iraq nor Iran seem to the Europeans to present problems that another war will solve.

The Israel-Palestine issue is highly divisive. Needless to say, the notion that Western Europe suddenly has become anti-Semitic is propaganda (whose theme is that criticism of this Israeli government equals anti-Semitism). It is no more anti-Semitic than the United States (and has better reasons not to be; that is why the European Union has never had a Middle Eastern policy).

Europe's immigrant Muslim minorities are anti-Israeli and have been responsible for attacks on synagogues and other Jewish premises, but that should surprise no one.

The European governments and public are more sympathetic to the political claims of the Palestinians than are most Americans, which in part is a result of the wartime European experience of foreign occupation. But as Mr. Perle says, "on these dossiers the United States is not going to change its positions." The same has to be said for the West European governments, with the result that the Europeans are being forced into a degree of foreign and strategic policy consultation and coordination that a year ago would have seemed highly improbable.

One of the biggest complaints Mr. Perle and other American officials voice is that the Europeans are building their own satellite global positioning system and their own military aircraft rather than buying American. The reason is obvious. They wish to be independent.

Once again, as so often in the past — but this time without intending to do so — Washington is giving a big boost to European unification.

May 26, 2002 — President George W. Bush finished his European journey with U.S. foreign policy in deepening confusion. The crises between Pakistan and India, and Israel and the Palestinians, are slipping beyond American control. The European trip did nothing to add to the administration's credibility.

Speaking in Paris on Sunday, the American president admonished Pakistan's President Pervez Musharraf to "show results" in stopping incursions into the Indian-controlled part of Kashmir.

His demand got no better response than his angry and peremptory order in early April to General Ariel Sharon to immediately halt Israel's military offensive against the Palestinians, withdraw from the occupied territories and end the settlements.

That was simply ignored. Expansion of the settlements, terrorist attacks and retaliatory incursions and assassinations have all since resumed.

Mr. Bush's inability to control his own protégés (and financial dependents) in the war on terrorism undermines the administration's credibility. It lends weight to the accusation that U.S. policy in practice disrupts international order.

The risk of another India-Pakistan war, conceivably nuclear, is now considerable. President Musharraf's enforced cooperation with Washington's war against terrorism in Afghanistan has so destabilized him in his own country that he seems to have lost control of the extremist elements in Pakistan's army and intelligence services.

Their efforts to liberate all of Muslim Kashmir from Indian control have stoked a virulent Hindu nationalism in India, and within the government in New Delhi, which has been relying on Washington to keep Pakistan in check.

Israel has this week rejected Washington's plan to reform and integrate Palestinian security forces under CIA director George Tenet's guidance, meant to rebuild a foundation for Israeli-Palestinian peace negotiations.

This scheme was unrealistic from the start. It serves nothing to tell the Palestinians to reform a Palestinian authority that Israel has spent the last three months destroying. Negotiations would be a charade so long as Israel insists on colonizing the territories and the Palestinian terrorists insist on destroying Israel.

The administration's favored solution for the Middle East is to attack Iraq, but another generals' revolt, this one in Washington, has become the obstacle to that. While President Bush was away, the U.S. Joint Chiefs of Staff made it known that they are unanimously against a military move against Iraq this year, and harbor serious doubts that such an attack should take place at all.

In leaked stories to *The Washington Post* and other newspapers, spokesmen for the Joint Chiefs argued that it is an illusion to think that someone else, with a little American help from the air, is going to fight and defeat Saddam Hussein on behalf of the United States.

They say that American forces numbering at least 200,000 would be needed to overturn Iraq's government, requiring a lengthy buildup and bases in a region hostile to such an undertaking.

The chiefs say there is serious risk of chemical or biological weapons used in defense, and they fear high-casualty urban combat to take Baghdad. They see the political outcome uncertain at best, and at worst as producing an even more hostile successor regime in Baghdad.

Until now, the Washington policy debate has been dominated by civilian hawks in the Defense Department, promoting the idea of a painless war that would lead to pro-American forces' taking power throughout the region, turning the Middle East into what would amount to an American protectorate.

Those who really believe this — Defense Department civilians; General Wayne Downing, the White House anti-terrorism coordinator; and the neo-conservative press — have not backed down, so Mr. Bush faces a Washington politico-policy struggle bigger than any his administration has faced yet.

Nothing happened in Europe to counterbalance these negatives. The arms control and NATO agreements with Moscow were mainly successes for Vladimir Putin's foreign policy, giving him a place at NATO and, it seems, tacit American acquiescence in how he runs his war ("against terrorism") in Chechnya.

Light notes were provided by President Bush's reiteration of personal confidence in the Russian president, assured this time not by looking into Mr. Putin's soul but because Mr. and Mrs. Putin "loved their daughters."

His rather bad-tempered appearances in France with his friend "Jacques" produced faintly ironic, or possibly amused, responses from the French president, similar to those Mr. Bush had already received, if perhaps not registered, from his other great friend, Vladimir.

The president's final meeting was with still another great friend, Silvio, and other new and old great friends from the NATO countries, meeting in Prime Minister Berlusconi's travertine-painted plywood edifices, built for the occasion on a secure military air base near Rome.

There were 15,000 troops and police present, to protect NATO and President Bush from al Qaeda and the rogue nations.

Madrid, June 13, 2002 — The head of the European Union's Institute for Strategic Studies, Nicole Gnesotto, wrote recently of the European anxiety "to keep NATO just as it used to be, European Security and Defense Policy as it was to be, and America as it no longer wants to be."

One of her colleagues, Julian Lindley-French, has written that the division of labor between allies implicit in current Washington practice has rhetorical multilateralism on the political side and a cool and decisive unilateralism on the military side. "Implied therein is a division of labor that Europeans must sternly resist if they are to avoid ceding the control of the strategic agenda to the United States. It will not be in Europe's interest simply to become America's garbage collector."

The Washington position nonetheless seems to be that Europe is incapable of providing the United States with much help other than peacekeepers to replace fighters, plus foreign aid for the objects of American military intervention, as in Afghanistan today — a job that amounts to picking up the pieces, as well as the garbage.

That was the implicit message of a senior Washington figure to a Madrid conference on transatlantic relations last weekend. He said Washington is debating whether it is worth cultivating European support. The general administration opinion, he suggested, was that the European impulse is always to appease threats, and such advice is irrelevant or even a nuisance to the United States, as it carries on the war against terror.

There was no aggressiveness in what he said, merely the implied judgment that transatlantic relations now are not all that important, plus a conviction that the United States understands world problems better than do Europeans, needs no advice, and will do what should be done whatever others think.

The Europeans, playing hosts, were polite, but a little more forthrightness might have been useful to both sides. The Europeans have three problems in dealing with Washington's current policy (apart from their annoyance with American complacency).

The first problem, as the European Union foreign relations representative, Javier Solana, said when introducing the conference, is the difference between European and American views of the terrorist threat.

The Europeans generally do not believe that it is as dangerous as it is made out to be by Washington. They have nearly all dealt with their own terrorists in the past, less spectacular than al Qaeda, but more dangerous in that they came out of alienated sectors of their own societies, and were revolutionaries. Al Qaeda simply wants to hurt the United States.

Second, the Europeans don't see the same remedies. They are not enamored of the military approach, which they think tends to generate new instabilities without eliminating old ones. This already has been the case in Afghanistan, Pakistan, India and among the Muslims of the southern Philippines (not to speak of Israel's "war against terrorism").

The third problem is that the Europeans do not have the courage of their convictions. As another of the Madrid participants said, Europeans are doing their best to live without a foreign policy, since it's more comfortable that way.

They criticize the United States but nonetheless let themselves be drawn along in America's wake — complaining all the way. That is one of the main reasons the European governments and their views are not taken seriously in Washington. Only in economic matters does Europe effectively defend its own views and interests.

The failure of the European governments to be serious about building the structure and supplying the money for an independent foreign and security policy is another demonstration of this.

The overall level of European military spending continues to be very low. Only Britain and France spend more than 2 percent of GDP on defense (2.6 percent and 2.4 percent, respectively), as against a programmed 3.5 percent in the United States next year.

Several of the low-spending European countries are actually spending a significant part of their military budgets to finance American projects (the Joint Strike Fighter program), rather than on European-controlled military technology.

The policy disagreement between Americans and the European allies has been greatly deepened by the war on terrorism. The division is serious between the foreign and security policy elites of the two sides, as was clear in Madrid, but it also is growing between the European governments and the U.S., although that generally is politely hushed up.

It almost certainly is a trend that will continue, since even after the Bush administration is gone, with its particular policy obsessions, the commitments made and the imbalance of military power will continue to confirm a transatlantic drift.

This is only beginning to be faced in European political circles, since it is politically unpalatable to raise the issue. But eventually it will have to be addressed, and that will make serious difficulties for everyone.

Paris, July 2, 2002 — The Fourth of July was once, from the American boy's point of view, right behind Christmas as the very best holiday of the whole year.

Why? Because of the noise and danger. Still in bed, you heard the random *bangs!* beginning in the neighborhood. They went on until dusk, when fathers set up Roman candles and nailed the Catherine wheels to trees in the front yard, lighting thrilling displays that children rushed to from up and down the street.

But the wowsers are always among us in America and helped by the annual casualty rate — fingers gone here and there, the occasional eye — they managed to stamp out all of that. Fireworks were taken away from the children who loved them and handed over to responsible adults in locations like town stadiums, where the volume of the noise increased but the danger and joy were removed.

After that, the businessmen, who don't like floating holidays, lobbied the legislators to turn what began as patriotic exuberance into a weekend featuring Fourth of July sales; and with that the patriotism went out of the holiday, and the United States became a drabber place.

At this point the columnist must get down to his real subject, which is the question of what has happened to that American patriotism? Once confident and jubilant, now it is defensive, lugubrious and seriously paranoid.

The paranoia has been on display all week as Washington has done its best to break the international consensus supporting the International Criminal Court on war crimes that came into existence last Monday. This campaign started in the Pentagon and Congress during the Clinton administration, which initially had supported the treaty. It turned into a crusade when George W. Bush took office.

Its intensity is hard to account for in rational terms, since the probability that any American acting in an official capacity would come before the court is slight. It is well insulated against malicious political exploitation, and only individuals, not governments, are subject to indictment.

Washington nonetheless threatened this week to wreck the UN's peacekeeping apparatus if Americans were not exempted from the court's jurisdiction. It said it would veto renewal of the UN peacekeeping mission in Bosnia and bluffed that it would block UN peacekeeping overall.

To do the latter would either terminate or remove from American influence the UN peacekeepers in southern Lebanon, allowing Hezbollah to reoccupy the Israeli border. Israel's situation is obviously at the core of Washington's concern, since its settlement of the Palestinian territories is illegal in terms of UN resolutions and the relevant Geneva conventions.

Ending the UN mission in Bosnia would not automatically affect the larger peacekeeping force there, set up under NATO authority as part of the Dayton Treaty that ended the Bosnian war. Washington could veto the UN-linked NATO role in both Bosnia and Kosovo, at the price of a crisis with its NATO allies, who would probably continue under European Union rather than NATO authority. However, that would mean curtains for NATO (which some hard-liners in Washington might not regret).

This legal approach to war crimes and genocidal acts can be questioned on grounds of practicality and political realism. Making those responsible for such crimes subject to international arrest does not necessarily solve problems. In some circumstances it can make things worse.

However, most of Washington's democratic allies believe the court is an important advance in building a system of international law that already has been a valuable asset in dealing with conflicts that might otherwise have ended in war. The U.S. itself has backed the criminal prosecution of Slobodan Milosevic and others for acts committed in the Yugoslav succession wars.

The historical American response to international disorder has been to strengthen and extend international law — the country's modern policy from the first Theodore Roosevelt government to the second Clinton administration (which initially supported and signed the war crimes court treaty).

The contrary policy of the Pentagon, Congress and the Bush administration seems motivated by fear, but fear of what? Of America's allies themselves? I suppose, in a sense, that is partly the case.

The administration's implicit demand is for a totally free hand in acting internationally. To put it in other language, it wants a grant of unaccountable power. No one is going to agree to that.

Fear has been the principal theme, and the justification offered, for administration policies and public statements ever since September 11. A different America would have scorned such fear.

Indeed, a different America did. Confronting the power of the British Empire, nearing its peak in 1776, the American Declaration of Independence was an act of calm defiance. The war it provoked could easily have ended with the Declaration's signers shot, hanged or in prison. That is why they concluded their Declaration with their mutual pledge of "our lives, fortunes and sacred Honor."

Their courage and the nobility of their sentiments were what we really were celebrating with those fireworks, many years ago.

Samos, Greece, July 16, 2002 — A note of frustrated anger is now audible in European criticism of the Bush administration's foreign and economic policies.

American defiance of what Washington likes to call "the rest of the world" ...meets European objections to the administration's repudiation of arms treaties and the new international war crimes tribunal, as well as criticisms of the implausibility and contradictions in U.S. Middle East policy.... Former President Bill Clinton, who was recently on Samos for a seminar led by Greek Prime Minister Georges Papandreou, offered his own story on what went wrong in the Middle East, while suggesting that nothing went wrong with America's international economic policy on his watch, except for the odd mistake.

The most effective critic of that policy, Nobel Prize laureate Joseph Stiglitz, once an economic advisor to Mr. Clinton, had a great deal to say about the economic constraints imposed on countries like Argentina, today on the verge of economic collapse thanks to the implacable demands of the IMF for deflationary reform in an economy needing growth.

He said that the European Union should itself have intervened in the Argentine crisis, reminding Washington that in the globalized economy (of American creation), the Monroe Doctrine no longer applies. The EU could have supplied credits allowing Argentina to shift to expansionary policies and begin again to create jobs and restore growth.

To do so, however, would have meant policy confrontation with Washington, and while the Europeans are generous with criticism, their governments consider themselves powerless to challenge the United States.

There is an irony in this, since many Americans currently accuse the West Europeans of defeatism or appeasement. This supposed defeatism concerns terrorists and rogue states, which only Washington is supposed to have the courage to confront.

The U.S. critics resist the notion that Europeans generally discount the reality of a universal terrorist threat. The Europeans' defeatism actually lies in their unwillingness to say as much to the United States.

The Bush administration's case against the international criminal court, to take another example, is merely the Republican elite's rerun of the populist right's old fantasy of UN troops landing from black helicopters to impose a sinister New World Order on the United States.

As such, it is nonsense, but nonsense from which American politicians are unlikely to retreat, given the Pentagon's determination to be free from international legal and political constraints.

The Europeans nonetheless gave the U.S. the yearlong exemption from the court's jurisdiction that it demanded, notwithstanding pressures in Europe that "this time" Europe stick to its convictions and call the self-defeating U.S. bluff to veto future UN peacekeeping missions (which could be mounted, without the United States, under other international auspices).

In trade matters, Europe displays its strength. The European Commission consistently challenges the United States on trade and competition issues, and often wins. In response to recent Bush administration sanctions on steel imports, it went so far as to threaten to target reprisals against U.S. exports from Florida and other states crucial to the Republican congressional campaign this autumn. (President Bush was reportedly outraged, describing this as a "personal attack.")

At another level, however, a political and intellectual cringe still marks European policy. European officials sometimes seem to think that criticisms of U.S. policy are valid only when they come with the endorsement of an American dissenter (which is itself a version of the cringe).

Thus, Stiglitz has provoked enormous interest with his attack on the Washington economic consensus, dominant in American academic economics, as well as in the policy of the government and the U.S.-dominated international lending institutions, since the Reagan years.

He was chief economist of the World Bank and entered into dissidence, so to speak, after witnessing the application in poor countries of ideologically motivated IMF policies that frequently left them even poorer.

Argentina was the IMF's star protégé for seven years, accepting deflationary measures that tied it to an unrealistic exchange rate, producing severe unemployment, poverty, and social and political crisis. The IMF pitilessly insisted on continuing contraction.

Stiglitz thinks the Europeans would do the world much good if they could bring themselves to offer the international community independent European initiatives that provided alternatives to American unilateralism. In that way, it would be within their power to restore a measure of multilateralism to an international scene rather in need of it.

Paris, July 23, 2002 — Tension and distrust now are the most important factors in America's relations with its European allies. The initial European reaction to last September's terrorist attacks on New York and Washington — a tightening of alliance links — has been wasted.

The American press is given mild and conciliatory messages about the underlying firmness of transatlantic cooperation in the war against terrorism and the unimportance of European criticisms, but these reassurances are not borne out by conversations with European leaders or in analyses in the mainstream European press. Criticism and apprehension about the consequences of U.S. policies prevail. In private, there is consistent criticism. In public, nothing serious is said or done by the European governments, other than useless complaints that Europe is being ignored.

It might seem that Americans could therefore reasonably go on ignoring what the Europeans think or say, in the belief, borne out by experience, that European objections to U.S. policies make no difference. The Europeans will eventually fall in line. They have no real alternative.

This time, that might be a dangerously complacent conclusion because the Europeans do have alternatives, explosive ones. They could overturn the post-Cold War alignment tomorrow, and do so to their own probable political and economic profit.

They do not themselves understand their power. Few in Europe's leadership seem to grasp that if the European NATO governments and public indeed object to a U.S. attack on Iraq, as they say, they can prevent it, or at least block it for many months, while accomplishing a fundamental transformation in the Middle Eastern situation to their own advantage (and possibly that of the Israelis and Arabs, as well).

Few understand that the European Union does not have to wait until it has built up its feeble military forces in order to have an independent world policy, with independent international influence to rival that of the United States. The world today is not one in which military forces are automatically the relevant, or most effective, means of power.

This already is evident in the commercial and economic relations of Brussels with Washington. Washington cannot dismiss European corporate strength and economic competition. It is compelled to deal with the European Union as a powerful trade rival, to whom it has to make concessions.

The same thing could be accomplished in political relations if the European NATO allies, or even some of them, were to take a simple but decisive step: to reaffirm that, as its founding treaty states, NATO is an alliance of independent and politically equal countries.

They could refuse American use of NATO's European assets in an attack on Iraq, on the grounds that such an attack does not fall under the agreements on countering terrorism that produced NATO's Article Five resolution of last September.

To do this would not destroy NATO. It might even save it by re-creating in it a political equilibrium. Sooner or later, the European powers will have to deal with the consequences of U.S. unilateralism, and if the European public feels strongly about Iraq (and indeed about the Israeli-Palestine situation), now could be the best occasion to act.

The fundamental reason that NATO will not be destroyed is that the United States needs NATO more than Europe does.

This is not widely understood. NATO no longer serves to protect Europe from any threat. The threat is gone. For the Europeans, NATO is an expensive relic of the Cold War.

For the United States, NATO has to exist. Washington may be indifferent to allied opinion, or in no need of allied military support, but it has to have the European alliance because NATO provides the indispensable material and strategic infrastructure for U.S. military and strategic deployments throughout Europe, Eurasia, the Middle East and Africa.

NATO gives the United States a military presence, usually with extraterritorial privileges, in every one of the alliance member-countries, and in most of the former Warsaw Pact and former Soviet countries that are members of the Partnership for Peace.

Washington needs NATO because without NATO the United States has no legitimate claim to a say in European internal matters. Richard Holbrooke once said (to some European indignation) that the United States is a European power. So it is, so long as NATO exists.

A polite mutiny by some or all of the European NATO countries on the question of war with Iraq would certainly produce what Saddam Hussein might describe as the mother of all transatlantic rows, but in the end the United State would back down. Even this article's suggestion that there might be a European NATO mutiny on Middle Eastern issues will probably produce a row, but it will also weigh in Washington's considerations.

After such a mutiny, NATO would be a different alliance. After that, the European allies would certainly never again have reason to complain that Washington was paying no attention to them. But do the Europeans really want this? Or is it all talk?

July 25, 2002 — Since last September, the Bush administration has invoked measures unknown since the world wars and the Civil War — and others entirely unprecedented in American constitutional history — to protect the United States from terrorism....

It now wishes to "reexamine" use of the U.S. Army for civilian law enforcement, which has not occurred since the Reconstruction period following the Civil War and which, because of the abuses of that period, was forbidden by Congress in 1878. Congress was then acting in deference to the U.S. Constitution's explicit restrictions on standing armies (ignored since the Cold War began) and the exercise of military power in civilian society.

All of these extensions of centralized state power by the Bush administration are presented as necessary responses to "international terrorism."

Consider now a case study provided by Greece, which has been identified by the U.S. State Department as the country in Europe containing the greatest terrorist threat.

On June 29, in the Athens coastal suburb of Piraeus, a bomb went off, seriously injuring the man who was manipulating it. He proved to be a 40-year old painter of religious icons, the son of an Orthodox priest.

His fingerprints were those found on a car used in the 1997 murder of a Greek businessman. He was in possession of a pistol used to shoot at police officers in a 1984 robbery. Bomb-making equipment was found in his apartment.

Evidence led the police to a second apartment, rented by a man said to live with the icon painter's former wife. There, an automatic pistol was found that Scotland Yard scientific police officers believe was used in six other terrorist killings. (Scotland Yard has for two years been collaborating with the Greek anti-terrorism police.)

The bomb-maker's brother has now confessed to participating in the murders of a Greek publisher and a police officer in 1985, an industrialist in 1986, the U.S. Embassy's naval attaché in 1988 and an American army sergeant in 1991. A family friend has admitted to taking part in other robberies and bombings.

A second brother of the bomb-maker confesses to having collaborated in the 1997 businessman's murder and in the assassination, in 2000, of the British military attaché in Athens.

During the week of 14-20 July, police commandos on the Aegean island of Lipsi arrested a university professor named Alexandros Yotopoulos as he was about to board a ferry for Turkey. He has a house on the island and teaches in Paris. Two other people were arrested on a second island. Five people were imprisoned or indicted on July 21.

Police now believe that they hold most of the members of the 27-year-old terrorist group that has called itself "November 17," in reference to a suppressed student demonstration against the U.S.-supported generals' coup d'etat of 1967, which placed Greece under military dictatorship for the next seven years.

"November 17" has been responsible for 23 murders since 1975, all in a supposed struggle against "imperialism." The membership thus far would appear to have numbered something like 20 people, most of them related to one another or friends of the same family.

The group's presumed leader and theoretician (who denies this), Alexandros Yotopoulos, is the son of a prominent Trotskyist of the 1930s. He was active in the Paris student radicalism of the 1960s, remained abroad after the 1975 generals' coup and is well known in leftist circles.

The terrorist movement deemed the most dangerous in Europe thus seems to turn out to be a family affair — together with a few of their friends.

This is consistent with the record of other left-wing West European terrorist groups in Italy, Germany, France and elsewhere: usually small groups of people brought together by circumstances, school experience, and ideology.

The Greek story is a minor one in the international press, and not a story at all in the American press outside metropolitan centers.

That is too bad, because it could teach Americans something about terrorism as it really exists, with its real activists and in its real dimensions. The lesson is to have a sense of proportion about terrorism. If you don't have that, you, and not the terrorists, may become the problem.

July 30, 2002 — A new and reassuring metaphor has been introduced into the transatlantic dialogue, portraying Europe as enjoying a "Kantian paradise" made possible by the United States's ordering of a Hobbesian world.

Europe, by virtue of its wartime and postwar experience, is said to have established "a post-historial paradise of peace and relative prosperity, the realization of (the German philosopher Immanuel) Kant's 'perpetual peace.'"

This benign achievement causes West Europeans to recoil from the use of force, and to see international problems generally as open to rational and negotiated solutions.

My quotation, and the argument, are from Robert Kagan of the Carnegie Endowment in Washington, whose widely promoted views have been reprinted in a number of foreign journals and are having a marked influence on how West Europeans see their own society.

Mr. Kagan goes on to say that Europeans can enjoy this happy condition because a sober and illusion-free United States patrols the frontiers, beyond which lies the Hobbesian world where lions and tigers prowl, and good intentions unaccompanied by power can prove fatal.

An attraction of the metaphor is that it compliments both societies to which the argument is addressed. The Europeans are congratulated on having put their bad past behind them (while reminded that it was American intervention in two world wars that rescued them, and American Cold War power that spared them Soviet domination).

They also are congratulated on wishing to deal with the conflicts and problems beyond Europe with dialogue and persuasion. One day, they are reassured, that might even be practical. It is their "mission civilisatrice" to try to make that ambition come true.

Meanwhile — in the world as it is, as Mr. Kagan continues — international order is maintained by an unsentimental United States, too wise to indulge illusions about dialogue and compromise in dealing with international society's thugs, dictators, rogue governments and terrorists.

Mr. Kagan was also an early promoter, in 1996, of the proposition that as circumstances have placed the United States in a position of world hegemony, this "hegemony must be actively maintained, just as it was actively obtained. ... Any lessening of that influence will allow others to play a larger part in shaping the world to suit *their* needs."

He collaborated then with William Kristol, the neo-conservative editor and advocate of American foreign policy unilateralism who has probably been the most important single outside influence on the George W. Bush administration.

In 2000, the two observed that American hegemony is not only to American benefit, but that of the world, since the United States "does not pursue a narrow, selfish definition of its national interest ... and infuses its foreign policy with an unusually high degree of morality."

This is not an argument to which all will assent. One can make a better argument that American policies today are frequently the cause of international disorder and destabilization, and that they are more often driven by domestic advantage than by altruism.

Currently, Washington is debating whether or not to attack or invade Iraq in order to overthrow and replace that country's unsavory government. This cannot possibly promote stability in the Middle East in the short term, or in the longer run, other than by resort to a forecast — which most specialists would classify as amateurish wishful thinking — that Saddam Hussein's overthrow would cause democratic governments to spring up in his country and throughout the region. Why?

A second Washington debate is whether to make a unprovoked attack on Iran to destroy a nuclear power reactor being built there with Russian assistance, under inspection by the UN International Atomic Energy Agency, within the terms of the Nuclear Nonproliferation Treaty, of which Iran is a signatory.

It is again impossible to interpret such an action as promoting international order, or to justify it other than by way of a highly speculative scenario of Iranian nuclear attack on a neighboring country or on the United States.

No other government in the world would support such an action, other than Israel's. Israel would do so not because it expected to be attacked by Iran, but because it (not unreasonably) opposes any nuclear capacity in the hands of any Islamic government.

The Bush administration's policy of providing virtually unqualified support — out of essentially domestic political motives — to Israel's policies in the Occupied Territories and Gaza is a self-evident source of potential regional disorder, as every government in the Near and Middle East and the Maghreb, from Turkey to Morocco, has already advised Washington.

The argument that the United States today protects international society from Hobbesian disorder is untrue. Washington acts as Mr. Kagan in 1996 urged it to act, to protect a hegemonic position that serves its political and economic interests, and its perceived security.

There is indeed a Hobbesian world out there. It is one in which the United States is a determined and self-interested player, not noticeably inhibited by its "unusually high degree" of national morality.

Paris, August 8, 2002 — George W. Bush is talking himself into a position where he will have to go to war against Iraq, even though there is no convincing argument that war would be good for the United States, or even good for Mr. Bush.

The military are certainly not convinced that war is a good idea. The U.S. Joint Chiefs of Staff have made that clear through a series of leaks to the press. They are wary of a war whose objectives — beyond Saddam Hussein's overthrow — remain murky, and for whose aftermath no serious policy exists.

Generals, of course, are always reluctant to go to war. They know what Hitler knew, who said that every war "is like opening a door into a darkened room. One never knows what is hidden in the darkness." Soldiers pay for what may be behind that door.

Generals are against war, but amateurs are for it. Who among the neo-conservative polemicists and op-ed writers baying for war against Saddam has personally spilled blood, or seen it spilled, or even heard shots fired in anger?

Few were anyplace but in an office, a graduate school (or grade school) or a stateside National Guard billet during the Vietnam War. The president himself, thanks to his father's friends, was flying a National Guard fighter to defend the State of Texas against the Viet Cong.

The leading hawks in the administration made their records as Defense Department bureaucrats. Donald Rumsfeld was a peacetime naval flyer, but the only administration heavyweight who has actually fought in a war is Colin Powell, and he is the Bush administration's leading dove.

The hawks' scenarios of rebuilding a defeated Iraq (or Iran, and now Saudi Arabia) — "just as we rebuilt a democratic Germany and Japan after the second world war" reek of amateurism and ignorance of what actually went on then — and during the war — in Germany and Japan.

That coven of hawks, the Defense Department's Policy Board, presided over by Richard Perle, last week was briefed by the hitherto unknown Laurent Murawiec of the Rand Corporation. He told them that Saudi Arabia is America's enemy, fosters terrorism "at every level in the terror chain," is "the kernel of evil, the prime mover, the most dangerous opponent" of the U.S. in the Middle East.

He recommended that the U.S. issue an ultimatum to the Saudi government to "stop all anti-U.S. and anti-Israeli statements in the country" — a preposterous demand — or see its oil fields and overseas financial assets "targeted," which would seem to mean seized by the United States.

Henry Kissinger, the intelligent member of the Policy Board, was the only one to demur, refusing to speak of the Saudi Arabians as strategic adversaries.

Law doesn't come much into amateur discussions since it is taken for granted that the United States — given (as the president said) "how good we are" — is justified in doing pretty much as it pleases. This administration has consistently insisted on exemption from international law and refuses the inconvenient constraints of treaties signed under previous administrations....It seems to regard the United States as exempt from the laws of war and from the traditional norms governing just and unjust war.

These have only philosophical or moral authority, but were taken seriously in American government as recently as the 1950s and 1960s in policy debates over nuclear war.

The norms of just war rest on the principle of proportionality in the use of violence, and ask not only whether the war is politically justified, but whether the harm it will do is proportionate to the good that can reasonably be achieved.

Is there an alternative this war? Have all of the alternative courses for achieving the goal been exhausted? Is war the sole and necessary means to a just goal? What is the disposition of those conducting the war: to do good with a minimum of harm? Or to aggrandize their own and the nation's power and standing at the expense of the lives or legitimate claims of others?

The Rand Corporation used to wonder about such things. It would be much better for Rand's reputation as an intellectually responsible organization to send briefers on just war to Washington, rather than promoters of aggressive war and international illegality.

However, a measure of consolation for what the Bush people are up to can be sought in what Walter Lippmann once wrote: "A policy is bound to fail which deliberately violates our pledges and our principles, our treaties and our laws. The American conscience is a reality."

August 20, 2002 — The death in Baghdad of the Palestinian terrorist Abu Nidal conveys another lesson generally neglected in today's American war against terrorism.

The lesson is that Middle Eastern terrorism has been around for a long time and has been worse in the past than it is today. It has never been "defeated." Americans did not notice, because they were rarely the victims. Americans noticed Al Qaeda because Osama bin Laden made them notice last September 11, and he declares the United States his enemy.

For Abu Nidal, there were two enemies: Israel and the Palestinian leaders who were prepared to consider a peaceful settlement with Israel. The current violence in Israel and the Palestinian territories has been an appalling form of war between two defined national entities, the Palestinians and the Israelis, with the two sides using the weapons available to them, high tech on the Israeli side, suicide on the Palestinian.

Abu Nidal's organization, in contrast, practiced terror for power and profit. His Fatah Revolutionary Council killed or wounded nearly a thousand people in 20 countries between 1973 and 1994. Had he thought of crashing airplanes into office towers and found the people to do it, he undoubtedly would have killed many more than Al Qaeda has done. His seeming obsession was the destruction of Israel. His actions, overall, tended to suit Israel's tactical interests.

Some in the Arab world accused him of cynical secret collaboration with Israel, contributing to the subversion of the Palestine Liberation Organization and providing a pretext for Israel's invasion of Lebanon in 1982 (in an unsuccessful effort to destroy that organization, which then had its headquarters there).

Israel's creation had ruined his father and family, before 1948 one of the richest and most successful in the old British Mandated Palestine. His father was said to have controlled 10 percent of pre-1948 Palestine's produce exports to Europe. The family's agricultural properties were expropriated by Israel.

He joined Yasser Arafat's Fatah. After the 1973 Yom Kippur War, when Israel had been shocked by its initial defeats in simultaneous Egyptian and Syrian invasions, Arafat gave his first indication of possible compromise with the Israelis. Abu Nidal broke with him. He began killing those PLO officials who approached the Israelis about peace.

He was responsible for the murders of PLO representatives in London, Brussels and Rome. His people killed the PLO delegate to the Socialist International (who was Arafat's link to the Israeli peace movement) and attacked Arafat deputies and associates in the organization's exile headquarters in Tunis. Some credit Abu Nidal's attacks on PLO moderates as having disrupted and seriously, if not fatally, delayed Palestinian implementation of the peace program launched in Oslo in 1993.

He also believed in indiscriminate terror. His organization attacked passengers on a Greek tourist ship, worshippers at Sabbath services in a Turkish synagogue and the passengers on a TWA flight from Israel to Athens in 1986. It destroyed a Pan Am flight at Rome airport in 1973 and a TWA airliner over the Aegean in 1974, and hijacked an Egyptian airliner to Malta in 1985 and a Pan American flight at Karachi airport in 1986. In 1982, his militants bombed a well-known Jewish restaurant in Paris. In 1985, on the same day and at the same hour, they machine-gunned crowds at El Al counters in Rome and Vienna.

Some in the Middle East concluded that he was a psychopath, a victim of a paranoia that eventually caused him to murder some 150 of his own followers, suspected of dissidence. He was sentenced in absentia to death in Italy and was wanted by courts or investigators in the United States, Britain and France. The PLO condemned him to death.

His presence in Iraq has been one reason given by the United States for calling that nation a "rogue state." The State Department once described his group as "the most dangerous terrorist organization in existence." However as Washington for years considered him mainly Israel's problem, no "war" or international mobilization was launched to stop him. He has been quiet for the last 10 years, either forced into silence by his host, Saddam Hussein, or too sick or too abandoned by followers to go on.

Now he is dead, a suicide according to initial Palestinian reports. If so, it was suicide by "multiple gunshot wounds." Possibly Mossad got him. Possibly Saddam Hussein decided that he was an inconvenience. But other than his enemies, few even remembered him during the last years before he died. However in his day he did a lot of harm and was a big man — like Osama bin Laden today.

August 27, 2002 — It is hard to judge whether the generational split on the Iraq issue — between Republicans who governed under the first President George Bush and those in Washington today — is more likely to block a war or speed its coming.

The young George Bush and his neo-conservative advisors and cheerleaders want the war, but opposition is widening and solidifying, in public opinion, as well as within the Republican party.

It is possible that the administration will feel compelled to go to war while it can. Gallup poll findings released Friday say that only 20 percent of Americans support a U.S. attack made without allies.

By now, the public has also taken note that members of the war party and their main backers in the press seem, without exception, to have arranged to be elsewhere while the last serious fighting was done, in Vietnam.

The "chicken-hawk" issue is not simple demagogy. It justifies asking if those planning this war are serious, and if they know what they are doing. "Sweet is war," wrote Erasmus, "to those who know it not."

James Baker, formerly the senior President Bush's secretary of state, is the latest from the father's administration to tell that president's son that while fighting against "rogues like Saddam ... is an important foreign policy priority for America," there are some conditions to be met.

The United States must have allies. To have allies, it must respect international law. UN Security Council backing is needed for an attack. This means a new UN demand that Saddam admit inspectors, with time for him to react (or even accept).

Next, the Palestine problem has to be out of the way before attacking Saddam. That requires an end to Palestinian suicide bombings, Israeli withdrawal to last September's positions and an immediate end to Israeli settlement activity.

Therefore Mr. Baker's actual message to the younger Bush is that the United States can't go to war, either now or in the near future. These conditions have not been met, and the last of them possibly cannot be met.

A Palestine-Israel truce or settlement is impossible without the United States abandoning the policy of unqualified support for Israel that the younger Mr. Bush has followed since he came into office.

Until now, the hawks have simply insisted that war is necessary because Saddam Hussein is a murderous and dangerous despot, and because the world would be better off without him. Few disagree with the description, but many disagree with the proposition, since there are many such figures in the world and the Bush administration coexists comfortably with most of them.

The only occasion I can recall when Washington found the sordid character of a foreign leader sufficient to justify a war was in 1989, when George Bush senior invaded Panama to seize General Manuel Noriega.

That operation, not the Gulf War, seems to be what the younger President Bush wants to repeat. However, Iraq is bigger, and presumably better defended than Panama, and the political context is explosively different.

In any case, the justification for a war has nothing to do with a war's feasibility. Overturning Saddam Hussein could simultaneously be a good cause and a bad idea.

It is reasonable to argue that the foreseen human casualties, and the foreseeable international political backlash to a unilateral U.S. attack on Iraq, could outweigh the advantages of getting rid of the Iraqi leader.

This administration and its supporters argue as if the feasibility issue can be resolved by willpower or "resolve." If you question the feasibility of the project, you must somehow be on Saddam's side.

If you think it is desirable to overturn Saddam, you are required to think that most of his army will run away when Americans arrive, and that the people will cheer the United States in the streets of Baghdad. It is not allowed to imagine that the Iraqi army might fight simply because it is the nation's army.

The public is listening when James Baker, Brent Scowcroft, Lawrence Eagleburger and other senior Republicans say that realism requires that plans to invade Iraq accommodate the possibility of a big and expensive war, significant casualties and major negative political backlash.

They are making it necessary for the younger George Bush's administration and its backers to give up the irresponsible arguments they have been using. But they almost certainly have not convinced them, and by complicating their situation, they could be forcing them toward what George W. Bush has already threatened, a preemptive war — which in this case would be a war of domestic political preemption.

August 29, 2002 — ...A number of constitutional questions have been raised in the "war" against terrorism, which is not really a war in a formal sense. Background to nearly all of them has been an intention to conceal what the government is doing. This is justified as keeping precious information away from the enemy, a rationalization always offered when governments impose exceptional measures of secrecy.

As everyone knows who has experience of government, and of the political context in which governments function, classifying information usually means hiding things that are at best politically awkward or bureaucratically compromising, and at worst are illegal.

Officials may protect the nation against the enemy, but they also protect themselves against interference by the American public, Congress and the judiciary. This is what the Bush administration has been doing.

Military operations in Afghanistan, for example, have been under tight, effective censorship since the start of operations last year. Why? U.S. operations are no secret to the enemy.

Most of what Americans even now know about what went on in Afghanistan during the war comes from foreign reporters, including the Arab press and television, and from non-governmental organizations (the NGOs).

The contrast between this and the detailed, front-line press coverage of the second world war, Korea and Vietnam is breathtaking, including the American press's willingness to accept this censorship. Most of the American public got all the information it has about the Afghanistan war from Defense Secretary Donald Rumsfeld.

Today, in the debate about attacking Iraq, documented fact about Iraq and its capacities is almost completely absent.

To Vice President Dick Cheney, Iraq will soon be a nuclear power taking over one country after another through nuclear blackmail. To his critics, that country is weak and isolated. Both sides assert as fact what suits their partisan arguments.

The same is true about al Qaeda. The only serious investigative reporting I have seen on al Qaeda since the Afghan war has been in the news pages of *The Wall Street Journal*. It does not give the picture Washington gives.

Nearly always, government secrecy is intended to prevent Congress and the press from interfering with the executive branch.

I was involved with the CIA-sponsored Free Europe organization in the late 1950s. A few of us were solemnly let into the secret about who we really worked for, but this was no secret to the Soviet Union, the Warsaw Pact governments, or to the anti-Communist political exiles at Free Europe itself (who had not been born yesterday).

The main (although not only) reason for the secrecy was fear of McCarthy-like congressional interference.

The retired U.S. ambassador William R. Polk recently circulated a note on the Internet observing that while it now is well known that both al Qaeda and the Taliban were CIA creations to fight the Afghan-Soviet war, this was never a secret to the Russians, Afghans or Pakistanis — only to Americans.

The U.S. supplied satellite intelligence and military advice to Saddam Hussein during the 10-year war that followed his 1980 invasion of Iran (when, incidentally, he used poison gas against the Iranians). Of the concerned parties, only the American public didn't know.

Governments like secrecy because it gives them latitude to act as they want. It gives them a space of unaccountability. But the basis of democracy is accountable government. That is why the Bush administration is making principled enemies.

Paris, September 10, 2002 — Americans are uncomfortable with foreign policies that are not given a visionary or idealistic formulation. They are accustomed to having foreign policy placed in a more generous framework than is currently offered. Where would victories over Iraq and al Qaeda lead?

The absence of vision is particularly noticeable this week, as memorial observances for last year's lost lives included readings from Franklin Roosevelt's Four Freedoms, the Gettysburg Address and other idealistic past statements of American purpose, intended as a kind of rededication of the United States.

Mr. Bush spoke of America's "moral vocation." But his administration has at the same time been making its most strenuous efforts yet to convince Americans and their reluctant allies to go to war against Saddam Hussein's Iraq. There is discordance here, which more than one American has found troubling.

Ever since communism's collapse left the United States in a position of unchallenged world power, there has been much discussion of how this power should properly be used, or how it could be abused.

Articles and books have described the American situation in terms of "global hegemony," and have recommended that the United States take advantage of its extraordinary position.

This ordinarily was accompanied by the disclaimer that American interests nonetheless serve the world's interest because of the high ideals of the United States. The administration's problem is that a war against Iraq does not comfortably fit into the model of progressive and essentially benevolent national policy.

Now there is an effort to supply a remedy. A part of the neo-conservative and pro-Israeli communities influencing Bush administration policy argue that a war against Saddam Hussein should be seen in the context of a long-term American policy for transforming the Muslim Middle East.

It identifies "regime change" in Iraq and the campaign against al Qaeda as necessary steps in a decades-long American program to replace virtually all of the existing Middle Eastern governments and install social and economic reform.

The entire Middle East, plus Central Asia, Afghanistan and Pakistan, would be included in an American policy that its authors compare with the remaking of Europe ("by America") after the second world war.

Descriptions of this new project have been provided by Michael Ledeen of the American Enterprise Institute and by others. The program itself will shortly be published in *Policy Review* magazine. Its authors are Ronald Asmus, formerly of the State Department, and Ken Pollack, formerly of the Clinton administration.

It envisages a remade post-Taliban Afghanistan; an Arab-Israeli settlement on terms acceptable to Israel; "regime change" in Iran, as well as Iraq; and backing for civil society throughout the region, "particularly among current allies" (meaning Egypt, Saudi Arabia and probably the Gulf emirates).

Other advocates of this approach insist that eliminating Saddam Hussein will release existing but suppressed democratic forces, radically changing the

Middle East. (The eminent British military historian Michael Howard wrote last weekend that to believe this "demands a considerable suspension of disbelief.")

There is nothing wrong with having a theory about reform in the Muslim world. A serious government is expected to have a strategic outlook. The new Washington proposal rests, however, on the progressive myth that mankind would be peaceful and democratic if it were not the victim of false ideologies or evil dictators.

It rests as well on an inherently contradictory notion that foreign intervention — above all, foreign intervention by the United States, currently identified in the Muslim world as Islam's enemy — is capable of solving the Islamic world's distress. In any case, there is no chance whatever that Congress would authorize or pay for such a program.

Europe was "remade" after the war because Europe was an advanced society before the war. It simply needed money to reconstruct.

To justify his war against Iraq, Mr. Bush needs a demonstrated grave cause (not speculation about what Iraq might do in the future); reasonable prospects for success, and legitimacy in the opinion of the American public and that of his allies.

He has yet to prove his cause. If he did, the UN could provide the legitimacy. But a theory that rests on the suspension of disbelief does nothing for him or for the debate. It tends rather toward the characteristic evil of the twentieth century, which has been to kill people because of a fiction about the future.

September 17, 2002 — Checked by Saddam Hussein [who accepted new UN inspections], but not checkmated, the Bush administration will now do all it can to get a new Security Council resolution on Iraq whose terms Saddam will reject.

Iraq's avowedly unconditional acceptance of renewed inspections has succeeded in re-creating the Security Council divisions that existed until President Bush's challenge to the UN last week to enforce its own past resolutions.

It is, of course, imaginable that Baghdad might astonish all by demonstrating that it has nothing to hide. There are some Western experts who think this is possible. The Iraqis might even agree to permanent UN monitoring, since that would provide some protection against attack from the United States.

Alternatively, Baghdad may have hidden so well what it has to hide that the inspectors will be unable to find it. However the UN team under Hans Blix is forewarned and will function without the handicap of infiltration and manipulation by the CIA, which as Washington has conceded, was the case with previous teams.

There may be no time for that. The Bush administration is determined to see "regime change" in Baghdad, and simple inspections will not satisfy that demand. However, regime change is not the UN's business, as Kofi Annan said last week.

Why the administration wants so badly to be rid of Saddam is a more complicated and less easily answered question than it seems, but certainly oil and grudge both have their parts in it, as they did in the Gulf War in 1991.

Israel is a crucial influence. It's not the supposed threat of Iraqi attack that makes Israel want Saddam overturned. (There are no positives for Iraq in an unprovoked attack, only fatal negatives).

The Sharon government wants a U.S. invasion because war between the United States and Iraq will bring the U.S. into the Middle East in a big and probably permanent way, and that would give an expanded and prolonged security guarantee to the Jewish state.

If some on Israel's political right were to have their way, war would provide an opportunity to rid the occupied territories of their Palestinian population, and possibly Israel of its Arab minority.

Elements of the Israeli right have always said that Jordan should be made into "Palestine," at the expense of its existing Hashemite monarchy. Some of Washington's more fanciful geopolitical draftsmen, or re-draftsmen, have already suggested giving back Iraq (or part of a newly dismantled Iraq) to the Hashemite royal family, who ruled Iraq from 1921 until a military putsch in 1958, which murdered King Faisal II.

Ideas floating about Washington envisage regime change in Saudi Arabia, as well, with a redistribution of regional oil resources according to how the major oil-consuming countries vote on forthcoming UN resolutions. The Bush people have already reclassified the Saudi monarchy ruling Arabia, for nearly 60 years an American ally and principal supplier of oil to the United States, from friend to potential enemy.

As the Washington press reported last week, the president's speech at the United Nations "marked the start of intense behind-the-scenes negotiations to see what inducements will help convert countries that so far have been balking, at least publicly, at joining the anti-Hussein campaign."

American domination of the oil production of Iraq, as well as that of Saudi Arabia, would give Washington control of U.S. energy costs, and presumably guarantee its oil supplies for the foreseeable future, with corollary influence over energy supplies to present or potential rivals among the industrial nations.

This at least is what the Arab Middle East thinks, as well as quite a few people in Europe and in the former Soviet Union. The overall opacity of Bush administration motives for going to war against Iraq, and on policy for Iraq after such a war, lends itself to conspiracy theories. In view of this administration's connections with the U.S. oil industry, these theories don't have to be fetched very far.

Less easily understood (possibly even in Bush administration circles themselves), is what the United States would, on balance, gain by trying to set up what would amount to a new Middle Eastern empire, or system of hegemony, in tacit partnership with Israel.

One might think that the downside in such a combination of implausibility and quicksand would intimidate even the Pentagon. However the Pentagon seems to have less influence on the White House these days than the neo-conservative press. For that reason, whatever Saddam Hussein does, it seems likely that Iraq will be invaded.

What Saddam has done is probably assure that the invasion will be an American invasion without a UN mandate. That would be a not inconsiderable American defeat, although it will do Saddam no good.

September 19, 2002 — The electoral calculation that has prompted both German Chancellor Gerhard Schroeder and his challenger, Edmund Stoiber, to refuse Germany's backing to George W. Bush's projected attack on Iraq, reflects the German public's wish to have no foreign policy at all — least of all a war policy.

This has been the case since 1945, disguised by the fact that the Germans' postwar American occupiers provided Germany with a foreign policy they couldn't refuse. Moreover, it seemed to offer security, and obviate the need to think.

They would be part of NATO, together with all the other West Europeans, and would follow where Washington led. There was incidental resistance, but nothing serious, and so it was done. Germany has since been the indispensable member and base for American-dominated NATO.

This was acceptable to Germans because there was deep and widespread confidence in the United States, seen generally in Western Europe as fundamentally trustworthy, a balanced and responsible custodian of international order, despite occasional aberrations.

The election campaigns of the chancellor and the conservative Mr. Stoiber now give evidence that German public confidence in the United States — or, at a minimum, German confidence in this American government — is badly shaken. The Germans do not want to go to war against Iraq alongside the United States, and they have little sympathy for the war itself.

Thus, Mr. Schroeder has said, to apparent public approval, that even the chemical and biological defense units Germany has had in the Gulf for many months will be withheld from a war between Washington and Baghdad.

Even permission for American military overflights of Germany remains in question, although it is hard to imagine any German government that emerges from this election, whatever its composition, taking so drastic a decision as to prohibit them. A significant fraction of the leftist electorate nonetheless is against allowing them.

American officials and editorial writers who have been warning that the two party leaders have "isolated" Germany, and that if the winner of the election does not change Germany's policy on Iraq the United States will retaliate, do not fully appreciate the situation.

We know that history is read only selectively in Washington, but someone should look up what happened in 1966, at a time when NATO's headquarters were at Fontainebleau in France and there were important NATO bases in that country. It cannot be emphasized enough to Washington that in today's world the United States depends on Western Europe, above all on Germany; it is not Western Europe that depends on the United States.

General Charles De Gaulle decided to withdraw France from NATO's military committee, which meant an end to French military integration in the alliance, while maintaining France's alliance commitment to mutual defense. NATO had to move its headquarters to Belgium and close down its airbases and other facilities in France.

The same option is open to Germany if it really has lost confidence in the United States or believes that the United States no longer observes Article 1 of the NATO Treaty, which commits the allies to avoid "the threat or use of force in any manner inconsistent with the purposes of the United Nations."

Germany might then be isolated, but in an important respect the United States would be isolated, too.

However, that would worsen Germany's foreign policy problem. Instead of no foreign policy, Germany would suddenly have a frighteningly dramatic foreign policy, fraught with uncertainties.

Would the European Union supply Germany with a substitute policy? Currently, it has no foreign policy itself, other than a generalized commitment to international law and multilateral solutions. This may not prove a very solid shelter from the storms that may arrive.

A foreign policy that goes beyond mutual security assurances and a commitment to the United Nations requires a degree of national confidence singularly lacking in the European Union.

An English writer, Clifford Longley, argued recently that England's national confidence, in its days of glory, derived from the conviction that the English were God's chosen people. Christianity had claimed that role in succession to the Jews, and English Protestants were convinced they were the true Christians. Longleysays the English "firmly believed that the Bible was primarily about them."

Via the Puritans, Americans then claimed the same role; and the people now in charge in Washington still believe it, in a secularized version.

No one else in modern Europe has confidence like that, except the French, who believe they created the modern age with their Enlightenment and Revolution. Americans, needless to say, dispute that claim.

France's confidence, in any case, cannot solve Germany's problem, nor Europe's. That is one reason the European Union remains at a disadvantage, confronting the United States.

PART FOUR

FROM OCTOBER 2002 TO MARCH 2003: THE U.S. DISCARDS ITS ALLIES AND DEFIES THE UN

Paris, October 1, 2002 — There has been oddly little comment on the fact that the new American National Security Strategy document issued September 20 is an implicit denunciation of the modern state order governing international relations since the Westphalian Settlement of 1648.

That agreement, ending the Thirty Years War, recognized the absolute sovereignty and legal equality of states as the basis of international order.

The principles of sovereignty and equality have been generally recognized ever since (if often in the breach). The consensus among governments and jurists has been that without acknowledging national sovereignty as the foundation of law, the world risked anarchical power struggle.

The National Security Strategy statement is thus a radical document, whether Condoleezza Rice, reputedly its main author, understands this or not.

There was another declaration of this kind, made 154 years ago, the Communist Manifesto. It denounced the existing international order of monarchies and "bourgeois" republics in the name of a new and superior legitimacy, that of the proletariat.

It claimed this to be a universal and liberating legitimacy.

After the Russian Revolution, the new Soviet Union set out to put this new principle into practice in its relations with other governments. It declared all other governments illegitimate. This is why Soviet policy so disturbed the international order. Its claim was absolute and, in principle, nonnegotiable.

Karl Marx's "scientific" interpretation of historical processes, the intellectual foundation of Communism, claimed that history is driven by the struggle of classes, and that only workers' states were ultimately legitimate, since the industrial worker embodied the productive forces of modern industrial society. There was only one workers' state, Bolshevik Russia.

All governments except the Soviet Union usurped power that history had determined should belong to the proletariat. Therefore those other governments sooner or later had to be replaced.

Now the United States has stated that it will no longer respect the principle of absolute state sovereignty. It does not do so by substituting some new universalist and allegedly liberating principle, but in order to assure American national security, to which it implicitly subordinates the security of every other nation.

It says that if the United States government unilaterally determines that a state is a future threat to the U.S., or that it harbors a group considered a potential threat, the United States will preemptively intervene in that state to eliminate the threat, if necessary by accomplishing "regime change."

We already have been given an initial list of such states, those of the "axis of evil."

The administration says that it is simple common sense to preempt threats. It would seem common sense to agree, if it were not for the principle of the thing. This American initiative is meant to supersede the existing principle of international legitimacy.

Now international law is not law at all. It is a system based on a accumulation of treaties, conventions, precedents and other commitments over many years, by which governments have attempted to limit war, keep the peace, and adjudicate their conflicting claims and interests to their mutual advantage and security.

It is not law because no authority issues it. No one enforces it, other than through cooperative actions among nations. The United States, as it happens, has over its two and a quarter centuries of existence been one of the nations most active in building up the structure of international law that the Bush administration now is engaged in knocking down.

The Charter of the United Nations is one of the principal existing agreements making up international law, and was drafted largely by the United

States. The "threat or use of force against the territorial integrity or political independence of any state" is outlawed by the Charter. "Preemptive" war was specifically treated as a war crime at the Nuremberg trials.

One can say that the most powerful states have always made the rules. The United States has intervened in small countries many times. However in the past Washington always claimed some form of legal justification. It acknowledged the principles of sovereignty and non-intervention.

Now it jettisons those principles, substituting the claim that its own perceived national security interest overrides all.

It also asserts its intention, and its right — by virtue of its own rectitude — to military domination of the entire world.

This all is pretty dramatic. It would be better if Congress does not simply take it as decided. It needs debate, as its consequences may in the longer run prove unpleasant.

October 3, 2002 — A good deal of printer's ink has been spent debating anti-Americanism during the past year, both in and out of the United States.

The latest instance came after Germany's recent parliamentary election, when Chancellor Gerhard Schroeder's party coalition won a narrow victory, credited by analysts to his stand against German participation in any U.S. attack on Iraq.

The chancellor's lèse-majesté provoked outrage in the Bush administration, a freeze on White House relations with him and an arrogant invitation to him to resign, offered by Richard Perle, chairman of the U.S. Defense Department's advisory Defense Policy Board.

Donald Rumsfeld said that U.S.-German relations had been "poisoned," and there were anti-German noises elsewhere in American neo-conservative circles, including a warning that it will be a half-century before Germany will have recovered "the trust" of the United States, and resume being an important state.

In fact, from the European side of the Atlantic, it seemed that Mr. Schroeder's stand added to Germany's international stature, Germany previously having tended to be seen as a satellite of Washington rather than a nation with a mind of its own.

Since a majority in German public opinion already opposed an attack on Iraq, and Mr. Schroeder merely profited from supporting the majority, the

Germans can probably expect to receive the same press and propaganda treatment in coming days that France got a few months ago.

Then, when the Palestinian-Israeli conflict provoked an arson attack on a French synagogue and other anti-Jewish and anti-Israeli acts, the neo-conservative press in the United States declared that the French as a nation had revealed their inveterate anti-Semitism and pro-Nazi disposition.

The subject of anti-Americanism can, however, be intelligently discussed, an example being a recent exchange between a French writer with a long record of sympathy for the United States, Jean-François Revel, and a younger colleague with family connections to the United States and a British education, Emmanuel Todd.

Todd maintains that the United States today actually is displaying a kind of fitful weakness. "I have always had a positive vision of the United States...[and] taken for granted that it was a reasonable power," he says. But now "I have the sense of a disquieting semi-bellicosity, an agitation, a feverishness."

He puts this down to an actual but unacknowledged sense of vulnerability in the United States, caused by its budget dependence on European and Japanese investment and its lingering strategic anxiety about Russia and China. Current American emphasis on military and diplomatic action against weaker "rogue" states, he suggests, is a kind of compensation for this anxiety.

Thus, embargoes are imposed on countries incapable of defending themselves, and tribal armies and "disarmed civil populations" are subjected to high-tech bombardment. (He presumably has Serbia in mind.)

Revel responds that blaming America has always been a reflex of European intellectuals. He says that American politicians are given to hyperbole that should not be taken too seriously, and that Europeans have only themselves to blame for today's American predominance, since Europe's own failures in the twentieth century made a gift of global power to the United States.

He also says that the French themselves would be "obsessed" with terrorism if suicide planes had simultaneously attacked the Paris Opera, the Arc de Triomphe and other prominent sites (although he himself mentions the series of attacks on crowded Paris stores, and on train and Metro stations, in 1995 that were met without panic).

It strikes me that the two are actually discussing two separate kinds of anti-Americanism. The old kind, which Revel stoutly opposed, was influential some 30 years ago, when news of the Gulag was only belatedly being admitted by a French intelligentsia traditionally disposed to uncritical support for the left.

Then, every American Cold War measure was attacked as if it were an unprovoked provocation to the Soviet Union.

The new kind of anti-Americanism is the one Todd talks about, and is a reaction to the post-September 11 policies of the Bush administration, which he takes as revealing deep-seated anxieties in American society that have economic and demographic structural causes — a fragile economy and loss of the old sense of national identity.

He also argues that Washington's preoccupation with the rogue states and China, actually a weak state, and its concern that they might become allied with Russia, avoids looking at the real strategic threat: that a nuclear Russia would ally itself with the two most important real power centers outside the United States: Europe and Japan.

This analysis is not one that seems to concern Washington, which makes much of the symptoms of anti-Americanism in Europe while its own actions actually worsen it. Chancellor Schroeder did not "whip up" anti-Americanism in Germany. It was there already. That is what should worry Washington.

October 10, 2002 — Earlier this year, in the Hoover Institution journal *Policy Review* (published in Washington), Robert Kagan offered a not unsympathetic but ultimately patronizing description of contemporary West Europeans as over-civilized practitioners of international legalism, accommodation and, when necessary, appeasement of tyrants — leaving to America the responsibility, indeed the obligation, to police the world alone.

In the current issue of the same magazine, two former officials of the Clinton administration, Ronald Asmus and Kenneth Pollack, disagree, insisting that continuing European-American cooperation is essential to deal with the "new scourges" of terrorism, weapons of mass destruction, and rogue and failed states.

A distinction was once made in American literary criticism between Pale-faces (Emerson, Hawthorne, Thoreau and the other New Englanders) and Red-skins, the literary frontiersmen following from Mark Twain.

The same distinction can be made in the foreign policy debate. Policy Pale-faces are looking for alternatives to war in the Middle East (they actually would probably have Mark Twain on their side, as he was a great enemy of whatever passed as the conventional wisdom). But the Redskins are in charge, planning to

117

reinstall and extend that New World Order that the first president George Bush proclaimed but then "put back on the shelf" (as his aides said) as too complicated and too dangerous. No Redskin he.

But his son, albeit another Skull and Bones man from that leading institution of the pallid East, Yale, has dug up the hatchet, influenced by a neo-conservative set of policy theorists. (These might be called Redskin wannabes, since their enthusiasm for war has come only since the Vietnam War, which they all managed to avoid.)

However supporters of the "new" New World Order include Clintonian liberals, since what this policy comes down to is an armed version of the Wilsonian ideas with which the United States attempted, and disastrously failed, to reorder international society in 1919.

Foreign critics are inclined to see Bush administration policy as imperialist. It is widely assumed in Western Europe (and unanimously in the Arab world) that President Bush wants to invade Iraq in order to take control of Iraq's high-quality and easily extracted oil. This would end Saudi Arabia's domination of the international oil market.

For this administration, control of Iraq's oil would actually seem merely the byproduct of a much vaster regional transformation, recently set out in several versions in Washington, its latest formulation that of Asmus and Pollack.

They argue that the "Greater Middle East" (which for them extends from North Africa to Afghanistan and Pakistan) must be rescued from its indigenous crisis of development, and its extremism. America and Europe together, they say, can do it. It is not really a military problem, even though Israel's security is a primordial Bush administration concern.

"[We] need to change the dynamics" responsible for the region's problems, they say, by providing it with "a new form of democracy ... a new economic system ... helping Middle Eastern societies come to grips with modernity and create new civil societies that will allow them to compete and integrate into in the modern world without losing their sense of cultural uniqueness."

They modestly add that "this is a tall order" but express confidence that it can be done, beginning in Afghanistan. Then must come Arab-Israeli settlement, on which they have nothing more to suggest than "a common approach" by Europeans and Americans (which actually would be most unwelcome in Israel).

Next needed is NATO cooperation to remove Saddam Hussein (NATO involvement is an unwelcome idea in Washington, which is having enough trouble getting agreement among Americans). After that would come European and American "help" for "the process of regime change" elsewhere in the region.

To critics who suggest that such a program to remake Islamic Middle Eastern and Central Asian society partakes of utopian fantasy, the authors reply that it was no less utopian in 1949 to suggest that all of Europe could be recon-structed and freed from Communist control.

They are mistaken and should consult George Kennan's April 1951 *Foreign Affairs* article called "America and the Russian Future" (written four years after his article in the same journal setting out the policy of containment). Kennan calmly and confidently proposed in 1951 exactly how Europe's, and Russia's, lib-eration could be accomplished: which proved to be how it actually happened.

There was nothing utopian about planning Western Europe's economic reconstruction. In 1940, Europe had been an economically and technologically more advanced society than the United States. (All the decisive wartime tech-nical innovations, including radar, rockets, jet aircraft and the atomic bomb were originated by Europeans).

In 1949, Europe only needed money. The United States had plenty of that.

It is irresponsible to draw an analogy between Europe's reconstruction and the cultural and religious crisis today afflicting the region from Afghanistan to Algeria. Cultural and religious crises are solved by the people involved — if they are solved at all.

October 15, 2002 — Even before recent newspaper reports of an American plan for lasting military occupation of Iraq, on the model of the post-second world war occupation of Japan, the debate over war with Iraq was awash with unchecked fantasies about the future.

The debate has mostly consisted of unproved assertions about Iraq's weapons or lack of them; about the threat that it does, or does not, pose to its neighborhood, or to Israel, or the United States; and about its connection, or lack of connection, with international terrorism.

It is a highly emotional argument untroubled by much fact. The outcome will apparently be decided by whoever last has the president's ear. The Senate, constitutional custodian of the power to go to war, has abdicated to George W. Bush, conceding to him greater discretion than any president in history.

This is not the conduct of a serious government or a serious nation. War is a grave matter even for a country that fancies itself invincible. One does not attack another society, inflict destruction upon it, kill its soldiers and people, and send one's own soldiers to death on the basis of speculation, hypothesis and partisan theories about the future.

The United States has never before gone to war without a clear and factually uncontroversial casus belli. In the Gulf War, it was Iraq's aggression against Kuwait. In Vietnam, it was Communist insurrection against a recognized government. The merits of America's intervention in these wars were certainly controversial, but the fact of aggression, and the fact of insurrection, were there.

Today there is as yet no incontrovertible fact that justifies war against Iraq. That is why there is such a controversy. Sending the UN inspectors back might produce some facts to replace speculation. One might think the inspectors more likely than not to find evidence to support Washington. Yet Mr. Bush and his advisors seem too little confident of their position to allow the UN inspectors to test it.

Their supporters now have offered a new theory about American-led peaceful revolution in the region, its democratization and peaceful economic transformation, with reform of Islamic religious thought so as to reconcile Islam with modern Western culture.

The newly disclosed plan for military occupation of a defeated Iraq makes up part of this theory. The occupation will reform and "re-educate" Iraq, supposedly in the way imperial Japan and Nazi Germany were remade after 1945.

Only people who know little about Japan and Germany in the 1940s could make such an assumption. Historical ignorance, however deplorable, is not considered an impediment to policymaking in today's Washington....Europe after 1945 simply needed to have its economy rebuilt. That is what Marshall Plan money accomplished. The Marshall Plan did not reform or transform European society, nor was it expected to do so.

Japan, like Europe, had an advanced industry in 1941. It would not otherwise have been able to put up a ferocious three-and-a-half-year defense against American offensives in the Central and Southwestern Pacific, and against the British/Indian advance in South Asia.

Japan in 1945 was also an intensely corporate, authoritarian and hierarchical society. By leaving the emperor in place — and acting with his consent and authority — the MacArthur occupation was able to conduct a peaceful reform of the Japanese government, economy and educational system. The Japanese authorities policed the country, not the American occupation.

There was no resistance. Would there be resistance to American occupation of Iraq? It is another agreeable fantasy to think that American soldiers would be cheered as they arrived, and be encouraged by the Iraqis to take over their country.

What would Mr. Bush do, though, if the Iraqi army put up a serious fight, and the Iraqi public resisted an American occupation? What Ariel Sharon is doing?

Vienna, October 22, 2002 — When the U.S. government sets forth a national strategy statement declaring its aim to be permanent military domination of the world, so that no rival should "even think about" challenging it, the inevitable result is to make people think the hitherto unthinkable.

They don't think about challenging the United States. They think about deterring the United States. The policy statement issued last month by the Bush administration risks doing more for nuclear proliferation than anything that has happened since 1945.

A government might reasonably consider how to construct a minimal nuclear deterrent that raises enough uncertainties to keep any hostile foreign power at bay, even the United States. North Korea now says that it has done this.

Consider Washington's different reactions to North Korea's newly announced nuclear program and Iraq's supposed one. Washington is eager to go to war against Iraq, but not against North Korea.

There are some 40,000 American troops in South Korea, and a single North Korean nuclear missile could kill a very large number of them. That is not to mention South Korean victims and the North Koreans who would die in retaliation.

Such a scenario is highly improbable and implausible. It is not a fully rational one. But it is enough to make even the flock of hawks currently in residence at the Pentagon and White House think again.

That has undoubtedly made Saddam Hussein, and others, to think as well. Nuclear nonproliferation currently is applied only to those who do not already have nuclear weapons. When the United States announces that it has no intention of giving up its nuclear advantage, but rather of enlarging it, as Mr. Bush has said, then any prudent government has cause to consider purchasing for itself a small but secure nuclear deterrent.

No one envisions a military challenge to the United States, which would be hopelessly expensive and provoke wholly unpredictable reactions in the American political class. It would also be a waste of money for quite another reason: this kind of military power is only marginally relevant in today's world.

People are being forced to think about the nature of power, and to wonder if the United States is really as powerful as it claims to be. They note that since George W. Bush was elected and began to assert American military "hard" power, America's "soft" power has shrunk.

Soft power — apart from economic power — encompasses diplomatic influence and political persuasion, cultural influence and prestige, and other qualities that cause others to respect a country, wish to become associated with it, and to accept its values and views. Joseph Nye of Harvard University has recently written about this in terms of the importance of soft power to the United States.

But soft power can also be used against America, particularly when the U.S. is in its Bush administration hard-power operational mode. France has been using its soft power to block the American demand for a single UN Security Council resolution that would authorize the United States to attack Iraq whenever Washington judged this appropriate.

The French maintain that international law requires that the Security Council authorize whatever retaliation follows Iraqi obstruction of inspections.

The American position was never popular with other governments, and in a low-key but persistent and unyielding way, the French have mobilized that international opposition. France has UN veto power but never threatened it, understanding that veto power, like nuclear power, is much more important unused than used.

The United States now has provisionally agreed to return to the UN before any attack on Iraq, although at this writing negotiations (notably with Russia) continue on the wording of a resolution acceptable to the five permanent Security Council members.

As for hard power, no other country imagines trying to construct as huge and versatile a military force as the United States possesses. What purpose would it serve?

No government today imagines fighting a full-spectrum war against the United States. No other government except the American has the least interest in deploying its forces worldwide, with bases in scores of countries.

The U.S. reaction to the September 11, 2001, attacks included establishing new military bases and deployments in Central Asia, South Asia and Southeastern Asia, while naming as new enemies a variety of Islamic extremist movements or factions in these regions, as well as bandit and kidnapping gangs, and separatist groups, all described as part of a vast axis of terrorism.

This served chiefly to multiply the number and geographical distribution of identified enemies, not previously perceived as important forces even in their own countries. This certainly has not improved matters for the United States, which risks becoming identified as at war not only with the Muslim world, but with the non-Western world as a whole.

Paris, October 24, 2002 — The twenty-first-century destiny of the United States has proved to be global hegemony, but is this to be a hegemony well assumed and acknowledged as legitimate, or is it to be illegitimate, resented, resisted and short-lived?

The question is urgent because of the decision made early in the George W. Bush administration to break with the traditional multilateralism of American policy.

Mr. Bush's government from the start was deliberately and provocatively hostile to treaties constraining American freedom of action, arms limitation and environmental agreements, and the rest of the apparatus of international constraint, cooperation and international law that previous American administrations had helped to construct since 1945.

The hawkish coven of neo-conservatives who supply the administration's thinking seems to have believed collaboration in any of this an unmanly stance for the nation they now led. They preferred unilateral action — and against Iraq, war.

Yet no one elected this war party. The country elected George W. Bush, who promised that the United States would conduct a "humble" foreign policy that would respect the good opinion of mankind.

Had he offered the electorate a platform incorporating the views of the leading figures of the neoconservative camp, who now make foreign policy for him, one may think that he would have lost in more states than Florida.

The crucial element being ignored is that any hegemonic power must be perceived as legitimate if it is to succeed in the long term.

In *Critical Views of September 11* (New York, The New Press), one of two valuable post-attack books just published under the auspices of the Social

Science Research Council, William Wallace of the London School of Economics writes about the combination of coercion and consent that underpins any successful claim to international domination.

"States can secure temporary supremacy over their neighbors," he writes, "through the use of overwhelming force and the utilization of superior technology, underpinned by the expenditure of the necessary economic resources." He goes on to say that "longer-term supremacy, however, depends on at least a degree of acceptance by those dominated of the legitimacy of the dominant power."

This was the case with Napoleon's "modification of the ideology of the French Revolution into a doctrine of popular mobilization and administrative modernization" in the early nineteenth century. Later in the century, Britain's defense of the gold standard, free trade and international law, and its suppression of the slave trade, legitimated its global domination.

In the case of the United States, when the second world war left it the dominant power, Washington became the prime mover in creating the liberal political and economic institutions that shaped modern international society.

Its leadership of the West was consensual. Not everyone agreed with all that the United States did, but even those hostile to specific U.S. initiatives or policies acknowledged that the American position was defensible and principled, and they respected its overall stance.

The much-cited example of this was General Charles DeGaulle, who ousted NATO bases from France and opposed the United States on many issues, but stood with it in such crises as the Cuban missile confrontation.

Today's leadership in Washington appears to believe that the legitimacy of its power will be established by making war on rogue and failed states, and by bullying the rest. The opinions of America's allies of the past half-century are dismissed as those of societies whose nerve has failed: who have abandoned a responsible and effective role in international affairs and can be ignored.

The day approaches, according to Robert Kagan, a celebrant of the administration's "Hobbesian" employment of power, when "Americans will no more heed the pronouncements of the European Union than they do the pronouncements of the Association of South East Asian Nations or the Andean Pact."

Washington has just given an ultimatum to the UN Security Council to approve its resolution on disarming Iraq or make itself "irrelevant." Its logic is that relevance for the Security Council lies in conforming to what the United States demands.

A clear theme in administration policy is that the United States neither needs nor particularly wants the good opinion of the states it dominates. It is indifferent to the legitimacy provided by the respect of other peoples. It is content to rest its claim to international leadership on the exercise of its power.

That certainly is not what the electorate voted for two years ago. It is why George W. Bush will almost certainly be a one-term president.

October 29, 2002 — Vladimir Putin vows to pursue terrorists even beyond Russia's borders, emulating George W. Bush. He is on board for the worldwide fight against terrorism.

An observer can only offer both Presidents Putin and Bush good luck. Terrorism has always been a force in history and society, as well as in the depths of individual human motivation — as Americans have just again been instructed by events [a series of anonymous sniper shootings] in Maryland and Virginia.

It was a fateful mistake for President Bush to have declared his war a "war against terrorism" after September 11, 2001. That made it a war that can't be won. At the same time, it aligned the United States with governments around the world engaged in suppressing nationalist, regional, religious or ethnic separatism, too often by methods of social and political injustice.

The recent outrage in a Moscow theater was committed in the cause of Chechen national independence. The attacks in New York and Washington last year were committed by members of an international movement made up of individuals who hate and fear the United States and its influence, and who acted for a number of clearly identifiable reasons, religion and nationalism prominent among them.

The latter group, allied around al Qaeda, can with patience eventually be tracked down and contained, if not eliminated; the problem it poses is within the competence of intelligence and police services. However, while it can bombed out of a headquarters, as in Afghanistan, it is not easily bombed out of organizational existence.

The nationalists and separatists pose a different problem, one theoretically open to political solution, as it concerns the condition in which a political nation is to be allowed to exist.

The claims of the Chechens can be repressed for a long period of time, at heavy cost to the Chechens, as well as to Russian standards of national justice, and military morale and efficiency — but those claims will go on being asserted.

The war between the Russians and the Chechens has been going on since 1783, when Catherine the Great proclaimed the Caucasus to be Russia's, and Russian troops began to try to enforce that claim in what until then had been a region of tribal societies and tribal authority (as in Pakistan's North West provinces today, where Osama bin Laden is reported to have found refuge, and where tribal authority prevails). The Chechens and their Ingush minority were her most ferocious opponents.

They fought conquest until 1859, fought Russian occupation until 1917, were an autonomous region and then an autonomous republic under the Bolsheviks, but collaborated with the invading Germans in World War II. Stalin then deported many to Central Asia. They were allowed to return only in 1956, when he was dead.

When Boris Yeltsin in 1991 declared the U.S.S.R. finished, and invited all Russia's subject-peoples "to claim as much autonomy as they can absorb," the Chechen parliament took him at his word and declared national independence.

It was an independence they failed to handle, allowing instead anarchical conditions in which kidnapping and smuggling gangs and other criminal groups absorbed much of the power available.

This disorder opened the way to Islamist influence. Saudi Arabia was propagating the Wahhabi version of Islam in the Caucasus, and the United States was not displeased with the Saudi program, which put another obstacle between Russia and control of the Caucasian oil fields. The United States also lent support to Georgia, near Chechnya, which now has been implicitly threatened by Vladimir Putin's offer to carry the war beyond Chechnya.

September 11 gave Putin the opportunity for a smooth countermove against Washington's interest in the Caucasus. He announced that his war against Chechen independence was part of George W. Bush's great war against global terrorism. If, as Mr. Bush insists, we are all either for or against terrorism, we all must be against Chechen separatists.

This gave the United States a moral involvement in Russia's bloodiest and potentially most dangerous internal crisis. It widens the war, not against "terrorism," but against Muslim Chechens, now provided reason to identify the United States as still another of their enemies.

The Bush decision to call America's enemy "global terrorism" may have been only a speech writer's flourish, but it reflected the administration's determination to tie last year's attacks to what already was on their agenda: Saddam

Hussein's overthrow and support for Ariel Sharon's repression of the Palestinian national movement.

Adding the Russian war against Chechen independence to the mixture was not on their agenda, but Vladimir Putin has put it there. How the administration will eventually manage all this is something the U.S. public might worry about as it goes to the polls next week.

Paris, November 5, 2002 — Washington and London officials are warning that the NATO summit in Prague at the end of November will decide whether NATO remains "relevant" to today's concerns....The United States says that to give NATO continued relevance, the Europeans must create a strike force with modernized arms "to wage offensive operations alongside Americans anywhere in the world."

But in what respect would these be NATO operations? Washington would insist that they be operationally detached from NATO, as neither the White House nor the Pentagon imagines submitting U.S. strategy to the consensus views of the permanent North Atlantic Council, which sits in Brussels and is NATO's own decision-making body. Nor, since Kosovo, have the U.S. Joint Chiefs indicated willingness to submit U.S. military operations to NATO staffs and command structures.

In these circumstances, the new strike force would look very much like a self-financing foreign legion for the Pentagon. This is not an arrangement likely to win approval from NATO's principal continental European allies.

It might be acceptable to the Blair government in Britain, and to some of the smaller European allies, but even then, it would be controversial.

It is clear what Washington wants from the alliance. It is less clear what the other allies get from giving Washington what it wants, particularly the new Washington of the Bush administration. To the United States, NATO remains an immensely valuable instrument of Washington's policies. It is indispensable to American military operations throughout Europe, the Middle East, and western and central Asia. NATO provides Washington with a sophisticated and comprehensive military infrastructure and base network in Europe, largely financed by the allies.

Europeans generally seem not to appreciate the extent to which the United States depends strategically upon them. The United States would be crippled were NATO to collapse. Washington sees NATO European forces as a proven body of peacekeepers available, as in the Balkans and Afghanistan, to relieve the United States of non-combat responsibilities in crisis or post-crisis situations.

Washington also has more than the obvious reason to want a modernized European NATO strike force. It offers added value to Washington in two respects:

First, it would preempt resources and energies that could otherwise go into the European Union's independent rapid-reaction force, also under development.

And, second, its modernized weapons systems and structures would be integrated into American command, control and communications systems, with the effect that they would function in degraded mode outside U.S./NATO operations.

These are not unimportant considerations in the eyes of some hawkish Washington policy thinkers who consider Europe the only possibly future challenger to U.S. global predominance, other than China. The initiatives of the European Union to reclaim independent security responsibilities are received with coolness in official Washington....

The Baltic States and certain of the East Europeans undoubtedly harbor long-term concern about what Vladimir Putin's Russia may become. These are not politically correct anxieties, to be voiced in a Brussels where the new Russia enjoys a privileged relationship with NATO. They nonetheless provide the residual European security significance of NATO, which will persist for some years to come. The Article 5 guarantees to new NATO members should not be sacrificed to Mr. Bush's war against terrorism.

NATO has been an important vehicle of transatlantic cooperation and security since 1948. Europe has a huge organizational, as well as political investment in it, even if the utility of the alliance to Western Europe has faded.

However a new force is at work, which European politicians cannot afford to ignore. There is much popular, as well as elite, hostility in Western Europe to what generally is called U.S. unilateralism, and particularly to American policy in the Middle East.

When a German chancellor, to be elected, needs to adopt a platform explicitly renouncing cooperation with a U.S.-led war in Iraq, this has to be taken seriously by European politicians. This has much more to do with NATO's "relevance" than a new strike force.

November 19, 2002 — NATO is supposed to be recast this week to meet the threat of terrorism, but no one has yet offered a clear explanation of what NATO can do to prevent new attacks on Western targets by highly motivated individuals or bands of Islamic militants, determined to punish Westerners for what history has done to the Muslim world.

I do not say "history" to imply fatalism. The situation of the Islamic states today has much to do with the world wars and Cold War, Zionism, imperialism and American and British oil politics.

It has even more to do with the Islamic peoples themselves: the failure of Mediterranean and Near Eastern Islamic civilization to develop systems of effective self-government to replace the Ottoman Turkish system that collapsed in the first world war.

What happened after 1918 did not have to happen. Turkey was not annexed by a European empire, as were the Arab societies. That fact has its political, military and social explanations. But people are responsible for what happens to them: The Turks produced one outcome; the Iraqis produced another, with which they now have to live.

The NATO debate has included warnings disconnected from real threats and policy proposals irrelevant to their solution. America wants help in carrying out a policy fatefully influenced by the notion that conquering Iraq will permit Washington and Israel to take control of the Islamic Middle East and its peoples — and that this will have a happy ending.

Germany's Chancellor Gerhard Schroeder recently asked for someone to clearly explain to him how we got from the New York and Washington terrorist attacks to war against Iraq. The answer is in part the tyranny of means. If a government's largest and bureaucratically most influential policy instrument is its armed forces, it turns to them in an emergency. But armed forces can't solve the terrorist problem.

What they were able to do was overturn the Taliban government that harbored the terrorists. They today offer to overturn Saddam Hussein. Doing these things provides a distraction from the failure to solve the terrorist problem. It provides a virtual solution, so to speak. When the followers of Osama bin Laden strike again, the Bush administration will answer that it won a war against Afghanistan and expects soon to win one against Iraq. The widows and orphans of the 9/11 victims will have to be satisfied with that.

A Middle East resident was recently quoted as saying to an American that "it's not you that we are afraid of. It's your fear that frightens us." Particularly in recent weeks, there has been a running barrage of official statements warning the North American and European publics against supposedly impending terrorist attacks.

These warnings reflect what police and intelligence services have been discovering about the projects, ambitions and wish lists of the militants who are members, followers, or would-be emulators of the Al Qaeda conspiracy.

Such threats are not connected with Iraq. The warnings, in the United States at least, nonetheless coincided with the Bush administration's campaigns to get congressional approval for an attack on Iraq and to win a UN Security Council resolution that might provide international approval for such an attack. It now has both.

The cumulative warnings seem, though, to have given a significant fraction of American public opinion an unreasonable conviction that the United States now is in danger of an attack, employing mass destruction weapons, either by Osama bin Laden or by Saddam Hussein.

There is to the best of specialist opinion no scenario by which the American public is plausibly threatened by rockets, nuclear weapons, gas attacks or biological warfare of Iraqi origin. The mechanical means are not there, even if such an attack offered any rational advantage to Saddam Hussein.

Western countries undoubtedly are threatened by possible new attacks by individual or groups of Al Qaeda terrorists, but the risk to a given individual in any such attack is statistically infinitesimal — much lower than the risks everybody runs in the course of everyday life.

The implication of the policy statements coming from Washington has been that terrorism and Iraq's past or present possession of mass destruction weapons are linked phenomena, and that a war against Iraq will somehow lift fear from America.

This is not true. The threat to the United States and its allies comes from an Islamic radicalism that will be intensified by war with Iraq. It is necessary to understand that "solving" Iraq is overwhelmingly likely to worsen the terrorist threat to the Western countries.

November 26, 2002 — The attitude of the George W. Bush administration, and of the neo-conservative policy community that supplies its ideas, is condescending at best to those who question its actions.

The members of the administration and their backers claim a moral realism that their critics, specifically their European critics, allegedly lack. The Washingtonians are "grown-ups" (in one particularly unfortunate recent formulation).

Their "realism" consists in believing that there are evil leaders and governments in the world. They are under the impression that their critics are moral relativists, who do not recognize this.

They interpret a reluctance to go to war against Iraq, and potentially Iran and North Korea, and an unwillingness to follow the United States in making radical government reorganizations, and restricting civil liberties in an ill-defined and thus far conspicuously unsuccessful war against terrorism, as evidence of this moral relativism.

One might think it evidence of good sense or an informed prudence, but the Bush people believe themselves more farsighted than others. This is a recurrent fallacy in Washington. It was Madeleine Albright, secretary of state in the Clinton administration, who provided this belief's most complacent statement when she said that the United States "sees farther" because it "stands taller," being more virtuous than other countries.

George Ball, an immensely respected U.S. diplomat of the postwar period, argued in the 1960s that the United States is "unique in world history" because its foreign policy is disinterested. Europeans, he added, "have little experience in the exercise of responsibility divorced from ... narrow and specific national interests." He said this in explaining why the United States would win the war in Vietnam.

Naturally this attitude does not always go down very well in other countries and has become a particular irritant in American relations today with Europe.

The serious formulation of the neo-conservatives' argument says that while the United States acts on moral realism, the West Europeans have adopted an idealistic view of international affairs that may be appropriate in dealing with the concerns of the European community but is irresponsible as an approach to an international order threatened by rogue states and anarchic failed states.

It contends as well that the European view reflects a lack of courage and a deplorably selfish willingness to allow the United States to defend the international order while Europeans appease rogue rulers and seize shady commercial advantages that the United States high-mindedly scorns.

In the past year, France and Germany have also been accused of displaying anti-Semitic sentiments, expediently concealed since Nazi and Vichy times but now rampant, ignored by a European leadership which in this respect is no better than that of the 1930s.

In part, all this reflects old cultural attitudes tied to the complicated relationship of Americans of European descent to the countries their ancestors left in the eighteenth and nineteenth centuries, and in the case of the neo-conservatives, many of them Jewish, in the attitudes of children and grandchildren of the Nazis' victims. Not a great deal can be done to change any of this.

It also presents, in an intense form, the same disagreement that has separated American governments from their European allies on a number of previous occasions. This, by analogy at least, is a theological disagreement.

Dualism has always been a powerful tendency in religion, the unmistakable good — light — confronting darkness and evil. Both Calvinism and the seventeenth-century Catholic heresy of Jansenism were affected by theological dualism, preaching predestination and the corrupting force of material goods and pleasures.

Both had great influence on the American consciousness, the first through the seventeenth-century Puritanism that shaped American Congregationalism in the eighteenth century, and the evangelical Protestantism of the nineteenth and twentieth centuries.

They preached that the world was replete with Satan's snares, and they took an activist approach to doing something about this (remember not only Prohibition but Carrie Nation and her hatchet). The Jansenist influence reached the United States via Irish Catholicism, deeply Puritan in outlook.

Manicheism has become a generalized term (usually of abuse), but the religion itself originated (not far from Baghdad) early in the second century of the Christian era and was a synthesis of Zoroastrianism and Christianity, with several other Asian religious influences.

Its dualism was of eternal war between God and Satan, light and darkness. It held that evil was physical, not a moral thing. Believers fell into two classes: the elect, or perfect, bearers of light, and their followers, who could hope to merit rebirth as elect. All others were sinners, destined to hell.

Manicheism itself had largely disappeared in Europe by the sixth century, although it influenced the medieval heresies of the Cathars, Albigenses and the Bogomils.

Its dualism is an interpretation of existence that has proven persistent and seductive. In the United States its religious expression has weakened, but its larger influence on the American mind, as it addresses foreign affairs, is stronger than ever.

132

Paris, December 3, 2002 — A part of the neo-conservative intelligentsia in Washington is attempting to turn the Bush administration's "war against terrorism" into a war against Muslim civilization and the Islamic religion.

Such influential figures as Eliot Cohen of the Johns Hopkins School of Advanced International Studies in Washington and Kenneth Adelman of the Defense Department advisory policy board, a former Regan administration official, criticize President George W. Bush for his efforts to assure Muslims that his war is against terrorism, not against their religion.

The Bush critics say that Islam itself is America's enemy because Islamic religion and civilization are intolerant, hostile to Western values, proselytizing, expansionist and violent.

Their implied argument is that Islam was hostile to the West before Israel came into existence, hence that the Israel-Palestine conflict has nothing to do with Islam's crisis with the West. This is a novel argument likely to leave many unconvinced.

A segment of the evangelical Protestant community in the United States adds to this an assertion that Islam is "evil." That is the view of a clergyman who officiated at the Bush inauguration in 2001.

Cohen, Adelman and their fellows in the U.S. policy community have yet to explain what they mean about war against Islamic civilization — against the second largest religious community on Earth, with more than a billion adherents on six continents. One would have thought that Mr. Bush already has his hands full with Iraq and Al Qaeda.

These intellectuals have fallen into Samuel Huntington's pernicious fallacy that civilizations, which are cultural phenomena, can be treated as if they were responsible political entities. They identify the members of Islamic civilization not in terms of their actions but in terms of what they are.

One can legitimately go to war against Iraq and Iraqis because of what the Baghdad government does, since Iraq's citizens have to accept responsibility for their government, even if it is a despotism.

The same can be said about Iranians, Saudi Arabians, Egyptians, Indonesians, Pakistanis — and Americans. The American people bear an ultimate responsibility for what their government does even if citizens individually oppose those actions. The obligations of citizenship are negative as well as positive.

However, neither Muslims nor Americans deserve to die because they are the product of their civilizations, whether those civilizations are admirable or otherwise. To think otherwise is totalitarian thinking. It is the equivalent of racist thinking. The enemy is an enemy not because of what he or she does but because of what he or she is. The Muslim is our enemy — man, woman and child — because of his or her cultural and religious identification.

Germans six decades ago were called on by their leaders to make war on Jews because Jews were Jews. They were the alleged racial inferiors and enemies of Germans. What these Jews actually did or who they were was a matter of indifference. Jews collectively were identified as Germany's enemies and were to be eliminated.

Communists during the same period were being told to exterminate aristocrats, "Kulaks" (prosperous peasants), shopkeepers, capitalists and professionals, "deviationist" party members and eventually Jews as well. The murder of all these was justified because they were "class enemies."

To call this totalitarian thinking is a grave accusation, heavily charged with the weight of the genocidal experience of the twentieth century. In this case it is justified.

Adelman, Cohen and those who agree with them are putting a culture, which has no political existence, in the place of identifiable and responsible political actors: governments, leaders, individuals. To do this disregards political responsibility and announces historical fatality.

If wars are cultural and religious they have no solutions. They are un-negotiable and unresolvable. If the Muslim is an enemy of America and Europe because he is a Muslim, and Westerners are his mortal enemies because of who they are, all have lost control over their futures.

But all this is simply untrue. Today's clashes between America and elements of Islamic society reflect a power struggle inside Islamic society between fundamentalists and others; between obscurantists and progressives; between traditionalists and political fanatics.

Identifiable Muslim groups and governments are in conflict with the government of the United States over the future of Israel and the Palestinians, the control of oil, and American power and presence in Arabia, the Gulf and now in Central Asia.

These clashes between Muslims and Americans are important, dangerous and potentially even more violent than they have already become. They are not a war of religion, and it is deeply irresponsible to try to turn them into one.

134

December 10, 2002 — In the months following the terrorist attacks of September 2001 it was politically taboo to say that the United States had in some way brought these attacks upon itself. Television talk-show hosts and print journalists lost their jobs for suggesting such a thing.

Yet anyone with any serious knowledge of American relations in recent years with the Moslem Middle East knows that it is true — even if it is only part of the truth.

The Israel-Palestine conflict is a self-evident source of the alienation of Arab Moslems from the U.S. since 1948, and particularly since 1967, when Israel occupied East Jerusalem and the West Bank.

The essential cause for conflict, however, is one that commentators are trying to get at when they talk about the "crisis of modernization" in the Islamic world. It is the incompatibility of values between Islamic society and the modern West.

The power and material dynamism of the West seems inseparable from a value system that demands that Moslems give up their moral identity. The British conservative writer, Roger Scruton, has in a recent book asked why we should blame Islam for trying to reject "western technology, western institutions, western conceptions of religious freedom" when all of these "involve a rejection of the idea on which Islam is founded — the idea of God's immutable will, revealed once and for all to his prophet, in the form of an inviolable and unchanging code of law?"

Why indeed? The West takes for granted that the existing religious assumptions of Islamic society have to be overturned, not only because they don't suit the West but because the West believes that they are unsuitable for the Moslems themselves.

There is constant western pressure on Islamic governments to conform to western conceptions of human rights and promote free and critical religious and political thought. In short, they are to become us.

We in the West are inclined to think that everybody must eventually become like us. Standard American discussion of American destiny and the "end of history" takes for granted an eventual benevolent Americanization of global society. To the orthodox Moslem, that means apostasy, immorality, and God's condemnation.

Westernization, to westerners, means liberation. Americans do not conceive of themselves as inheritors of a western legacy of Promethean violence.

For people in other societies, westernization frequently means destruction, social and moral crisis, with individuals cast adrift in a destructured and literally demoralized world.

Cultural and political disorientation, violent resistance to the intruder, and attempts to recapture a lost golden age are natural reactions to this. We see all of this today.

The violence of the shock is intensified when the foreigner establishes military bases and tries to shape an Islamic country's policies. This has been Pentagon policy during the past decade, with regional commanders for all of the world's major geographical zones and expansion of the U.S. worldwide base system.

The New York Times a few days ago wrote about the rising importance of ultraconservative or radical Islam in Saudi Arabia, and acknowledged that its growing influence has been directly connected to the presence of American troops in that country since 1990.

Originally the bases were temporary, needed for the U.S. campaign to drive the Iraqis out of Kuwait. It was a moment when the Saudis believed they needed protection from Iraq.

However when the Gulf war was over, the U.S. rashly pressed a reluctant Saudi monarchy to allow permanent American bases. The September 11 attacks, carried out mainly by Saudis, avowedly were revenge for the "contamination" of the Islamic Holy Places by those bases.

Relations between Washington and the Saudi monarchy today are so strained that the U.S. will likely be denied use of the bases for an attack on Iraq; almost certainly this will be so if there is no UN mandate for the attack.

The United States now has extended its base in Kuwait to nearly a third of that state's territory. There are new bases in the other Gulf monarchies. The Afghanistan intervention has left U.S. bases in that country, and in Uzbekistan and Kazakhstan. The war against terror has expanded American troop presence in Georgia and the Moslem southern Philippines. A long military occupation of Iraq is envisaged by Washington.

Every base conveys the contamination of "infidel" modernization as well as the oppressive suggestion of foreign military occupation. Washington remorselessly expands its military presence in the Islamic world, in order to fight the anti-American terrorism that its presence causes. No one in the government seems to see a contradiction in this.

December 17, 2002 — The meeting last weekend in London of members of the Iraqi external opposition proved more of a demonstration of disagreements than a display of unity on the principles and practical compromises necessary to make a plausible Baghdad government out of Iraq's exile groups and factions.

It ended with a declaration supporting federal government and tolerance, but while the group asked the international community to help them by liberating Iraq, its text rejected "any form of occupation of Iraq, any military administration either foreign or local, or any foreign mandate."

Most published American policy speculation has envisaged indefinite American military occupation and "reeducation" of Iraq (indeed of the Arab Mideast as a whole, plus Central Asia in the more extravagant theories), on the supposed example of the postwar Allied occupation of Germany and Japan.

One assumes that given the sweeping military victory Washington is counting on, military occupation could keep an expedient coalition of political groups in power for a considerable time, just as now is the case in Afghanistan. Whether such a coalition would survive without foreign support is another matter.

In the longer run, the fissures in Iraqi society (as in Afghanistan) would almost certainly reappear. These are the religious and ethnic divisions separating Sunni and Shi'ite Muslims, Christians and Kurds; and the political rivalry between the secular political forces of the Ba'ath party and orthodox religious forces (which Saddam Hussein has been appeasing).

They are the fractures responsible for minority revolts in Iraq in the 1930s, and for seven military coups between 1936 and 1941, all during a period when the country — in origin, three distinct Ottoman provinces — was a British protectorate.

Another military coup in 1958 overthrew the British-sponsored monarchy, murdered the king, crown prince and prime minister, and installed a republic (with Islam the official religion).

The secular Ba'ath party came to power in still another coup in 1963. Saddam Hussein took power after more unrest involving the (legal) Communist party, the Kurds, Iranian interests and Iraq's Shi'ites, who are the majority in the country (even though the government has always been Sunni).

Whether this country is ready for federal unity and peace remains to be seen (as is whether the United States Army will be welcomed with cheers).

The answers will come after Iraq's expected defeat by the United States and its yet to be determined coalition partners. The coalition's make-up will be known when Washington makes its decision on whether to await further UN action or concludes that it has grounds to invade, disarm and replace Iraq's government on its own authority.

Certainly, Iraq and the world would be better places with Saddam Hussein removed from power. The question of principle is whether the world would also be improved by Washington's putting into practice its declared policy of preemptive intervention.

The notion that the "international community" (an entity of admittedly inexact definition) has a right or obligation to intervene in situations of catastrophic evil has been gaining ground in recent years. David Rieff writes in the indispensable handbook *Crimes of War* that the idea of humanitarian intervention is both "immensely powerful and terribly imprecise."

It was inspired, of course, by the slaughters of the wars of Yugoslav succession and attempted genocide in Rwanda. It presents a relatively easy intellectual and political problem of diagnosis, but a hard problem of policy, as demonstrated in the U.S.-led UN intervention in Somalia.

Its other difficulty is that it challenges the principle of absolute national sovereignty, the basis of international relations since 1648, with long-term implications very difficult to foresee.

The United States today is promoting the notion of preemptive military intervention, which again undermines the Westphalian system.

Washington claims that states can be and (sometimes) should be invaded, with "regime change" carried out when they have, or might in the future acquire, weapons of mass destruction, and might use them against others.

This causes international uneasiness because intervention rests on an argument about what the state involved might do in the future.

The uneasiness is strengthened in the Iraqi case because the object of intervention is a country where the United States has an economic interest in intervention, and because most of Iraq's immediate neighbors, other than Israel, seem more afraid of the military intervention and its consequences than they are of Iraq.

Humanitarian intervention is carried out to halt crimes already under way. There is a *corpus delicti*. In the Washington's plan, there is only the rogue nation — so designated by Washington.

December 19, 2002 — Christmas arrives under the shadow of a war that both sides seem determined to interpret as a war between civilizations, even though it is not.

It is only a war between governments and people.

It now seems that war between Iraq and a UN-mandated coalition is all but inevitable, due to the conduct of the Iraqi government. Iraq would like this interpreted as a war of aggression by the West against Islam, as many in the Islamic world will do.

The war at best will do no more than decide who will be Saddam Hussein's successor in ruling Iraq, and in allocating its oil. At worst, of course, it may do a great deal of harm to both sides.

War is not a positive option, despite the pressure for war against Iraq that has been exercised in Washington over the last year by a neo-conservative ideological faction convinced that a radiant future lies on the other side of the battlefield.

No time is more dangerous than when intellectuals acquire the power to impose their ideas on world affairs. "It is only those who have neither fired a shot nor heard the shrieks and groans of the wounded who cry aloud for blood...vengeance, desolation," as U.S. Civil War Gen. William Tecumseh Sherman said in 1879.

War in Iraq will do nothing to solve the challenge of terrorism. A report just submitted to the UN Security Council reports that new volunteers have been swelling the numbers of that loose network of activists who identify with al Qaeda and share its convictions.

This is not a traditional terrorist organization and does not function according to the logic of such organizations as the IRA. It is more like a missionary religious movement, or even a millenarian sect.

Its dynamism is a product of nationalism, as well as religion. It considers itself at war against the United States because its members are convinced that America has allied itself with Israel to dominate the Arab world and capture its resources.

Its war, however, unlike war in Iraq, offers no prospect of a military victory. The essential damage al Qaeda can do to the United States has already been done, by sowing an irrational fear among Americans — irrational because of the actual material limit on what al Qaeda's militants could do to a society as huge, populous and well defended as the United States.

That fear has provoked the U.S. government into limiting civil liberties, suspending the rule of law with respect to designated citizens, creating courts of exception and special prisons, and has inspired abdication by the Senate of its constitutional war powers.

Al Qaeda represents radical Islam. Its own objective is to punish the United States and its allies so as to force the West's military and political withdrawal from the Islamic world.

Radical Islam, a religious movement, aims to reform and "purify" Islam itself.

The Bush administration's attack on Afghanistan, and a war against Iraq, can do little to counter the latter movement, which promotes itself through religious channels of influence throughout the Muslim world, and in Europe, the United States, and non-Muslim Asia.

Its ambition to transform the Muslim world is a familiar one in the modern history of non-Western societies reacting against the moral, cultural, and intellectual challenge of the West. Unable to deal with the West on its own terms, radical Islam tries instead to revive a past when Islamic power was great — supposedly because religion was pure and people then were obedient and devout.

But as you can't go back, and since the countries where the strict version of Islamic law, or Shari'a, is already installed, society's practical problems are not noticeably improved, the radical solution inevitably will eventually lose its appeal. One saw how grateful many people in Afghanistan were to get rid of the Taliban, who earlier had promised a solution to their problems.

In Iran, where modern Islamic fundamentalism succeeded, the power of the radical clergy is already undermined by student and popular resistance to clerical repression. An evolution is under way that will eventually return Iran to the ranks of "normal" nations.

What people have to understand is that in matters like this we are dealing with deep currents in history that have to work themselves out over many years.

Like the totalitarianisms of the last century, the political and strategic manifestations of today's radicalisms may have to be contained. War is the worst way to do it, since war damages everyone. But circumstances dictate choices, and war it now looks to be in a New Year that for many will not be happy.

December 31, 2002 — A nation with the power and ambition of today's United States owes to itself, and to the world, to recognize facts. Knowing what

140

actually happened, rather than myths about what happened, would seem essential to avoiding error about what may happen in the future....

A senior official in the White House was quoted last week in *The Washington Post* as saying that America has assumed "an almost imperial role" today because its responsibilities are the same as when "America [was] standing between Nazi Germany and a takeover of all Europe."

Britain, not the United States, stood between the Nazis and the takeover of all Europe. The United States did nothing substantial to oppose the Nazis until 1942. Churchill pleaded for help, but an isolationist Congress denied it.

Jews fleeing Germany were refused American refuge. The U.S. government rejected a French government appeal for help in mid-June 1940. The French republic collapsed, and the Battle of Britain began. A handful of American volunteers went to join the RAF's Eagle Squadron.

The only practical aid for Britain that Franklin Roosevelt was able to get from an isolationist Congress was to exchange 50 obsolete destroyers for 99-year leases on British bases in the Western Hemisphere.

Lend-lease was a system of war supplies delivered on credit, which Congress demanded be eventually repaid (as much had to be, which is one reason the British Empire came to an end after 1945).

Even after the Japanese attack on Pearl Harbor, the United States did not declare war on Germany. It did so three days later, after Germany had declared war on the U.S.

Look back a century. In January 1903, the world was at peace and Britain was the sole superpower. It was the greatest empire ever known. Britain's First Lord of the Admiralty in 1903 would have looked with contempt at challenges from the feeble "rogue states" that preoccupy Donald Rumsfeld and Dick Cheney.

Britain had not only the capacity to wage simultaneous naval wars against its two greatest rivals, France and Germany, but could have fought the combined navies of the United States, Germany, and Russia. In 1903, Britain had 67 battleships in service. France had 37, Germany and the United States 27 each, Russia 18, and Japan 5.

The Boer War had been settled the previous May, after nearly 6,000 British casualties and 16,000 losses to disease, as against Boer losses of 4,000. (This was the British Empire's Vietnam war — an intimation of decline.)

141

The great-power peace of 1903 was to end in 1904, when Japan, with its five battleships, went to war with Russia and sank virtually the entire Russian fleet. The first Russian revolution followed.

Also in 1903, less widely noticed, the Wright brothers flew a powered aircraft on a North Carolina sandbar. The Russian Social Democratic Party split into Menshevik and Bolshevik factions, the latter led by V.I. Lenin.

Thirty-six years later, Lenin's Russia joined Nazi Germany to divide and conquer Europe, followed by Nazi Germany's attempt to destroy Soviet Russia. Two years after that, in a campaign lasting five months, Japanese naval air power drove all the great powers out of the western Pacific — ending colonialism by doing so, and bringing the United States into the world crisis.

The United States, four years later, essentially unharmed, more powerful than it was before the war, picked up the pieces. The United States is where it is today because of what other nations did to ruin themselves. Being the world's sole superpower is not a permanent appointment.

Paris, January 7, 2003 — President George W. Bush continues to repeat moral arguments for a U.S. attack on Iraq because his domestic political advisor, Karl Rove, has convinced him that the "moral clarity" of his declarations about the war against evil and the wickedness of Saddam Hussein have proven a decisive electoral asset.

However, his current difficulties in consolidating U.S. and international opinion behind an invasion of Iraq lie in the realms of reason and evidence. His speeches have, in those respects, offered nothing new to demonstrate that the United States should attack Iraq here and now, with or without a new UN mandate.

No one needs to be convinced of Saddam Hussein's iniquity. Scarcely anyone in the western world defends him or pretends that international society would not be a better place if the Iraqi dictator were gone.

But speeches such as the one the president gave at Fort Hood in Texas last Friday, again claiming that "either you're with those who love freedom or you're with those who hate innocent life," say nothing to those who need to be convinced that military intervention in Iraq will actually leave the Middle East better off than before.

The president's critics include pacifists who are against war itself, and others who defend international law by opposing cross-border interventions, or at least those not warranted by some immediate and overt offense against international norms.

Genocide in Africa, and barbarous tribalisms and nationalisms there and in the Balkans, have in recent years made a widely accepted case for military interventions that offer a high probability of doing more good than harm — which is the traditional philosophical justification for "just" war.

However, the administration has failed to answer the people in the United States and in allied countries, who are numerous and who want prudential, political and practical evidence to convince them that intervention in Iraq provides such a case.

Take the weapons inspections. There has been a steady, critical commentary by administration officials concerning the UN inspectors, even though, supposedly in order to protect U.S. intelligence sources, the inspectors are not being given the evidence the U.S. claims to possess about the location of mass destruction weapons and facilities.

Accordingly, notwithstanding its failure to account for certain stocks of chemical and biological agents, Iraq's strategy of accepting inspections and allowing full access to its installations has thus far lent a certain plausibility to its claim to have renounced mass destruction weapons. One would have thought that in order to justify its policy, the Bush administration would do better to help the inspectors.

It surely can do the administration no good to have the inspectors come in at the end of this month with a report consistent with Iraq's claims. Even if Washington then makes dramatic new accusations, if these too are undocumented the United States would fail to make its case.

Critics of the administration's policies are concerned about the balance of harm and good reasonably to be expected from a war, and about the war's likely long-term consequences for American foreign relations.

They would like a more intelligent discussion of strategic outcomes than unsupported assurances that the Arab world, including the Palestinians, will welcome "liberation" by the United States, allied with Israel.

Senator Chuck Hagel, the influential Nebraska Republican and a friend of President Bush, is one such person. He came back from a Middle Eastern trip in mid-December to tell the Chicago Council on Foreign Relations that invading Iraq "will neither assure a democratic transition in Iraq, bring peace to Israelis and Palestinians, nor assure stability in the Middle East." He specifically rejected the argument that "the road to Arab-Israeli peace" goes by way of Iraq's invasion.

There are almost daily Washington press reports that claim the contrary. They describe how an Iraq war would successfully be fought, how post-intervention Iraq would be governed and how regional peace would prevail. All this is given the press by interested parties.

Attacking another country to accomplish "regime change" is a grave matter in human terms, and in the effect it will have on international norms and legal precedent.

An attack on this particular country, in these particular Middle Eastern political circumstances, against a culturally charged background of Islamic-American relations and difficult U.S. alliance relationships, demands much franker, more open and more serious debate than President Bush's policy has received until now. If the affair goes badly, the administration and the Republican Party will pay; but the American nation may be done lasting harm.

New York, January 16, 2003 — The UN inspectors have found 12 chemical weapons shells rather than a smoking gun, opening an argument as to whether the former amount to the latter.

The argument has already been made that if the inspectors find concealed weapons, their discovery and destruction prove that the inspections are working and should continue.

Until now, the New York foreign policy community has seemed persuaded that the war with Iraq is going to be postponed or might even not take place at all. The obstacles to a military intervention have grown steadily more complicated and persuasive as U.S. public support for unilateral attack falls and allied opinion remains overwhelmingly against it.

President Bush has made a huge political investment in "regime change" for Iraq and has launched a costly military buildup that will be hard to suspend and awkward to reverse, but has thus far shown himself both unreflective and stubborn in defending his case.

Unreflective, in that he seems to have failed to grasp that the public in the U.S. and abroad need to be convinced intellectually that a war would have more positive than negative consequences. He simply repeats that Saddam Hussein is an awful man, as if his critics were disputing that. Saddam's actual threat to the United States is asserted but neither explained nor documented.

This lack of clarity about intentions and political strategy is why his public support has faded and why Britain's foreign secretary, Jack Straw, has joined

France (and Germany) in asking for another Security Council debate and resolution after the chief UN inspectors make their provisional report on January 27.
It is why all the allies now talk about giving the inspectors more time, and post-
poning any military intervention until the end of the summer.

Washington's failure to make a structured and supported case for intervention has disquietingly echoed Mr. Bush's testy answer to a recent query
about the timing of the war. He said, "I get to decide that." It suggests that he
personally will decide on war and postwar policy, according to his hunches and
what he has called his "good instincts."

On the consequences of a war, the president's neo-conservative supporters
have offered futuristic theories about a transformed region and a modernizing
shock to the Muslim Middle East. They and anonymous administration officials
have given the press proposals for military government in postwar Iraq, or some
form of UN administration, or a new government by returned exiles or regional
leaders, or even for dismembering the country.

But we still have nothing official about the administration's intentions. The
president cannot expect wide international support until he says what, once
Saddam Hussein has been driven from power, he intends to do with Iraq (and its
resources, a cause of much current suspicion)....

If the discovery of chemical weapons components is accompanied in the
UN inspectors' January 27 report by other evidence of continuing Iraqi violation
of UN resolutions the president can go to the Security Council for an
endorsement of military intervention in Iraq and is likely to get it.

Lacking that, the administration might act because Mr. Bush has made so
large a personal and political investment in doing so. In those circumstances, he
would have little NATO help, no American use of Turkish or Saudi Arabian
bases, no foreign money to pay for the war and an immense wave of foreign criticism, as well as much domestic dissent.

Much as he might dislike it, the Security Council provides the way to go.

Paris, January 23, 2003 — The crisis between Americans and the Germans and
French over war in Iraq only superficially arises from the Bush administration's
determination since 2001 to attack Saddam Hussein. The two West European
governments have seen the Iraqi dictator as a minor international problem, and
war against him as likely to do more harm than good.

The difference in views derives from historical experience. The West Europeans, generally speaking, do not share America's visions of vast global reform, or of bringing history to an end. They had enough of that, and its consequences, with Marxism and Nazism.

They are interested in a slow development of civilized and tolerant international relations, compromising problems while avoiding catastrophes along the way. They have themselves only recently recovered from the disasters of the first and second world wars, when tens of millions of people were destroyed. They don't want more.

American commentators like to think that the "Jacksonian" frontier spirit equips America to dominate, reform and democratize other civilizations. They do not understand that the indefatigable American confidence in self comes largely from never having had anything very bad happen to the United States.

The worst American war was the Civil War, in which the nation, North and South, suffered 498,000 wartime deaths from all causes, slightly more than 1.5 percent of the total population of 31.5 million.

The single battle of the Somme in the First World War produced twice as many European casualties as the United States suffered, wounded included, during the entire Civil War.

Washington does not really possess the authority to explain Europe's reluctance to go to war in condescending terms of a supposed European reluctance to confront the Realpolitik realities of a Hobbesian universe.

The difference between European and American views is more sensibly explained in terms of an irresponsible and ideology-fed enthusiasm of Bush administration advisors and leaders for global adventure and power, fostered by people with virtually no experience, and little seeming imaginative grasp, of what war means for its victims.

It cannot be emphasized too often that not one of the principal figures associated with the Bush White House's foreign policy, with the exception of Colin Powell, has any actual experience of war, most of them having actively sought to avoid military service in Vietnam.

Their inexperience and ignorance could not be better displayed than by Defense Secretary Donald Rumsfeld's recent comment that draftees have added "no value, no advantage really, to the United States armed services over any sustained period of time." Who does he think fought the Second World War — the Regular Army?

The American Regular Army has never been truly effective until large numbers of flexible, brainy and nonconformist wartime civilian solders are integrated into its command, staffs, and ranks.

This has been true from the Civil War to Vietnam — when the system of egalitarian civilian service was finally destroyed by draft evasion by the privileged in American society, and the Army was brought close to mutiny.

Germany's current resistance to President Bush's war coincides with the reemergence in Germany of memories of exterminatory bombardment, pillage, population expulsions and mass rape, suffered in the final months of the second world war.

This devastating experience has deliberately been repressed in the German consciousness, in acknowledgment of Germany's responsibility for the war and the crimes committed by German forces.

In recent months, a series of books and articles have at last recalled what the Germans themselves call "taboo" subjects, at a time when the youngest generations of those who experienced these events are mostly still alive.

This has not been to argue the merits, justification and minor actual effect on the German war effort of Allied saturation and fire-storm bombing of German cities — which is a fruitless argument — but in order to establish a moral and aesthetic coming to terms with events that, together with the fire-bombing of Japan's wooden cities, rank among the worst things ever done in, or by, western civilization.

Next to this, the intellectually claptrap war rhetoric of the Bush administration seems unbearably unimportant, evidence only of how remote the political class in the United States has today become from the rest of the world.

January 30, 2003 — Javier Solano, the European Union's High Representative in foreign affairs, spoke recently about what he saw as a confrontation between a religious vision of world affairs in the White House, and the secular and rationalist vision of the Europeans. ...

According to U.S. policy and political intellectuals quoted by contemporary historian Timothy Garton Ash in the latest *New York Review of Books*, Europeans are "weak, petulant, hypocritical, disunited, duplicitous, sometimes anti-Semitic and often anti-American appeasers." The president has said (rashly assuming to himself the words of Jesus [Matthew 12:30]), "He who is not with me is against me."

Yet the religion — or religiosity, to make a distinction not usually made today — of the Bush administration is only one strand in modern American Protestantism, although currently an important one.

It derives from the Puritan/evangelical (which is to say, Calvinist) dualism in American Protestantism, dividing mankind between those who are Saved and Born-again, and the sinners. This view of a moral universe riven in two is easily transferred to foreign policy.

While George Bush himself is "born again" and his White House includes many evangelical Protestants, it is hard to see the Donald Rumsfelds, Paul Wolfowitzes and Richard Perles of the administration as part of this. They are tough, power-oriented, bureaucratic operators and ideologues. On their side, the alliance must be a fairly cynical one.

Relevant to the transatlantic confrontation of political cultures, however, is a man now largely forgotten, who was the most important religious influence on modern American political thought, and specifically on its foreign policy thinking. This was the distinguished theologian Reinhold Niebuhr.

From the early 1930s on, he was concerned with the use of power in international relations. Religious people then tended to be uncomfortable with power, as they often remain today. They are inclined to respond to serious international conflicts of interest and ideology with a sentimental pacifism.

Niebuhr rejected this, as part of his coming to terms with what society had become after World War I, and with the rise of the totalitarian regimes of the 1920s and 1930s. He gave up "Christian absolutism" as a result of the pressure of world events, writing a deeply influential book called *Moral Man and Immoral Society*.

He was concerned with that zone where ethics and power meet, defending the necessity of power in ordering society, while refusing to yield on ethical standards. The historian and diplomat George Kennan called him "the father of us all," speaking for all who belong to the "realist" intellectual tradition in American foreign policy.

The tradition is all but absent in American government today. It is certainly absent from the Bush White House. But it also seems to have limited influence on modern post-Christian European political thought and practice, disposed toward what Niebuhr considered the illusion that institutions in and of themselves can reshape society.

The institutions of European Union have been unprecedentedly effective in reshaping West European society since the war. But they also failed completely in dealing with the Balkan crisis of the 1990s. The United States ignored that crisis, too — America had "no dog in that fight," as then-Secretary of State James Baker said — but eventually, under liberal popular pressure, the U.S. did force NATO to use its power to stop the war.

The Europeans had been held back by reluctance to make moral and political judgments. They wanted to keep their hands clean (and failed). As the French poet Charles Péguy once said, having clean hands can mean having no hands.

The problem with this American government is that its "realists" — the neo-conservatives — are not realistic at all, while the president and his domestic policy advisors are shallow and simplistic.

I say the neo-conservatives are not realistic because they are pushing the country into an attack on Iraq on the basis of stubbornly biased and ideologically based scenarios of an easy war and even easier democratic transformation of the Middle East. They exclude other possibilities.

They are also unrealistic in that they have no compassion or empathy for the enemy. This failure is ethical. It means that they totally underestimate what he represents. In this respect, the Europeans are more realistic, fearing what may come in the region. But the Europeans have no power, and they don't want power.

Paris, February 4, 2003 — Political destruction for Gerhard Schroeder and regime change in Germany seem to have replaced Saddam Hussein and Iraq as the immediate priorities of the Bush administration and its more ardent supporters in the press.

This is interesting since Mr. Schroeder is already a politically damaged figure because of Germany's economic impasse under SDP government. At the same time German popular hostility to military interventions abroad has always been well known.

President Bush may have been shocked that Chancellor Schroeder made opposition to an Iraq war part of his campaign platform in last September's parliamentary election, but he can hardly have been surprised: he too is a killer politician who knows a winning issue and how to use it.

However Washington and the conservative Republicans are indifferent to German opinion. They are concerned with what German government and politicians do. In their opinion the precedent set by the chancellor of running on an anti-American issue must not be allowed to stand. He must be humiliated as an example to others.

Germany (whatever its current difficulties) is the most powerful economy in the European Union, and no matter what happens will remain a leader of Europe. The neo-conservative theory that currently governs official thinking in Washington identifies Europe as the principal future rival and potential challenger of the U.S.

This is the first time that a German government has taken a stand against Washington and refused to back down. The chancellor who has done this must not, in the current Washington view, be allowed to get away with it. What Schroeder did was all the more dangerous to Washington because he expressed popular opinion across Europe.

British public backing for Tony Blair's support of George Bush is at its lowest point. Eighty-four percent of the British are now against an Iraq intervention without a UN mandate (changed from 68 percent ten days ago).

Jose Maria Aznar was one of the initiators of last week's letter from European leaders demanding Atlantic solidarity, but 74 percent of the Spanish are against any military intervention whatever in Iraq — with or without UN approval.

An intervention lacking UN endorsement is opposed by 79 percent of the Italians. Seventy-two percent of Portuguese opinion (as of ten days ago) opposes such an action, as does 79 percent in Denmark, 71 percent in Hungary, and even 63 percent and 61 percent respectively in Poland and the Czech Republic.

The letter signed by leaders from five of the 15 European Union members, plus three EU membership candidates, called for Atlantic solidarity and resolute application of Security Council resolutions, but did not endorse U.S. policy as such.

Its effect was nonetheless to align the conservative governments of Italy and Spain, and traditionally Atlanticist Britain and Denmark, with the U.S. in unspoken opposition to Germany and France.

It was meant to split Europe. It actually demonstrated that the split that exists is between politicians and public. While European governments do not have a common foreign policy, on some issues the European public does.

This is important. Prime ministers Blair, Berlusconi, and Aznar are (with qualifications) supporters of President Bush on Iraq, but the people are not. The people can elect new prime ministers, but the prime ministers can't elect new peoples.

There is another split in Europe, a permanent one, between those who want Europe to be a united and autonomous actor in world affairs, and on the other hand those who are frightened by the possibility that Europe might lose the Atlantic attachment. The latter is true for the former Communist countries, and some of the smaller West European states.

As there cannot be a wholly independent "Europe" which does not sooner or later clash interests with the U.S., it follows that only a small number of European states are serious candidates for a common European foreign and security alliance capable of playing an influential role in world affairs.

This group consists essentially of the core states of the old European Community, possibly without the Atlanticist Netherlands and Italy, and possibly including Spain — a nation with ambitions, an imperial history, and no great love for the United States.

The Europeans are wasting their time trying to create a single foreign policy (concerned with other than trivial matters) for a 25-member or larger EU. A union of core Europe might conduct a common policy, with France and Germany at its center. This is regarded by Washington as a threat, which in a sense it is. This explains why the Bush administration is determined to crush Germany's independent stand on Iraq.

[This article was reported in the German press as having convinced Chancellor Schroeder to stand firm against the United States on the issue of invading Iraq without specific UN authority.]

February 6, 2003 — The question implicitly asked of Secretary of State Powell at the Security Council was whether this war would be a just war.

It is the persisting question in the minds of people inside and outside the United States. Popular opinion may not know the criteria established for just war in the Middle Ages, as international law was struggling to be born. But common sense tells us whether or not a war makes sense.

The principles are that the war must have a grave cause and be the last resort, all peaceful solutions having been tried in vain. There is supposed to be convincing evidence that the war will do more good than harm. The "right intention" is supposed to exist: the country launching war is not supposed to be acting to serve its narrow political interests or for material profit.

Despite Secretary Powell's presentation, not only governments, but much of the public — certainly the Western, as well as Middle Eastern public — seems unconvinced that these conditions exist today.

People instinctively flinch at the prospect of the United States, with its 280 million people and most powerful economy and military forces on earth, launching a high-tech war on a nation of 23 million people, already weakened by a dozen years of UN sanctions. They feel this even when they simultaneously recognize that Iraq's regime is a repellent despotism that defies the international community.

If Secretary Powell had convinced them on Wednesday that Iraq posed "a seething threat to humanity," as some commentators have put it, they would undoubtedly agree that it should be attacked. Powell contributed much to the evidence that the Baghdad regime is wicked and duplicitous — but few have thought otherwise.

What he failed to produce was conclusive new evidence that Iraq is an active threat to international society, or even that it is a real threat to the United States. This failure has actually weakened the American position, since so much had been promised.

It was also a surprise, and a source of some skepticism, that the United States had taken so long to put together a detailed case against the Iraqi regime. Surely, intelligence sources would not have been compromised by earlier production of intercepted telephone conversations and defector information already hinted at in the press.

The inconclusiveness of the American case had been telegraphed several days earlier, when a State Department source told reporters that the president himself would eventually furnish the decisive evidence that justified military intervention, and that the secretary of state was simply preparing the ground for Mr. Bush.

Mr. Powell saw to it that George Tenet of the CIA was with him at the UN. He has not come as far as he has through the politicized jungles of Pentagon and White House bureaucracies without learning that in difficult circumstances, blame is better shared.

The real American problem derives from the moral question of proportionality. Is an attack on Iraq an act of justice — that is, is it a disinterested act to protect regional and international security?

To the extent that people close to the Bush administration have framed regime change in Iraq as part of a geopolitical strategy that primarily serves perceived American and Israeli national interests in the region, the other Security Council members, as well as international opinion, remain reluctant to see matters as Washington would like them seen.

International opinion may remain hostile to a war, but Washington is where the decision is going to be made, and the Bush administration seems set on intervention, regime change and the military occupation of Iraq.

It would like international endorsement. It needs allies to finance the war and take responsibility for civil reconstruction when the war is over. But it seems certain to go ahead, even if it goes alone.

For Washington, the argument over war or peace is settled. The only relevant arguments are how to maximize political support for the United States in waging war, and how to assemble practical and financial support for its vast project to remake Iraq — and the Middle East — after the war.

Mr. Powell's speech does not seem to have changed the situation. If more governments rally to the American cause, it will be pressure, not persuasion, that brings them over.

Munich, February 11, 2003 — The stalemate at NATO early this week was unnecessary and, in basic respects, irrelevant. The argument was only symbolically over military support for Turkey.

It was over Iraq intervention itself. By posing the issue in terms of defending Turkey against the consequences of a military intervention that formally has yet to be decided, the United States was trying to force the NATO allies to commit themselves to such an intervention.

The threat made by American officials in the corridors of the annual Munich strategic seminar last weekend — to transfer U.S. NATO bases in Germany to "new Europe," meaning formerly Communist Europe, so as to leave behind "old Europe" — was also empty.

Germany has no need of American bases on its territory, but the United States needs those bases. They are the logistical and operational foundation for the American strategic deployment in Europe, the Near and Middle East, the Horn of Africa and Central Asia.

The United States could well lease new bases in Poland or Bulgaria or Romania. They might even, for old times' sake, be called NATO bases. But they would be sovereign American bases. If forces based there were committed to operations that did not enjoy popular support in these "new Europe" countries, the United States would face the same problem it has now in old Europe.

NATO was created for the mutual defense of its members against the Soviet threat. The alliance has been moribund, for lack of a strategic purpose, since the Cold War ended. Its life-support system remained the popular support it has continued to enjoy in its member countries, based on agreement over common security interests.

The support system now has been disconnected because the agreement has broken. America's German bases now are part of a U.S. deployment that encompasses more than 40 nations and supports a foreign policy meant to establish an integrated international order with "the United States as the ultimate guarantor of order and enforcer of norms" (to quote Andrew Bacevich of Boston University). Iraq intervention is part of this.

By adopting this policy, the second Bush administration has opened a deep strategic divide between itself and Western Europe. This is why there is a transatlantic crisis. Public opinion in NATO Europe has turned against the United States.

Washington prefers to call this "anti-Americanism." This is not true. It is hostility to American foreign policy.

Donald Rumsfeld has claimed that the European governments making difficulties for the United States over Iraq are only three among 19 NATO members and are "isolated." Actually, NATO popular opinion is universally opposed to a war against Iraq not mandated by the UN. The dissident governments speak for something like 80 percent of West European opinion — and more than 70 percent of opinion in Eastern Europe, as well. Who then is isolated?

Rumsfeld arrived for his weekend in Munich confident that he would rapidly humiliate the German government and isolate France diplomatically. On Monday, France and Belgium blocked the U.S. proposals concerning war on Turkey's border, saying they were premature and compromising.

Later in the day, Russia joined the Germans and French in recommending an extended inspections program, and China did so on Tuesday.

So far as the Security Council is concerned, the relevant question until this week had been whether France would veto a resolution authorizing military intervention.

The question now has become whether the United States will be forced to veto a French or French-German resolution expanding the inspectors' mandate. German sources on Tuesday said that 11 of the 15 members of the Security Council supported the Franco-German position.

President Bush's great supporter, Tony Blair, is peculiarly vulnerable in this situation. His government would probably fall if he followed President Bush into a war that lacked UN endorsement. Mr. Bush is convinced that he can afford to go it alone; Tony Blair cannot.

The key to it all is public opinion. The Western public understands perfectly well that Saddam Hussein is a brutal and evil leader. But unlike Slobodan

Milosevic at the time of NATO intervention [against the Bosnian Serbs and in Kosovo], he is not waging war against neighboring societies or conducting ethnic cleansing.

Public opinion in Europe, and to a lesser extent in the United States itself, seems convinced — rightly or wrongly — that Iraq currently threatens no one outside Iraq's frontiers, and that such threat as it may pose in the future is containable at less human cost, risk and injustice than war would impose.

The Bush administration believes otherwise, and almost certainly will attack Iraq before the end of March, with or without UN endorsement, whatever public opinion may be in the NATO countries. This being so, not only was the argument in Brussels at the beginning of the week irrelevant, but so, now, is NATO itself.

Paris, February 18, 2003 — The second Bush administration is devoted to macho posturing with little consideration for the consequences. This could turn the current transatlantic confrontation into something for which Washington may eventually be very sorry.

The administration's effort to intimidate Germany and isolate France in the quarrel over military intervention in Iraq backfired on Friday at the UN Security Council and in the antiwar demonstrations of the weekend. Unless the inspectors find a mine shaft packed with drums of anthrax and nerve agents during the next few days, Washington is unlikely to win a mandate to go to war....

President Bush and his more hawkish advisors believed they could bully the Security Council's members and get what they wanted. They confided to reporters some days ago that objections by the French were already "fixed" and that Paris would fall in line, while the Germans would do what they were told.

France is accustomed to this treatment, but Germany is not. Germany is a very complex, and in some ways mysterious, nation (to Anglo-Americans, at least), and the pleasantries of Donald Rumsfeld, accompanied by the recent right-wing press campaign in the United States against Germany, have not only had a damaging effect on German-American relations but also have challenged the foundation of modern German foreign policy.

I was in Germany when Mr. Rumsfeld arrived in Munich earlier this month, after comparing German foreign policy to that of Libya or Cuba. A very senior retired officer in the German army (and NATO) asked me, "why are they doing this?"

He said, "You Americans have been telling us for 60 years that we must never go to war. You have made the Germans pacifists. We have accepted that war is never a solution. We believe that even more because of our own history. Now you attack us because Germans are against this war."

He made it plain that he was equally distressed that Germany should set itself against the United States. For half a century, Germans have resolved their fundamental questions of security and "purpose" with a dual anchorage in Europe and in alliance with the United States.

Until now, the dual anchorage has remained solid, despite developing tensions between the Bush administration and Western Europe as a whole on a range of political, environmental and economic issues.

The anchorage has also survived persistent Gaullist arguments that sooner or later Europe will have to declare its independence of the United States. This idea never found much support in Germany because it raised possibilities the Germans do not want to contemplate.

A split between Europeans and this administration has nonetheless been coming. It became inevitable when Washington declared its own national strategy to be "full-spectrum domination" of the world's affairs.

The split is potentially most dangerous in Germany. Voters clearly chose pacifism over "preventive war" five months ago, in the parliamentary elections. Chancellor Gerhard Schroeder might then, or since, have challenged his electorate, but had he done so (and still been elected), he would today be in the same position as Tony Blair — and Silvio Berlusconi and Jose Maria Aznar — all massively isolated from majority opinion.

The disagreement over Iraq did not have to be made into a bitter German-American confrontation. Alas, the Bush administration is led by bullies, convinced that threats, denigration, personal attack, and efforts to split the European Union are the way to deal with allies.

Defense Secretary Donald Rumsfeld now is reported (by London's *Observer*) to have told the Pentagon to prepare "to end military and industrial cooperation" between the United States and Germany, so as to "harm the German economy" and punish Germany's "treachery." Such is the Bush's government's conception of alliance leadership.

As an ironical coda, it surely will not have escaped readers that the insults currently flung at the French, Belgians and Germans as "cowards" come from an American administration whose principal figures are, with one exception, draft-dodgers, and from journalists who — if they respect the current advice of the

U.S. government — will have spent recent days crouched under their beds, surrounded by canned provisions, in duct-taped rooms, waiting for Osama bin Laden to cause the sky to fall on them.

February 27, 2003 — "[There is] but one response possible for us: Force, Force to the utmost, Force without stint or limit, the righteous and triumphant Force which shall make Right the law of the world...." That was Woodrow Wilson at the time of the first world war. As the reader sees, it's a short distance from him to George W. Bush.

Total victory in war commands total obedience from the defeated and opens the way to unhindered realization of political objectives. This is the traditional American position. The Bush White House takes total victory in Iraq for granted, and assumes that unhindered political possibility will follow.

Mr. Bush's advisors are prepared to concede the social and political complexity of the Middle East, but dismiss it by saying that in the end power trumps all. In this respect, as in others, they are the disciples of Ariel Sharon.

They say that what America did in Germany and Japan after the second world war to make new democracies can be done again in Iraq. Some of them already recommend that regime change in Iran should be the next American objective. Victory in Iraq will sweep democracy into the Middle East.

The Bush administration has said that military occupation of a defeated Iraq should last no more than two years, although the army chief of staff, General Eric Shinseki, shocked Congress last week by saying that "several hundred thousand soldiers" would be necessary to control the country. He added that Iraq's occupation would restrict the army's ability to do other missions and "maintain high morale."

The occupation of Germany was also supposed to last less than two years. Until a few days ago there were 90,000 U.S. troops still there. They are now in the Middle East, and speculation says they will stay there permanently, in new bases.

German's occupation was meant to be punitive. The April 1945 order of the U.S. Joint Chiefs to occupation commanders said they were to impose on the Germans recognition that they had brought their suffering onto themselves; to avoid all fraternization with them; to arrest and punish war criminals and take control of German war-making capacity.

Political reconstruction or "deNazification" got a bad start with distribution of thousands of questionnaires demanding the life history of everyone looking for a public post.

A nationalist writer, Ernst von Solomon, published his own savagely mocking answers to the form's 131 questions. It took him 541-pages (even in English translation and small print), and the book sold a quarter of a million copies in Germany.

DeNazification mostly was dropped with the start of the cold war, when Germany was somewhat awkwardly turned into an ally. Economic reconstruction seriously began with the Marshall Plan in 1948, but the Germans really reconstructed their country themselves. The German people turned off their memories and worked. Prosperity became their goal and NATO became their foreign policy.

This remained the German condition until very recently. George Bush, without noticing, awakened the Germans from their political slumber last year by calling for western war on Iraq.

About the same time, several new German books were having unexpected success. All reawaken suppressed memories, of the terrible bombings of German cities, the savage expulsion of Germans from East Prussia and other places where they had lived for centuries, the ravages of Soviet conquest and occupation.

All horrors brought on themselves, of course. But nobody in Germany has talked about them for 58 years.

The "democratization" of Japan was simple. Douglas MacArthur received the Japanese surrender delegates aboard the battleship Missouri in the harbor of burned-out Tokyo, and told them that he renounced the spirit "of distrust, malice or hatred." He said that the two sides "must rise to the higher dignity, which alone benefits the sacred purposes we are about to serve."

The Emperor listened by radio. He consulted with the diplomats present at the ceremony, and reflected. Then he informed his foreign minister that when General MacArthur was established in Tokyo, he would pay him a formal visit — as he did. The Japanese people then understood that they were to become democrats.

The dynamic and educated Japanese, like the Germans, reconstructed their own country. On MacArthur's explicit orders, they accepted educational and social reforms of so liberal a nature as would scandalize the U.S. Congress today.

The Korean war arrived, and with it military orders to Japanese industry. The economy was set on its way.

Germans and Japanese "democratized" because they had no alternative. They were threatened by Soviet Russia, and in the Japanese case by China, and America offered them security and rehabilitation within an international society dominated by democracies.

Iraq in the short term will have no alternative to formal democratization. A new Iraq government will not be threatened. As agent of American power, it will pose the threat to its neighbors. The Bush people place their confidence in power. Iraq is their critical experiment.

Paris, March 6, 2003 — The impending Iraq war has become a watershed event. It will permanently alter the American relationship to the Islamic Middle East. It has already provoked serious change in Europe's relations with Washington. It may have lasting influence on what becomes of American society.

American troops already operate inside Iraq, and President Bush and his people insist that nothing short of Saddam Hussein's abdication will now stop them.

Nonetheless, the Turkish parliament's failure to permit an attack on Iraq via Turkey came as a staggering and unexpected blow to Washington. Even if the parliament, under intensified pressure, were to reverse its decision, an old and important American alliance has broken.

The scale of international demonstrations against the war have shocked the White House. Congressional sources say that Secretary of State Colin Powell has told the president that if the U.S. returns to the Security Council next week for a new resolution authorizing war, it faces humiliating defeat — by "old Europe."

No one will have to veto the Anglo-American-Spanish resolution. It simply will fall short, possibly badly short, of the nine votes needed to pass.

Some in the White House are said to argue that last weekend's capture of a senior al Qaeda figure could be spun so as to shift attention away from Iraq and back to terrorism, while UN inspections were allowed to continue. This could save Tony Blair, reported on Thursday to want more time for the inspectors. It could mean wider support when and if the war does come.

But such a back-down before the French, Germans and Russians, after Washington's six-month buildup to war, and after all that the president has said, would itself alter the perceived international balance.

President Bush, in any case, seems much too committed for anything now to stop him. Anyway, he doesn't have to go to the UN. He claims the right to go to war without further Security Council action — even if that would mean too bad for Tony Blair and the president's other foreign allies.

His neo-conservative desk warriors assure him that the geopolitical conse-quences of victory in the Middle East and the effect on American relations with Muslims will be positive. It will promote democracy as the way to go, while pro-viding an intimidating display of U.S. power.

Pessimists, such as myself, say the consequences will be bad for the Middle East, for American interests and, in the long term bad for Israel (as well as for the Palestinians, as if anyone still cared about the Palestinians).

On past results, pessimism is where the smart money should go.

Certainly, the transatlantic relationship will not be the same after this. If the administration's Iraq gamble succeeds, Washington intends to divide Europe and build a new alliance with Central and Eastern Europe as the base for U.S. power-projection in the Middle East and Central Asia.

If the gamble fails, there probably will be a general American fallback toward an embittered version of the anti-internationalist and America-first pol-icies with which George Bush began his term two years ago.

A policy metaphor recently popular in Washington has been that of European Lilliputians unsuccessfully trying to tie down an American Gulliver. The effort supposedly is led by politically craven or vainglorious Lilliputian poli-ticians, unwilling to share the burden of global responsibility, ungrateful, longing for lost national glories, etc.

The recent Washington-inspired campaign against the motivations, persons and moral character of individual German, French and even Belgian leaders has been the most vicious in postwar transatlantic relations. The whole affair nonetheless has served to clarify a number of things.

One is that the Bush administration has, without understanding what it was doing, created a situation in which the majority of nations see the United Nations as the only institution that has the possibility of checking American power and limiting the consequences of American unilateralism.

In the future, shifting coalitions of the willing are likely to work through the UN and other major international institutions, and use the unprecedented means the Internet provides for mass mobilization (including inside the United States itself) to counterbalance or contain the United States on many economic and politico-military issues.

It may also be that the America will no longer be entirely free to set the international agenda. Rogue states, war against terrorism, anti-proliferation, trade globalization and other American causes may not automatically dominate international political and media attention.

Washington only now is discovering that its efforts to override or divide opposition to what it wants on Iraq have created a coherent international opposition that before was not there. It has diminished rather than affirmed its old international leadership.

March 11, 2003 — The door to war is not yet opened, but the unexpected has already happened. U.S. Defense Secretary Donald Rumsfeld's announcement Tuesday that British forces might not take part in the initial intervention against Iraq suggests that Britain may be out of the coalition.

The reason? The United States and Britain will almost certainly fail to get a Security Council resolution this week authorizing invasion of Iraq. If Tony Blair should go to war without it, he could lose the prime ministership.

Neither possibility was imaginable in Washington as recently as late February.

President George W. Bush finds himself in a huge international controversy that he thinks is about policy toward Iraq. Everyone else knows it is about the Bush administration and, beyond that, the future role of the United States in the international system.

Washington is unwillingly — and uncomprehendingly — grappling with the possibility that the UN is not irrelevant. Secretary-General Kofi Annan said on Monday that the United States really does need the legitimacy Security Council approval can provide. Without it, the United States must well and truly go it alone in Iraq.

Critics are perfectly right to ask why the UN — this organization of governments, few of them democratic, many if them lamentable in their respect for civil liberties and human rights — should pass judgment on the United States. The answer is that the UN is the only forum in which the world's nations can make any collective judgment on international matters.

The international system rests on the principle of absolute sovereignty of states. This has nothing to do with the merits or morality of governments; by trial and error, it has been found to be the least bad of international diplomatic and legal systems. The UN is the agent of this system, by which a form of international authority is exercised.

The United States, in the Iraq crisis, is proposing to break the system, and this is what the current crisis is really about. The Bush administration says that unless the Security Council gives the United States what it wants, America will ignore the UN and in the future do whatever it thinks right.

Thus, the United States has implicitly proposed a different international order and is making a claim to the sovereign right to intervene in, disarm and carry out "regime change" in other countries, subject to no external restraint.

In its National Strategy statement last fall, the administration stated its intention to maintain overwhelming global military superiority and take whatever action is necessary to prevent the emergence of a rival.

The logic in this is open to negative or positive appreciations. The hostile interpretations are all around us at the moment. The Iraq intervention is said to be a step toward seizing global energy control, hegemonic world economic and trade domination, or to assure Israel's expansion. There is even a claim that Mr. Bush sees himself acting out prophesies concerning the Biblical Apocalypse and the Second Coming as interpreted by certain marginal American Protestant fundamentalist groups that have his ear.

The positive interpretation of American intentions — the one made by most Americans themselves — is that the United States is a responsible nation with benevolent intentions, and that, in cooperation with its close democratic allies, it would use its great power to protect democracy and peace.

Iraq has become a crisis because members of the UN see the prospect of war as a test of unchecked American world power.

What they have seen is a United States that insists on its way and no other.

They have seen it unable to provide a rationale for its policy on Iraq that can convince the majority of the democracies, its natural supporters.

They have seen it denounce those who criticize it, and threaten serious and damaging material retaliation against democracies that actively oppose it — France, Germany, Belgium and Turkey.

They have, in short, seen Washington demand submission and take steps to obtain this through force.

This, to the rest of the world, is not reassuring, to put it mildly. Unchecked American global power has precipitously lost appeal.

Yet from the end of World War II to the collapse of the Soviet Union, the United States exercised international leadership with responsible policies and sensitivity to the demands of alliance.

162

For this reason, there has until now been relatively little concern over its emergence as the world's sole superpower. America continued to possess the confidence of the international community.

The Bush administration has managed to undermine, if not destroy, the American offer of benevolent and responsible international hegemony. With this Iraq affair, it has made the UN seem more relevant than ever.

One may add that by so doing, it has perhaps done a favor not only to the world, but to the United States itself. I myself am not of the opinion that the values of the American republic would survive the possession of absolute power. Lord Acton and all that.

March 13, 2003 — France until now has successfully defied the United States on UN approval for a war against Iraq, and even made Washington yield on some points. What comes next? Indeed, what has it really all been about for France, with what gains and losses?

The policy of the Chirac government has critics in France, although few defend U.S. policy. Most critics argue that because the Atlantic alliance is one of the foundations of the postwar order, and because George Bush is going to war despite any Security Council vote, opposing Washington has been futile and has resulted in net damage to French interests.

Why have the French done it? The two commonly heard British and American explanations cite vanity — French nostalgia for a glorious past — and French oil interests in Iraq.

The first explanation is puerile. I have yet to meet a Frenchman who thought lost glories have anything to do with French possibilities today. Every serious person in the country knows that France is a second-ranking international power. It's simply an ambitious one (unlike Britain or Germany).

As for oil, the French are not so stupid as to think they will protect their oil and economic interests in Iraq by being on the losing side. The United States will decide Iraq's oil contracts after the war, not Saddam Hussein.

One French critic, the historian Alain Besançon, suggests that Jacques Chirac's policy has expressed a certain French taste for the gallant gesture — for panache — often at the cost of French interests, and to the country's eventual regret.

He recalls Agincourt in 1415, during the Hundred Years' War, when the French barons, whose army outnumbered the exhausted British four to one, insisted on a glorious cavalry charge against British infantry armed with longbows. They thereby handed over the crown of France to the English king, Henry V.

The French have not gained the leadership of Europe by blocking the United States in the Security Council. They have had a great victory in global public opinion — overwhelmingly hostile to Washington — but such victories are ephemeral.

The German-French alliance against Washington resulted from the brutality of Donald Rumsfeld and American diplomacy after Gerhard Schroeder declared that Germany would not support the war. Washington drove the Germans, who needed an ally, into the arms of the French.

This alliance will probably last as long as the United States conducts itself as hegemon of the West, with a policy to divide Europe.

In theory, a German-French alliance provides the core for a politically united Europe with a common policy of counterbalancing American power. In economic matters, such a union now exists. In trade and industry, the EU deals with the United States on equal terms (or better).

In political and diplomatic matters, there still is no union for France (or France-Germany) to lead, even if the other Europeans wanted France to lead them, which most of them don't.

For the foreseeable future, a single European Union foreign policy is improbable, if not impossible, other than in reaction to extraordinarily hostile pressures from Washington (which, with this administration, cannot be excluded.)

Is there any future in the French-Russian alignment that emerged in the Security Council? One thinks not. The two simply have a certain shared interest in checking American power.

However, as Stalin asked of the pope, how many divisions (or in this case, percentage points of GNP) do Africa, the Arabs and the Latin Americans bring to such an alliance? Some in France wish that Paris could lead a new international alignment — of some European countries, the Arab states, Africa, Latin America and parts of Asia — to defend the UN and a multilateral international system.

In the end, real influence does not come from alliances, but from individual national quality. France, if it claims international leadership, must pay the price of such pretensions.

France's postwar period of greatest international influence was under DeGaulle. After he took power in 1958, he reformed public finances and the industrial economy, made the French franc a hard currency and paid back the money loaned France under the Marshall Plan, plus interest (no other country did so).

He ended the war in Algeria, reformed the army, built an independent nuclear deterrent and left the NATO military command while remaining a firm ally of the United States on basic issues, as in the Cuban missile crisis. He was not shy about telling the United States when it was courting disaster, as in Vietnam.

If Jacques Chirac made the equivalent domestic reforms today, increased high technology and military investment — visible elements of power — and kept the clear head DeGaulle possessed, France could have the leadership it wants. If all of Western Europe were to do the same, it and the world might benefit.

PART FIVE

MARCH TO JULY 2003: FROM WAR TO HOLLOW VICTORY

Paris, March 18, 2003 — And so we go to war, the United States, Britain and Australia — alone.

George W. Bush and Tony Blair see this as a Churchillian moment: Alone? So be it!

If their troops are received in Basra by surrendering Iraqi soldiers, and by Iraqi civilians cheering their liberators, they say all the rest will be forgotten. We shall soon know.

We can certainly expect the war to be run with more professionalism than the diplomacy that has led up to the war.

These past two weeks have recalled Freedonia going to war in the film "Duck Soup," except that the Marx Brothers meant to be funny. The lugubrious diplomatic nadir was surely the British proposal that war might be called off if Saddam Hussein went on television to say "sorry."

A final UN resolution and vote were abandoned by Washington and London, not only because they lacked the votes for a resolution authorizing war but also because they faced the possibility of a majority vote against them — sending them to war in actual defiance of the Security Council.

The problem was not the French veto. The United States and Britain had already said they would be satisfied with a moral victory, meaning a majority vote the French were forced to veto. In the event, they didn't even try to get it:

they were blocked by concern that Angola, Chile, Pakistan, Cameroon, Guinea and Mexico might vote against them.

This inability to persuade — or even intimidate or bribe — friendly or dependent countries on a matter so vital to the U.S. government is unprecedented in postwar history.

Washington has even had great difficulty in getting NATO Turkey to open itself to U.S. forces and overflights. To force this still-unsettled issue could provoke a crisis for Turkey's democracy, making Turkey, in this war, the first victim of friendly fire.

The failure of the United States to win international support for its position on Iraq is due in part to the weakness of its case. Few saw Iraq in its present condition as a threat to anyone, much less to the United States. Washington had no serious evidence linking Iraq to al Qaeda. The failure was also due to this administration's arrogance in its employment of American power.

However the hostility was already there, latent. It was there because history says that use (or abuse) of hegemonic power inspires challenge. The resistance may arise hesitantly, but a crisis can provoke convergence or consolidation of the individual elements of resistance, so that each reinforces the others. This is what has happened.

Germany's initial rejection of the war was the act of a politician in electoral trouble, responding to public opinion. It probably would have been unimportant had the United States not reacted as it did, and had Jacques Chirac not supported the Germans. Doing so, he catalyzed international opposition to American unilateralism.

France, moreover, offers the only coherent and relevant modern model of constructive resistance to U.S. power: the Gaullist model. Articulated in the Security Council debate, this found overwhelming support in international opinion.

The result has been a basic shift in international relations, which will affect the future configuration and policies of the European Union, no matter what happens in Iraq. Closer union and a common defense formerly seemed luxuries. This no longer seems the case.

A similar development, less advanced, is taking place in the Far East, caused by a U.S. policy toward North Korea that does not have the support of South Korea, Japan or China.

Something has happened that might be compared with the breakup of the Austro-Hungarian Empire in 1918. Before the first world war, tensions existed inside that empire, but the aura of benevolent imperial authority was intact, and the troubles could be contained.

The war, and Woodrow Wilson's doctrine of universal national self-determination, destroyed the aura, and the authority, of the empire, with results that contributed heavily to the outbreak of a second world war.

The war in Iraq is intended to establish U.S. authority over a democratic Middle East. Washington never imagined that it would be successfully challenged by Europeans and at the UN.

If the Bush administration's optimism about the course of the Iraq war proves justified, America's international authority will provisionally be re-established. But the aftermath, as the United States tries to control Middle Eastern developments, will automatically generate new forces of resistance and hostility.

We will still find ourselves in post-imperial disorder.

The American superpower has been the center of a solar system. Centrifugal political forces now have been set loose. These will be extremely difficult for Washington to deal with, so long as it remains on its current global course. They may also prove more dangerous than Washington, or anyone else, now thinks.

March 20, 2003 — At this moment, let us talk about soldiers, whose role is one of the most ancient in human society.

It is a role like no other because it is inherently and voluntarily a tragic role, an undertaking to offer one's life, and to assume the right to take the lives of others. The latter, morally speaking, is probably the graver undertaking.

The intelligent professional soldier recognizes that the two undertakings are connected, in that his warrant to kill is integrally related to his willingness to die.

Phillipe Morillon, a former commander of U.N. Protection Force in Bosnia, has remarked on the moral anomaly of the modern American military preoccupation with "zero casualties." He asks, "How can you have soldiers who are ready to kill, who are not ready to die?"

Against a weak or backward enemy, it is now feasible to wage war with few or even no casualties on the technologically superior side. This, obviously, is eminently desirable from the viewpoint of its soldiers (and airmen), who naturally wish to survive, but it worsens their moral situation as dealers in death for others.

Armies have always employed a strategy of rituals, myths, chivalries and vanities of uniform and unit to distance the soldier from the essential horror of war. This is part of the explanation of why men become soldiers. There is a further clue in the existence of elite formations in all armies. At Fort Benning in the 1940s, the members of the original American parachute regiments were deliberately selected as bigger, fitter and better educated than the average soldier.

The volunteers in the parachute units I knew a decade later were usually the opposite. The most powerful motive for an individual to volunteer for a combat arm or for an elite corps is to redress his own (conscious or unconscious) sense of inferiority or fear of inadequacy.

Combat or elite military training is a rite of passage, imposing an ordeal that allows those who endure it to believe they have proved their superiority to others. A primordial assertion of masculine identity is involved in this.

Therefore, the effort to turn an army into just another technical or civil service career path weakens it in its essential nature. This may seem to be a claim from another era, but I believe it is true.

The nature of the soldier's vocation is ordinarily to serve anonymously. The act of enlistment removes the choice of the cause for which the soldier is sent to fight. To die as a deliberately elected risk in the service of values consciously chosen is one thing. The soldier is trained to serve national objectives or policies that he may not understand or to which he may be hostile.

The professional soldier finds honor in what may be called the absurdity of this situation. The nineteenth-century poet and professional soldier Alfred de Vigny wrote of the soldier as "scapegoat" for a public "to whom, and in whose stead, he is daily sacrificed."

A form of moral stoicism is thus required of soldiers, ordinarily evoked by refocusing loyalty upon the unit and on comrades. This is notable, for example, in the U.S. Marine Corps and in the French Foreign Legion. The legionnaire is deliberately formed to give his loyalty not to the French nation, but to the Legion, composed of his anonymous fellows. They fight for the corps, not a cause.

The state secures itself by means that are not always moral. Yet the security of the state is a moral objective and, indeed, is its primordial political obligation, presupposed by everything else the state might do. The agents of the state, particularly those its military services, are caught in the middle.

170

This is why Vigny also wrote that the soldier is both executioner and victim. The army is a machine designed to kill but is also "a machine capable of suffering." What it does in the service of the state is at potentially fatal cost to its members.

Because it is a company of those prepared to die, it possesses the moral authority to set terms and a limit on the claims of the state. One thus is uncomfortable with a war instigated and directed by the military virgins who head the Bush administration — who would not understand any of this.

March 25, 2003 — Last Friday, the most prominent of Washington's neo-conservative policy groups, the American Enterprise Institute, held what one witness, the correspondent of London's *Financial Times*, described as a "victory celebration."

Richard Perle, corporate consultant and member of the Pentagon Defense Advisory Board, told the audience that the Iraq war is going well — that "there are more anti-war demonstrators in San Francisco than Iraqis willing to defend Saddam Hussein." The pro-American coalition was growing, he said, and Saddam Hussein's fall would be "an inspiration" to Iranians.

The members of the Washington group, which is described as the Bush administration's "ideological vanguard," discussed what to do about Iran, considered by them to be even more dangerous than Iraq, in terms of its nuclear weapons program.

Israeli Prime Minister Ariel Sharon has already told visiting American congressmen that Iran, Libya and Syria must be stripped of nuclear weapons, and U.S. Undersecretary of State John Bolton replied to him that it would be necessary to deal not only with Syria and Iran but also with North Korea. Israel's defense minister has already asked American friends of Israel to press for action against Iran.

An administration official was quoted Monday in a *New York Times* dispatch as saying that Iraq "is just the beginning. I would not rule out the same sequence of events for Iran and North Korea as for Iraq."

This enthusiasm for more war is familiar to those who follow neo-conservative arguments in the Washington debate. One might have thought, however, that the American Enterprise Institute would have been discreet enough to hold off its victory celebration until victory arrives and its cost is known. At this writing, the cost is proving more considerable than expected in neo-conservative circles.

Their celebration of victory at the war's start suggests to what extent these policy intellectuals, and much of the administration itself, live and act within a closed intellectual world, in what one commentator, Philippe Grasset, calls "virtuality" — where reality is both perceived and treated as they want it to be, not as it is.

For example, on the day the war began, the coalition command assembled journalists and television crews to fly to Basra in order to capture images of "flag-waving crowds hugging British and American soldiers." Thus "an immediate positive image" of the war could be given worldwide.

The war began the next night. A week later, as I write, Basra still has not been taken, British commanders are saying that reinforcements will be necessary, and artillery is in use to suppress Iraqi resistance. The port of Umm Qasr, an initial target of U.S. and Royal Marines, was declared captured last Friday — it is badly needed to land military supplies and humanitarian aid — but remained unsecured as the current week began.

The 3rd Infantry Division, on its way to Baghdad across "desert flats that U.S. planners expect to be defended lightly or not at all," is taking casualties and losing helicopters, and U.S. prisoners have been taken. The division has bypassed towns to avoid street fighting, a sensible measure, but one that leaves unknown and untested threats in the rear of the coalition forces. The attack on Nasiriyah has proved difficult.

Ominously, the supply train of the troops headed for Baghdad, which will eventually stretch to 500 kilometers — farther overland from their logistical base than American forces have ever before operated — has been attacked by what appear to be irregular forces who have sprung up elsewhere in southern Iraq.

The cheering crowds have not appeared. *The Wall Street Journal's* front-page lead on Monday said the coalition, "far from being hailed as 'liberators,'" has "faced deep hostility and gunfire" from civilians. It seems rather early to plan the next step in what Michael Ledeen of the AEI describes as "an epochal war....Iraq may turn out to be a war to remake the world."

It has, of course, already remade the world. It has divided the world between the United States and Britain on one side, and nearly everybody else on the other. Washington talks about its "ever-enlarging coalition" of indebted and impressed micro-states, but the reality was revealed by the UN Security Council votes and the General Assembly debates that preceded George Bush's decision to go to war.

The AEI meeting heard that the UN now is finished. It might be allowed some humanitarian jobs but is otherwise "irrelevant." In political and security matters, the United States will henceforth ignore it. Since in Bush ideological circles, more war is what we need in order to right the world and make it a better place, the president would waste his time going to the UN with his projects.

We Americans are on our own now, Lone Rangers, riding toward the sunset.

Amsterdam, March 27, 2003 — The current split between the United States and Old Europe is particularly painful for The Netherlands, not only a very "old" European nation but a founding member both of NATO and the European Union.

The Netherlands government has formally backed Washington's intervention in Iraq, but the public disapproves of the war. This leaves people in a secular nation of scrupulous Calvinist formation asking if they are not behaving hypocritically.

They would like to have reassurance that a divided conscience will not continue to be essential to membership in the transatlantic alliance, which is very important to them.

As a university professor put it, "the government and the people both want to be told that George W. Bush and Donald Rumsfeld are not really in charge. They want to believe that, somewhere in Washington, serious but silent people are really in control."

The Netherlands' experience during the past 50 years was of American leaders and officials who sometimes were difficult to deal with, but ultimately were responsible men and women with realistic views that commanded respect.

The idea that the neo-conservatives now promoting "benevolent" American global hegemony, and making war in order to make it come about, are the people running the United States makes the Dutch uneasy.

This is why Britain and Tony Blair are important to them. The British and the Dutch have in modern times been very close, and today the British prime minister is hopefully looked to as the person who can rebuild damaged European-American links. This expectation, however, rests on an assumption that the irreconcilable can be reconciled.

Prime Minister Blair was in Washington last week talking with George Bush about issues important to the West Europeans as a whole. He was looking for compromises President Bush clearly is not prepared to make.

He told the president that Iraq after the war must be submitted to a governing structure "specifically accepted and endorsed by the UN."

This amounts to a variant, less aggressively expressed, of the position taken by France, Germany and Russia. They insist that the UN, not the United States, must take charge of Iraq when all this is over, as representative of the international community as a whole.

However even as the British prime minister was on his way to Washington, Secretary of State Colin Powell was telling the House of Representatives that the United States has not done what it has done concerning Iraq without intending to have the dominant voice in what happens afterwards.

The prime minister also wants action on the "road map" for Palestine-Israel settlement that was agreed late last year by the so-called Quartet — the United States, the European Union, Russia and the UN.

Just before the Iraq war, Mr. Blair persuaded President Bush to announce that he would publish this detailed road map (which he has not yet done). The promise was made to appease Blair's domestic critics, and to respond to the drumbeat of international criticism of the Bush administration's failure to try to solve the poisonous deadlock between Israel and the Palestinians.

However President Bush has already suggested that when the road map eventually is published the Israelis can propose modifications, which was not part of the original agreement.

In addition, Prime Minister Ariel Sharon some time ago said that the Quartet's proposals are "dead." As he has the means to kill them, this may be taken as a statement of intention.

The Quartet demands that Israel withdraw from its colonies in the occupied territories. Sharon refuses this on principle. Nothing in the record or the known inclinations of the Bush administration suggests that it would do anything to sanction such an Israeli refusal.

Prime Minister Blair nonetheless declared last week that the prewar Bush promise to take action on Israeli-Palestinian peace was not "simply [an affair of] statements...made in the context of military action in Iraq, then forgotten.

"I can give my assurance that they will not be forgotten, they will be taken forward and they will be done. This will be a central priority of British foreign policy."

In saying this, Mr. Blair clearly expressed the wishes of the European Union as a whole. Unfortunately, so far as the Bush administration is concerned, it takes no special insight to say that he was wasting his time. This war is not being fought by George Bush to take the West Bank away from Israel.

Blair is not dealing with the Old America that people in The Netherlands remember with respect. He is dealing with a new America that has an ideological vision of the world, which few outside the United States accept or support.

Both Tony Blair, and America's friends in The Netherlands, have yet really to come to terms with this, and with its permanent implications for transatlantic relations.

Paris, April 8, 2003 — The Bush administration now has the bit between its teeth on remaking the Middle East by remaking Iraq.

Few had seriously doubted that the military forces of the United States would overcome Iraq's army in fairly short order. It was the administration itself that fueled contrary fantasies of military disaster caused by Iraqi weapons of mass destruction — weapons that might tomorrow be used against the American "homeland" itself.

The balance of conventional forces indicated that Iraq's defeat was a military inevitability; the single question open to discussion was whether Iraq's population, or a part of it, might rally to the invaders, or on the other hand support irregular or terrorist resistance.

However quick victory now is taken for granted in Washington, and the debate has moved on to two other matters: who will govern a conquered Iraq, and what country will be the next American target.

The president went to Belfast on Monday (identified as "Dublin" by his geographically-challenged press spokesman) to discuss the first of those questions. Tony Blair, who still believes that he can bridge certain now unbridgeable Atlantic differences, settled for a common statement that the UN will play a "vital" role in conquered Iraq.

That will not satisfy Europeans or others who insist on international law, which holds that military conquest affords only limited authority to alter the political structure and rights of a defeated country — and limits the disposition of such national assets and resources as Iraq's oil.

However even Secretary of State Colin Powell, internationalism and multilateralism's bulwark in the Bush government, has said that the United States has not come all this way in order to let some other authority dominate Iraq.

175

Given that possession is nine-tenths of the law, former General Jay Garner, the unilateralist Donald Rumsfeld's protégé, and his shadow cabinet of ex-diplomats and businessmen named as interim authority for Iraq, will undoubtedly take over the country's government.

The more important question is what country will be next. Until now the existence of a "next" has been in some doubt. But unless victory in Iraq is marred by a punishing irregular resistance, or a persisting political breakdown and factional struggle, the Bush administration seems likely to proceed with the neo-conservatives' program for remaking, by military means if necessary, the political culture of the Moslem Middle East.

That means building on the political reconstruction of Iraq to cause eventual "regime change," spontaneous or otherwise, in Saudi Arabia, Iran, Syria, Egypt and Libya. (North Korea is another problem.)

The neo-conservative publicist and Washington columnist Charles Krauthammer claims that if Iraq becomes "pro-Western and if it becomes the focus of American influence,...an American presence in Iraq will project power across the region, [suffusing] the rebels in Iran with courage and strength, and [deterring and restraining] Syria." (I am quoting a summary of his views recently published in the Israeli daily *Haaretz*.)

This will "enhance the place of America in the world for the coming generation." The outcome "will shape the world for the next 25 years."

Deputy Secretary of Defense Paul Wolfowitz is generally acknowledged as the man whose determination and bureaucratic skill turned President George W. Bush's reaction to the September 11 attacks into a decision to overturn Iraq's regime.

He calls the neo-conservative crusade to change the Arab world an application of "the power of the democratic idea." His critics call him a naïve and dangerous ideologue. However his program, at this moment of success in Iraq, seems the most important single influence on Bush administration policy.

This is not good news. There are three things to be said about the neo-conservatives and what they want.

The first is that they act out of fear. They are motivated by a fear of mass destruction weapons in the hands of terrorist bands, armed by Islamic states, that is politically, technologically and militarily highly implausible.

There is an element of hysteria in this fear, as there was a quarter-century ago when Washington convinced itself that a victory by peasant insurgents in

Vietnam would lead to world domination by "Asian Communism" and the isolation and destruction of the United States.

They are naïve. Krauthammer says it is "racist" to think that "Arabs" can't govern themselves democratically. The problem in the Middle East is not "Arabs." The problem is a powerful historical culture that functions on categories of value absolutes and religious certainties hostile to the pragmatic relativisms of western democracy. Military conquest and good intentions will not change that.

Finally, the neo-conservatives are fanatics. They believe it worth killing people for unproven ideas. Traditional morality says that war is justified in legitimate defense. Totalitarian morality justifies war to make people or societies better.

April 10, 2003 — Statements by both George Bush and Colin Powell at the start of last week made it clear that the United States does not intend to give the United Nations a political role of any consequence in postwar Iraq.

Washington says that as the U.S. and Britain waged and won the war (with a little help from their Australian and Polish friends), they will also manage the peace. The UN, a Pentagon official says, will have no role "in constructing a democratic Iraq."

The intellectual as well as political position of the administration and its supporters is that the United States, as sole superpower, legitimately defends international order because the UN has defaulted on this responsibility, having never in the past enforced its resolutions demanding Saddam Hussein's disarmament.

Unilateralism and preemptive war are said necessary measures to defend the United States, and to establish and maintain a democratic international order, which the UN cannot or will not do.

However Iraq is not that simple. The Fourth Geneva Convention imposes on the military occupier full responsibility for the well-being of the civil population. It severely restricts the occupier's right to make use of the occupied country's resources.

No one is going to stop Washington from doing what it pleases in Iraq, but if it goes against international law it will have to pay and stay. The Bush administration would prefer to have the international community pay for reconstruction, and have other countries' forces do the peacekeeping.

Otherwise some kind of deal will have to be struck with the members of the self-proclaimed "peace camp" in the Security Council, and with the European Union, the principal potential international source of reconstruction aid.

This confronts the United States with a problem the Bush administration is unwilling to acknowledge.

The United States has been the most powerful country in the world since very early in the twentieth century. Its use of its power has never been contested by the democratic nations because they saw the U.S. as essentially pacific in intentions, and a defender of international law and order.

From the first world war to the Gulf War, American foreign interventions were intended to restore peace and legality. Even the Vietnam war was conceived and waged as a counter to Communism's revolutionary threat to world order.

The Iraq intervention, a unilaterally decided preventive war, destroyed "the reputation the United States has enjoyed for so long as a benevolent power," to quote Robert A. Pape of the University of Chicago, writing in *The Boston Globe*.

He says that it broke the rule "that democracies do not wage preventive wars" by doing what no other democratic state has done in the more than 200 years of the American nation's existence.

The government of George W. Bush has made it American security policy to prevent any other nation from attempting to equal the United States in military strength. This is unprecedented.

It inevitably has produced a fundamental change in how other nations see the United States. It has forced other democracies to rethink their own positions, causing some of them to resort to certain classic counter-measures against a government newly perceived as a potential threat.

These measures are not military but diplomatic and economic, which are more relevant, and to which Washington is more vulnerable. Thus France, Russia, Germany, Belgium, and China used diplomatic methods to isolate the U.S. on Iraq.

The same methods may be used again in the developing controversy over a UN role in Iraq and over the contribution of the international aid community to war reconstruction.

Turkey and Austria refused U.S. military forces transit rights during the war, and Belgium is now expected to revoke the automatic transit rights accorded years ago to the U.S. in a secret treaty. U.S. bases and transit privileges are vulnerable in many countries.

Pape notes that the European Union now is a more powerful economic and trading power than the U.S., and argues that if there were a concerted effort to require oil suppliers to bill in euros rather than dollars, this would undermine the position of the dollar as a reserve currency.

A move out of dollars by Asian or European investors would contribute to making it impossible for the Bush government to continue to run its enormous budget deficit. The University of Chicago political scientist estimates that a fall of one percent or more in U.S. GNP could result.

By renouncing America's traditional foreign policy and adopting one of global military domination, the Bush administration has made a fundamental change in the international balance.

It seems proud to have done so. It seems not to understand that this has been to its own potential disadvantage, and to the American nation's future risk.

April 17, 2003 — We arrive at Easter and Passover in a season dominated by international hatred, the griefs of a war not completely over, and with Israel and the Palestinians more deeply mired in conflict than perhaps ever before — to take account only of matters currently on the front pages.

Passover and Easter both concern exceptional divine interventions into human history, the first to favor and protect the monotheist God's original followers, the second an incarnation of the deity as man, in order to erase the primal sin of all mankind. Those at least are what believers say these events were, and meant.

God caused his chosen people, the Jews, who marked their doorstep with the blood of a lamb, to be passed over by the avenging angel striking down their Egyptian oppressors.

The God incarnate in man, Jesus, whom Christians believe to have been the Messiah promised in the Old Testament, underwent humiliation and crucifixion as a sacrifice to atone for human sin and to open salvation to all.

Strange events, when you reflect on them. Even if you are not a believer and consider them myths, they are strange myths for human imagination or longing to have invented. Acts of mercy or liberation, to temper divine justice.

Justice responds to "evil," whose definition remains controversial. Is evil an active principle in human affairs, as the Manicheans held, and as is presumed in the story of the angels who rebelled against God in pride, and thereafter pursued man's corruption, proclaiming, as the poet Milton has it, "Evil be thou my Good...all good to me is lost"?

Or is it the negation of good, as the Thomist philosophers said: a disorder of free will? That seems an unconvincing argument, I would think, in the presence of the active wickedness of a Saddam Hussein, and of Hitler and Stalin and other prominent figures from modern public life, not to speak of private life.

Even without the theological, scriptural or mythological definitions of evil, one can see it as a back-formulation from empirical evidence. We are surrounded by evil and want to find an explanation that will help us deal with it.

The theological explanation that evil is a disorder of free will and a result of human freedom, since if there were no freedom man would not be free to do evil, suits the modern utopian in a perverse if unconscious way. If a human utopia could be created, evil would be made obsolete. The effort to create one has only produced further evil.

Isaiah Berlin has written of the great Russian writers of the nineteenth century, that "[w]hat was common to all...was the belief that solutions to the central problems existed, that one could discover them, and, with sufficient selfless effort, realize them on earth." That was the great progressive under-taking of the post-Enlightenment West.

Failing to find the solutions, the totalitarian utopians chose to ban the problems. North Korea, like Stalin's Russia and Mao Tse-tung's China, is, according to its leader, a society that is the culmination of human happiness and progress, an achievement that he celebrates in endless numbers of parades and pageants by its malnourished citizens.

Utopianism thus remains with us. But God's righteous wrath and Divine justice are conceptions that no longer seem to weigh heavily on western man, although I have always thought that Paul's recommendation of fear and trem-bling in contemplation of one's mortal course is realistic advice. Jefferson said of slavery that "Indeed I tremble for my country when I reflect that God is just." A fearful comment.

Certainly the fear of God's justice does not seem to feature in the happy-clappy religion and the self-realization pseudo-religions of the present day.

It nonetheless seems to me a consideration we should not neglect when we look about the landscape of oppression, ruins and hatred in which much, if not most of the world, today lives.

Even in the proclaimedly happy and successful United States, fear, hatred and vengeance have since the September 2001 attacks become a more powerful combined influence in governing circles than at any time in my lifetime, and it is national policy to do evil for evil.

The promise of both Easter and Passover is mercy — fortunately, of unearned mercy. We perhaps do not deserve it, but it is offered. This notion in both religions may reflect a common primordial sense of our ancestors that man, in his freedom, is profoundly vulnerable.

April 24, 2003 — Washington's threat to punish France for promising to block UN approval of the Iraq war echoes Jacques Chirac's threat earlier this year to the European Union candidate-members who supported Washington on Iraq [that "they had missed a good chance to keep their mouths shut"]. Both cases recall how dissent used to be handled in the Warsaw Pact.

Retaliation for resisting the U.S. is a novel development in a NATO alliance supposedly composed of equals. It seemingly is of little consequence, since as this week's semi-annual conference of the European Union Strategic Studies Institute on transatlantic issues seemed generally agreed, not much is left of the NATO alliance. Its security guarantees to the new members in Central and Eastern Europe presumably survive, and there is new Washington interest in installing its military bases in those regions.

American participants told the EU meeting that Washington neither needs nor particularly wants allies — even British allies, as Donald Rumsfeld indicated in March, when the going got tough in getting a second Security Council resolution on Iraq to help Tony Blair.

The "new" Europeans probably are wise to want those U.S. bases since they are a better guarantee of Washington's protection than promises. The latter these days tend to become forgotten. Neo-conservative Washington has shown itself inclined to cancel treaty commitments when they become inconvenient. That's playing hardball.

These EU-U.S. conferences in the past were usually occasions for American policy specialists and officials to give themselves a Paris weekend while providing European counterparts with the latest news from Washington, conveying Washington's expectations of its European allies and the things they were expected to be thinking. It was the Romans keeping their Greeks in the picture.

This time Americans were telling the Europeans that they went too far in opposing the U.S. on Iraq. Something has broken, and there will be consequences. It was not only "old European" government opposition, but public and press opposition in new as well as old Europe, that angered the Bush administration.

Western Europe is unimportant and irrelevant, the more severe of the meeting's American participants warned: Europe is economically stagnant, in demographic decline, and militarily insignificant.

NATO counts only as a toolbox for the Pentagon, making a few specialized European units available for Pentagon use, but otherwise of minimal value in composing the mission-defined coalitions of the future.

European participants were at the same time told (once again) that Europe must spend a lot more on arms to count in the world. This American emphasis on military capabilities as the measure of European "relevance" comes in tandem with the argument that the U.S. is so powerfully armed that it doesn't need any help.

Governments that want to be "relevant" and have influence in Washington were advised not to bargain, like Turkey, but to back the U.S. from the start of a crisis, and afterwards ask for a favor. George Bush might then fly to Belfast for them, just as for Tony Blair.

People in Washington listen to Tony Blair, the meeting was told. They don't pay much attention to what he says, but they like him on television with George W. Bush. He is on the team. They did not add that on television he explains American policy more clearly than the president does.

Europeans at the meeting countered with the "soft power" argument. They said that Europe today deploys much more soft power — economic influence, diplomatic and developmental experience, skills in nation-building and peacekeeping, cultural attractiveness — than the United States.

While there was no Rumsfeldian belligerence at the meeting, there was an angry undertone in much of what was said. The Americans were told that Washington efforts to split Europe will backfire. Even German trade union resistance to German structural reform was said to be breaking down because the unions see that Europe is under U.S. challenge.

Europe's commitment to unity and multilateral action was defended as a matter of principle. A German editor said that when he writes editorials today arguing that the European Union should not be built up against the Americans, he is flooded with e-mails and letters saying that this is exactly what European Union should now be about.

He said to the Americans, I think you do not understand how much hostility towards you now exists in Europe. This did not seem of much interest. The

American speakers seemed more interested in nuclear weapons in Iran, Pakistan, and North Korea — the next countries that need to be fixed.

Paris, May 1, 2003 — It has been announced that American forces will shortly be withdrawn from Saudi Arabia. These reports usually mention that the continuous presence of these U.S. forces ever since the Gulf War is what provoked Osama bin Laden, onetime CIA collaborator in the guerrilla war against Russia's occupation of Afghanistan, to launch a war of terrorism against the United States.

The objective of his al Qaeda movement was to get U.S. forces expelled from proximity to the Moslem holy places. I have not yet seen mention that Osama bin Laden now has won his war.

The moral complexity of the bin Laden story seems rarely discussed, even among American intellectuals. Yet Osama bin Laden, more than anyone else, is responsible for the enormous change provoked in the United States by the events of September 2001.

He enabled Washington's neo-conservatives, previously an intellectual sect of limited influence, to take control of American foreign policy and turn it from George W. Bush's "humble" program into one of announced global military domination and preventive wars.

This split the American intellectual community on unfamiliar lines, beginning with the conservative movement itself. A new magazine called *The American Conservative* was recently created to attack what traditional conservatives saw as a foreign policy of radical and destabilizing militarism and imperialism.

Calling themselves "paleoconservatives," the magazine's editors quote Edmund Burke: "I dread our being too much dreaded." The neo-conservative establishment has counterattacked by calling their paleoconservative critics "racist, nativist, anti-Semitic, and unpatriotic" — a polemical excess which the "paleocons" take as proof of their success.

On the American left, the new U.S. policy challenged a certain dogmatic pacifism and anti-interventionism already shaken a decade ago by events in Bosnia and Kosovo. War and bloody ethnic repression there had made military intervention seem a humanitarian obligation.

Some liberals saw it a logical sequel to attack the obscene Iraq regime. Leon Wieseltier of *The New Republic* has said to the Paris daily *Le Monde* that Iraq was a war justified by the values of the left. The day Baghdad fell "was the happiest day of my life since 1989."

Others accepted President George W. Bush's much-disputed contention that the war was necessary to prevent Iraq from attacking the United States. Amitai Etzioni of George Washington University says that while a war against terrorism always seemed to him legitimate, he backed the intervention in Iraq because he thought it right "to stop rogue states from possessing mass destruction arms." He adds that if such weapons are not found in Iraq, "my reasoning collapses."

Other American liberals told *Le Monde* that the outcome of the war retroactively justifies it. They make a post-factum application of the just war argument of proportionality. Freeing Iraq has made the human and political costs of the war worthwhile.

Hendrik Hertzberg of *The New Yorker* says the worst predictions did not come true, and he now leaves his office and crosses Times Square "less afraid of being shredded by a bomb."

This pervasive American fear in the aftermath of the New York and Washington attacks is one factor setting American intellectuals off from Europeans, prompting them to demand why Europe and particularly France "abandoned" the U.S.

Etzioni says that the transatlantic fracture now dividing Americans and Europeans because of the war "will take at least ten years to overcome." Wieseltier says that Europe is "historically exhausted," and that the differences between it and the U.S. on the use of force have become fundamental.

David Rieff, who was in Bosnia for much of the war there, accuses European intellectuals of being "virtuous, right-thinking and complacent" in allegedly thinking that international law can substitute for military power.

The philosopher Michael Walzer declares that discussions in Europe are never about what should be done; "they ask, what will the Americans do?; the Europeans do not see themselves as agents of change or as international actors." (Jacques Chirac might reply that Americans become furious when they do.)

David Remnick of *The New Yorker* agrees that the Paris-New York division has never been so deep. Etzioni adds, with concern about opinion beyond Europe, that he cannot remember "in all my life such universal condemnation" of the U.S.

Only one of those interviewed by *Le Monde*, Wieseltier, mentioned foreign concern that the Bush administration is set upon power hegemony or "empire." He scoffs at this. "We haven't the slightest idea how to run an empire."

Tony Judt of New York University, a British historian long resident in the U.S., hence an observer with a certain detachment, notes that U.S. literary and academic intellectuals have little contact with the Washington neo-conservatives, whose publications "are practically unread outside Washington."

He concludes his *Le Monde* interview by remarking, "for the first time in 17 years I begin to feel myself a stranger in America."

Paris, May 6, 2003 — Foreign ministers of the G-8 leading industrial nations met in Paris on Monday to affirm that terrorism remains a "pervasive and global threat."

Three days earlier, the U.S. State Department had announced that terrorism is at its lowest level in 33 years.

That news failed to reach the G-8 foreign ministers. One wonders if anything would have changed had it reached them. The war against terrorism, like the war against Iraq, functions in all but total indifference to facts.

A "senior Bush administration official" told the press last weekend that he would be "amazed" if weapons-grade plutonium or uranium were found in Iraq. He said it was "unlikely" that biological or chemical weapons material would be found. He said that the United States never expected to find such a "smoking gun."

What was the Iraq war all about? The official said that what Washington really wanted was to seize the thousand nuclear scientists in Iraq who might in the future have developed nuclear weapons for Saddam Hussein. He described them as "nuclear mujahideen."

The preventive war, according to this redefinition, was not directed against an actual problem but one that might have appeared in the future.

One might have thought the official's statement merely an alibi for why no mass destruction weapons have been found, but this time it is President George W. Bush who seems not to have been told. He has gone on assuring Americans that the illicit weapons will be found.

In its annual report to Congress on terrorism, the State Department said that last year's recorded 199 terrorist incidents represented a 44 percent drop on the previous year, and was the lowest total since 1969.

There were no terrorist attacks last year in the United States, 5 in Africa and 9 in Western Europe. Nearly all the rest were in Asia (99), Latin America (50), and the Middle East (29).

Forty-one of the total 50 incidents reported as terrorism in all of Latin America last year were bombings of a U.S.-owned oil pipeline in Colombia.

What the report actually indicates is that virtually all of the incidents the U.S. government identified as acts of "global terrorism" in 2002 occurred in four places: Colombia, the separatist war in Chechnya, the continuing low-scale war in Afghanistan, and the Palestinian intifada. Elsewhere, the Bali tourist bombing by Islamic extremists caused some 200 deaths.

Before September 11, 2001, virtually none of this would have been called terrorism. It would have been called civil insurrection or nationalist or separatist violence.

Since September 11, vast global significance has been attributed to such episodes. They have been made the rationale for state mobilization and civil liberties restrictions in the U.S. (and at the American penal colony at Guantanamo Bay).

Elsewhere methods of state repression have been rationalized that in the past might have won the concerned governments a place in another annual report the State Department makes to Congress, on international human rights violations.

The distorted account of terrorism has had extraordinary psychological effect on many in the United States, causing them to think they are exposed to a degree of personal risk that has virtually no foundation in statistics, or indeed in common sense.

The New York editor who recently said that since the fall of Baghdad he has, for the first time since 2001, felt himself secure from being "blown to bits" by a terrorist bomb while crossing Times Square, is one such case.

Thousands of New Yorkers, earlier this year, acting on federal government warnings, built themselves tape-sealed rooms stocked with provisions, water, gas masks, etc., for a prolonged siege by terrorists.

Polls indicate that American voters no longer really care whether mass destruction weapons are found in Iraq. The victory was not over a threat they really identified with Saddam Hussein. It was a victory over "terrorism,"

Now, in an official report few will read, or are expected to read, their government admits that terrorism is at its lowest level in three decades, and that the actual risk it poses is statistically negligible. At the same time the same government tells them they must live in fear of "appalling crimes" and mass destruction. Where is this leading Americans?

May 8, 2003 — The Bush administration decision to exclude the United Nations and "old Europe" from Iraq in the war's aftermath is petty, as we have come to expect, but is also in the long term a good thing.

It serves to clarify to other countries the administration's intentions, and enables the Bush administration's enemies and its newly favored friends to discover the consequences of choices already made.

This also casts some light on the international order Washington's neoconservatives would like to construct, in replacement to national power pluralism and the cumbersome and inefficient multilateralism of UN and WTO (as well as the constraints of existing conventions of international law).

The rogue nations would in this new order have been disarmed, with democratic institutions installed, by military means when necessary, and in its preferred version only the United States would possess weapons of mass destruction.

To get from here to there will be tricky affair, since the international institutions and the alliances to be discarded afford certain advantages lacking in the arrangements meant to replace them, and the nations supposed to rally to the new order do not always do so.

Administration sources have already suggested, for example, that the Czech Republic might receive American military bases which, to "punish" Germany (and save money), are to be moved to former Warsaw Pact countries. President Vaclav Klaus commented in response that due precisely to the Warsaw Pact experience, the Czechs prefer to be free of foreign military forces.

Take the case of Poland, which would like American bases because they seem to provide security, and they offer investment and employment.

Poland made support for Washington in the Iraq war its policy priority, even though this served Washington's interest in dividing Europe so as to isolate the German, French and Belgian opponents of U.S. policy.

It was a necessary choice, given that a choice had to be made. Poland's history is one of vulnerability and victimization. It is at the frontier of western, Catholic Europe and the Orthodox East. It has a comprehensible concern over what Russia might become in the future.

Washington now has rewarded Warsaw for its allegiance, and for having sent commandos to the war, by giving Poland military command of northern

Iraq. Washington wants, by the autumn, to reduce the American troop strength in Iraq to 30,000. It asked the Poles for a brigade (normally three to five thousand men) to replace American forces.

The Poles said that while they appreciated the honor they can't afford it. The U.S., or someone else, will have to pay. The country has serious economic difficulties and an army of fewer than 40,000 professionals (plus 100,000 12-month conscripts).

Warsaw can send 1,500 men now, and suggested that Germany and Denmark might like to help. Germany, understandably, said thank you but no. It resisted the temptation to say that Germany's army is committed to the service of German foreign policy, not the Middle Eastern policy of the United States.

Denmark's peacetime army, not counting conscripts and attached civilians, numbers 7,400 soldiers. Copenhagen did send a diplomat who is also a Moslem convert to administer Iraq's northern region. The Poles are now talking with Lithuania and the Ukraine.

Take another example. The Bush administration decided in recent days that Turkey might like to become once again an American strategic "anchor" in the Eastern Mediterranean (the other one is Israel).

Paul Wolfowitz, Donald Rumsfeld's deputy, told the Turks on Tuesday that the U.S. would "like to see a different sort of attitude" in Ankara. The Turks should apologize for their "mistake" and rejoin the American team.

Wolfowitz particularly criticized the Turkish military, saying that they should have shown "strong leadership" to reverse parliament's refusal to allow the U.S. to attack Iraq from Turkey. (What did that comment mean?)

Turkey's prime minister, Recep Tayyip Erdogan, replied that "Turkey, from the very beginning, never made any mistakes." The Turks have made recent diplomatic contacts with Syria and Iran.

In short, the "new Europe" on which the neo-conservatives count is neither as willing nor as able as Washington would like it to be. Abusing old allies for following democratic opinion doesn't pay. And administering Iraq without the UN and its experience and staffs is not as simple as it seemed in Washington before the war.

The administration has only now offered its draft Security Council resolution meant to lift sanctions and establish who has the legal right to sell Iraqi oil and use the proceeds. So long as title to the oil is uncertain, not even American companies will buy it. Getting agreement on a resolution is not likely to be easy.

May 13, 2003 — The trouble with American conservatism during most of the twentieth century was that it was not particularly intelligent. The Republican Party was and is a business party, anti-intellectual and to a considerable degree xenophobic.

The conservative movement created in the U.S. around the *National Review* magazine in the 1950s profited from the wit and repartee of William F. Buckley, Jr. but was otherwise largely pedestrian when not tediously reactionary.

The radical neo-conservatives, who appeared in the 1960s, are the first seriously intelligent movement on the American Right since the nineteenth century. They want to remake the international order under effective American hegemony, destroy America's enemies, and cripple or eliminate the UN and other institutions making a claim to international jurisdiction.

They have a political philosophy, and the arrogance and intolerance of their actions reflect their conviction that they possess a realism and truth others lack.

They include Paul Wolfowitz, deputy defense secretary and supposedly the main influence in the decision to invade Iraq; Abram Shulsky of the Pentagon Office of Special Plans, Richard Perle of the Pentagon advisory board, Elliott Abrams of the National Security Council, the writers Robert Kagan and William Kristol, among others.

The main intellectual influence on the neo-conservatives has been the philosopher Leo Strauss, who left Germany in 1938 and taught for many years at the University of Chicago, dying in 1973. Several of the neo-conservatives studied under him. Wolfowitz and Shulsky took doctorates under him.

Something of a cult developed around Strauss during his later years at Chicago, and he and some admirers figure in the recent Saul Bellow novel, *Ravelstein*. The cult is appropriate because Strauss believed that the essential truths about human society and history should be held by an elite, and withheld from others who lack the fortitude to deal with truth. Society needs consoling lies.

He held that philosophy is dangerous because it brings into question the conventions on which civil order and the morality of society depend. This risks promoting a destructive nihilism.

He said that the relativism of modern American society is a moral disorder that could block it from identifying and attacking its real enemies. "Moral clarity" is essential. The Weimar Republic's toleration of extremism allowed the rise of the Nazi party.

He made an intellectually powerful and sophisticated critique of post-Enlightenment liberalism. He saw the United States as the most advanced case of liberalism and thus the most exposed to nihilism.

His claim was that Greek classical philosophy, notably that of Plato, is more true to the truth of nature than anything that has replaced it. Some critics say that his interpretation of Plato is perverse, but he said that he had recovered the "real" Plato, lost by later Neo-Platonic and Christian thinkers.

He also argued that Platonic truth is too hard for people to bear, and that the classical appeal to "virtue" as the object of human endeavor is unattainable. Hence it has been necessary to tell lies to people about the nature of political reality. However an elite recognizes the truth and keeps it to itself. This gives it insight, and implicitly power, that others do not possess. This obviously is an important element in Strauss's appeal to America's neo-conservatives.

The ostensibly hidden truth is that expediency works; there is no certain God to punish wrongdoing; and virtue is unattainable by most people. Machiavelli was right. There is a natural hierarchy of humans, and rulers must restrict free inquiry and exploit the mediocrity and vice of ordinary people so as to keep society in order.

This obviously is a bleak and anti-utopian philosophy that goes against practically everything Americans want to believe. It contradicts the conventional wisdom of modern democratic society. It also contradicts the neo-conservatives' own declared policy ambitions to make the Moslem world democratic and establish a new U.S.-led international order, which are blatantly utopian.

Strauss was no friend of hegemony, American or otherwise. He said that "no human being and no group of human beings can rule the whole of the human race justly." His concern during the cold war was that Soviet universalism invited an alternative American claim to world rule.

His real appeal to the neo-conservatives, in my view, is that his elitism presents a principled rationalization for policy expedience, and for "necessary lies" told to those whom the truth would demoralize.

It obviously is impossible in the space of a newspaper column to give more than a glimpse of Strauss's thought, whatever its merits. His thought, however, is a matter of public interest because his followers are in charge of American foreign policy. In my opinion, he is better and more interesting than they are.

May 20, 2003 — One might think the French would be flattered that the Bush administration considers Paris dangerous enough to wage a disinformation campaign to undermine it.

At present the French are being discreet and "constructive" about a new Security Council resolution concerning the Coalition's occupation powers and Iraq's oil. Thus far the Russians have been the most robust critics of the draft resolutions Washington and London have offered.

The Bush people are nonetheless afraid of the French because France is the only European country that says American power should be contained. The French obviously do not have the means to do this themselves, nor have they any current chance of mobilizing the European Union as such to make such an attempt. But they give people ideas.

They are a bad example to the other Europeans. They have a coherent position, and a tradition of Gaullist independence that always stuck in the American government's craw, long before the power-obsessed Bush administration took office.

Washington's recent unilateralism and brutality have created conditions that encourage certain other governments to listen to the French. The Europeans are no longer docile allies. Consider the Germans and Belgians. This concerns Washington, and motivates the attacks on the French.

There are French political figures and businessmen uncomfortable about bad relations with Washington, or harmed by reprisals. The public seems superbly indifferent.

A recent poll listed a number of issues confronting the government and asked which of them should be immediate priorities for President Jacques Chirac and his prime minister.

Just 3 percent of those polled said that restoring good relations with the U.S. is the most important thing for the government to do. Only 6 percent thought that fixing transatlantic relations even deserved to be on the list of priorities. Six percent!

However at the same time the French public expresses warmth towards Americans. In the latest Chicago Council on Foreign Relations/German Marshall Fund poll of national attitudes, the French expressed roughly the same warmth of feeling towards Americans as did the Germans, the Dutch, and even the Poles. In other words, there's nothing personal in the French attitude. It's political.

This Washington doesn't grasp. The Bush administration says you are either with me or against me. The French say: with you on what?, to do what?, to go where?

And it's not just the French who are saying this, which is something else the administration doesn't grasp. In the long run, the French are on the winning side in this contest, which is not a popularity contest. It's a contest of national identities and autonomy.

The pre-Berlin Wall transatlantic relationship, in which the U.S. led, and the Europeans more or less willingly followed, is ended. The contract on that has been ruptured — by the U.S., but also by the passage of time and events.

The current Greek presidency of the European Union recently invited 25 academics and analysts who figure in the transatlantic policy debate to write memos to be given to all the European foreign ministers before an informal EU meeting on U.S.-European relations May 2-3.

Both Americans and Europeans were asked to contribute [myself included]. The contributions, in my opinion, were reasonably representative of the expert opinion currently heard on the European side of the Atlantic (although not the opinion generally heard in Washington). The organizer, Greek Foreign Minister George Papandreou, is American-educated and widely respected.

A few of the writers wanted to see something like the old transatlantic relationship reestablished. However only one memo said that the Europeans should be content as subordinates, and do their part by spending more on arms.

Others, in the guise of saying what Europe should do, actually talked about what the U.S. should do: Europe must somehow convince the U.S. to change its ways, recognize the merits of multilateralism, turn back to a "revived" NATO. Europe must try to influence the U.S.'s "better self." This is not advice likely to succeed.

All the other memos said in one way or another that the Europeans have to find an independent role on which they can unite. They might unite on defending the UN's role, or international law and justice. They might try to establish "an alternate beacon" in international affairs. They might concentrate on the Balkans and the European periphery. They might try to make themselves an equal but independent partner of the U.S.

But what they all really were saying was that they want what the French want: a Europe with an independent policy, exercising an equal influence on international affairs (probably through different means, primarily political and economic rather than military). That is just what the United States does not want.

May 29, 2003 — George Bush starts running his Gulf War victory lap at St. Petersburg's 300th anniversary celebration, offering Russian President Vladimir Putin tepid congratulations and advice to get back in White House good graces.

He goes then to Evian in France to drop in on the G-8 meeting of the major industrial countries, and on the next day to the Middle East....At Evian the president faces Europe's "old" nations, which happen to be three of the five most important industrial nations in the world. He undoubtedly will indicate his displeasure with the two that led the opposition to his intervention in Iraq.

He and his entourage think that pressure, punishment and displeasure — no Texas ranch invitations for the miscreant national leaders — will eventually force them back into line. (One might think avoiding the ranch visit a plus for the Germans and French, sparing them the usual press-conference charade in cowboy boots and 10-gallon hats).

This conviction suggests that the Bush government leaders don't understand the history of the cold war alliances. NATO prospered because American leadership was light and consensual, and everyone supported the cause.

Soviet alliance leadership was oppressive, intolerant, exploitative, and accompanied by military intimidation. It had had virtually no popular support in the Warsaw Pact countries. The system eventually collapsed, to much rejoicing.

Why? Nations with authentic national cultures don't put up with domination when the people don't accept the ideas of the dominator. When his power weakens there is nothing to hold the system together.

Washington has effectively if uncomprehendingly been trying to turn the transatlantic alliance from consent and consensus into a system of intimidation and pressures.

The Bush administration says that it wants U.S. representatives inside EU institutions. (What about reciprocal EU observers in Donald Rumsfeld's office?) It sees the European Union as a potential threat and wants to divide it. It has succeeded, up to a point. But in the long run it is up against nationalism.

A current example. Washington has for years been telling the Europeans to spend more on defense, meaning on NATO-integrated systems.

A week before the G-8 meeting, the Europeans took the following decisions:

Seven countries contracted to buy a total of 180 Airbus-manufactured military transports, the most ambitious military project yet undertaken in Europe.

The fifteen governments who are members of the European Space Agency agreed to launch Europe's own 30-satellite "Galileo" global positioning system, rival to the Pentagon-controlled GPS. Washington bitterly opposes Galileo.

The Space Agency also committed a two billion euro credit to the troubled Ariane space launcher, until recently global leader in commercial space.

This is not what the U.S. had in mind.

It demonstrated the reality of European "nationalism" and European self-interest. These are far more important than how France and Germany vote at the UN. They are not affected by Donald Rumsfeld's irascibility, or by who snubs whom at Evian, or even by who's invited to the barbecue at the Crawford ranch.

Paris, June 3, 2003 — From the start it has been hard to understand Tony Blair's conduct concerning the war on Iraq. Clearly he believed deeply in the moral case for unseating Saddam Hussein. He had nothing to gain politically from supporting George Bush, since the British public initially was against the war.

But he backed the president so obsequiously that he actually forfeited the influence he might have had in Washington, President Bush's pally treatment notwithstanding. He simultaneously reinforced Britain's reputation in Europe as incorrigibly Atlanticist and divisive.

Rodric Braithwaite, former chairman of Britain's joint intelligence committee, said of the prime minister's performance that "a junior partner who is taken for granted is a junior partner with no influence."

To have influence you must express opinions and national interests of your own, and indicate that on some issues you might break with the partner. It is no use playing Little Sir Echo. This conduct was particularly odd from a prime minister said to be obsessed with winning a place in history.

Blair remained faithful even after Donald Rumsfeld told him the U.S. didn't really need British troops, the administration subverted his independent effort to work with the Palestinians, and cut him (and everyone else) out of Middle Eastern road map implementation.

Now the prime minister is in trouble. It's charged that the war decision was taken in Washington last fall and everything that followed was expedient charade. London and Washington are accused of lying to get public support for the war and of faking evidence about Iraq's mass destruction weapons.

Paul Wolfowitz has given a candid and totally convincing explanation of how it began to the magazine *Vanity Fair*.

Implicit in his account is that the Bush administration last year wanted to go to war but had no excuse for doing so. The bureaucracies were called together and told to find an excuse. The only casus belli they could agree upon was Iraqi possession of mass destruction weapons.

That settled, it became the government's virtual reality that the weapons existed, even if the CIA, DIA and UN had not found them.

The mighty Wurlitzer of American policy, persuasion, and press was put to work to persuade the public and the world of the reality of this threat, so that America could go to war. Britain's modest harmonium joined in. The prime minister proudly furnished Washington with two dossiers of evidence on Iraqi weapons that subsequently proved very dodgy.

When the war was over, the coalition's failure to find the weapons had to be explained. First it was said that they had been smuggled to Syria. Then Donald Rumsfeld suggested last week that none exist. They were destroyed before the war and all evidence buried. This week he reversed himself and said they do exist, still are there, and will be found.

The U.S. military command in Iraq said the search may take several years since it is a big country. President Bush went back into virtual reality mode last weekend and told Polish television: "We found the weapons of mass destruction." On Tuesday, Secretary of State Powell expressed confidence that they will eventually be found.

Tony Blair's contribution last Friday was to say that the coalition has been too busy to look for the weapons.

In the United States, until now, few seemed to care, thinking that the war had been a splendid little affair. However Congress has interested itself in what the Senate and public had been told, and there will be joint hearings by the Senate and House intelligence committees.

There actually is not much pretense about what happened. Speaking by way of retired officers, the intelligence community says that Donald Rumsfeld's Defense Department cut the CIA out of the planning loop and substituted tendentious material coming from exile groups and pro-war Washington think tanks.

Britain used to have higher standards, and has a much more aggressive press corps and television. Prime Minister Blair's government has a reputation for "spinning" its public relations but not for the bare-faced lie. The prime minister himself has the reputation of a decent man.

His ex-foreign secretary, Robin Cook, has now demanded an independent inquiry. It seems likely that parliamentarians will investigate whether Downing Street's own flacks and handlers clumsily "improved" the material they had been given by MI6 before furnishing it to Washington, and will report to the prime minister's office rather than to Parliament.

However such discretion may not be possible if the American hearings stir trouble in Washington (and on television). The prime minister may come to regret having been so reliable an American partner.

June 5, 2003 — The Bush administration's plans for a new world rest on the progressive theory that mankind's ultimate and natural condition is universal democracy. Preemptive action against rogue regimes — such as Iraq — merely removes obstacles to the common destiny.

There is, however, an important ideological clash behind this within the Republican party right, and in conservative intellectual circles.

A considerable part of the Christian fundamentalist community in the U.S. has by now convinced itself that Islam represents evil, and that U.S. war with the Islamic world is part of the biblical plan.

This bigoted, theologically ignorant, and extremely dangerous idea has a sophisticated counterpart in the widely circulated proposition that Moslems are incapable of democracy.

Samuel Huntington's mischievous argument that the "next world war" will be a clash of civilizations included an assertion that Moslems are peculiarly and uniquely given to violence.

The scholar Bernard Lewis' best-selling book on Islam and modern history, *What Went Wrong*, ends on a "with us or against us" note that contributes to an intellectual climate of Islamic-western confrontation.

There is a pragmatic challenge to this idea in an article on "universal democracy" by Larry Diamond of the Hoover Institution, appearing in the forthcoming issue of the Washington Journal, *Policy Review*.

Diamond says that while democracy is indeed all but completely absent from the 16 Arab Middle Eastern countries, this is not true for the world's 27 other Moslem-majority countries, whose record on democratic development is little different from the international average.

His explanation is politically convincing. Since 1948 the Palestine-Israel conflict has become a paralyzing political obsession in the Arab world. It has generated "a powerful symbolic struggle over Arab identity and dignity. Until the fog of this struggle is lifted...genuine and lasting democratization will be unlikely in the region."

His argument is highly relevant today because the initial steps on the so-called road map to Middle Eastern peace were taken last week against a background of reports indicating that the Provisional Authority the United States has established to democratize Iraq is far from having a grip on the material and social disarray of that country.

It's not even properly functioning; it doesn't have the number of computers and telephones it needs for its own staff. They can't talk to one another because the satellite phones they brought with them don't work indoors — to their surprise.

The Authority still is dominated by security considerations, living behind barricades, its members staying indoors at night. Violence mounts in the Sunni districts of Baghdad and the Sunni-dominated regions in the center and north of the country.

The bureaucratic problems can be explained away, but are nonetheless surprising, given the Defense Department's pre-war promises to put the country back together within weeks, and to pull the Authority out in three months (and its often-expressed scorn for UN "inefficiency").

The authority seems even further away from winning a consensus among Iraqi political and religious leaders — existing or self-appointed — on how to launch political reconstruction.

Its new director, Paul Bremer, dismissed the leadership that first emerged as unrepresentative, and wants to appoint an advisory Iraqi "political council."

Existing political groups point out that the Security Council resolution authorizing the occupation says "the Iraqi people" are to form an interim authority "with the help" of the occupiers. That's not the way it's currently working.

This is a very important problem, affecting not only what will happen in Iraq but the credibility of the Coalition Authority, the Pentagon, the Bush administration, and the neo-conservative brain trust responsible for the U.S. decision to invade.

If Iraq's condition doesn't keep some people in Washington awake at night, the huge question of "remaking" and democratizing the Arab Middle East should. That is what Iraq's rapid reconstruction by the U.S. is supposed to provoke — to Israel's and the United States' permanent benefit, as well as to that of the region's people.

The situation thus is having an unexpected effect on the Israeli-Palestinian situation. Success in Iraq was supposed to make the latter work by influencing the Palestinians to follow the peaceful and democratic precedents being set in Iraq.

But if pacification and reconstruction in Baghdad remain bogged down, the Bush administration's plan for democratizing the region — and more to the point, its political prospects in the 2004 elections — are going to depend on getting Israel-Palestine agreement.

That will be needed to justify invading Iraq, and to keep alive the administration's sweeping promises of democratic reforms in the Arab world and beyond.

Como, Italy, June 24, 2003 — The most interesting aspect of this year's workshop of the Council for the United States and Italy, recently concluded, was the European participants' indifference to the new American policy of promoting Europe's "disaggregation," as if it were of no consequence.

Admittedly, the European participants were all from what Washington considers "old Europe," most of them from Italy, the oldest part of old Europe. The Italians have seen barbarians, internal or external to Europe, come, go — or even themselves become civilized.

The last is not a fate likely to overcome the official American representatives at this meeting, voicing the now standard Bush administration message: we are the most powerful; we are also the most virtuous, and even if we were not, might makes right; everyone else is either with us or against us.

This had been heard before. The German representation, small, but the largest European group other than the Italian, made the most important if least dramatic contribution to the discussion by noting that a basic change in German political culture has taken place. What happened as a result of the Iraq affair has proven a crucial change.

No doubt much has contributed to this: more than a century of an inculcated postwar pacifism combined with a certain external exploitation of German war guilt, German tedium with being taken for granted by the United States (and by its European allies), and a primordial German wish to express a national opinion and have a national policy. Whatever the case, there has been a quiet, unaggressive, German assertion of independent European identity....

Shortly before this Italian-American meeting at Lake Como, an American appeal for transatlantic unity was issued by the Center for Strategic and International Studies in Washington, signed by two former Democratic secretaries of state (Madeleine Albright and Warren Christopher) as well as by Zbigniew Brzezinski and a number of other cabinet-level or leading congressional figures from past Democratic administrations, and by Republican veterans of the first Bush and the Ronald Reagan administrations.

The statement expressed concern over how European Union institutions are evolving, saying that Americans want "to continue...to feel welcome in Europe."

To that end, it made a number of proposals. It suggested that U.S. observers be part of current EU constitutional deliberations. It asked that U.S. government officials have a role in European Council meetings (where European Union decisions are taken).

It asked for European unification within a formal transatlantic structure, so as to make the EU the political equivalent of NATO.

It warned against European defense spending and military measures that might seem a challenge to U.S. military predominance.

In short, it asked for the European Union to be subordinated to the United States. This has been heard before, but has been associated by Europeans with the Bush administration. This statement was important because it demonstrated that this is not simply the policy of the Bush administration, but is that of most of the "establishment" policy community in the United States, Democratic as well as Republican.

While the Como workshop was in progress, a reply to this declaration was published in the leading Italian daily, *Corriere della Sera*, and in France's *Le Monde*.

The signers were mainly former prime ministers or presidents from Italy, France, Sweden, Poland, Germany, and cabinet-level equivalents of the signers of the American declaration.

These included Giuliano Amato, Raymond Barre, Carl Bildt, Bronislaw Geremek, Valery Giscard d'Estaing, Felipe Gonzales, Douglas Hurd, Helmut Kohl and Helmut Schmidt.

The letter expressed appreciation for the Americans' concern over Europe's evolution but maintained that world problems "can only be dealt with in a multinational framework as provided by the United Nations," not in the unitary framework demanded by the U.S.

It implicitly condemned a U.S. policy directed to Europe's "disaggregation," intended to divide Europe, asserting that the EU "will soon be the main reference in transatlantic relations," and that "an effective European defense does not endanger NATO."

It drew a line between what mainstream opinion in Western and Central Europe wants, and what the United States wants. This was useful. The transatlantic political conflict has only begun. It will dominate the decade to come.[2]

Paris, June 26, 2003 — The only member of the United States Senate who voted against granting war powers to President George W. Bush, Robert C. Byrd of West Virginia, holds that lies were told by the president to justify the Iraq war, and that eventually truth will out. He said of truth, addressing the Senate in May: "The eternal years of God are hers; / But error, wounded, writhes in pain, / And dies among his worshippers."

One would like to believe it true. But while Senator Byrd will be vindicated in the long run, the culture of lies that prevails in the Bush administration is integral part of a larger culture of expedience and systematic dishonesty that dominates the present leadership of American political society and business. There is little reason to expect that to soon change.

Expedient lies have always been part of politics; and American business, at its higher levels, has often been crooked, but uneasily so, in conflict with the residual Puritanism of the American Establishment.

This Puritanism was contemptuously discarded by the profit-driven business ethic that took over in the 1980s. Thus no effort is deemed necessary today to mask the connections of members of this administration with corporate profit-taking from defeated Iraq.

The personal links of high officials, including the president and vice president, with the commercial interests and business sectors that expect to profit from Iraq's reconstruction and the privatization of Iraq's resources are not only widely known but largely uncontroversial. Even in the Gilded Age they would have been considered scandalous.

---

2. The text of the American declaration and of the European reply appear in an appendix to this book, as does an exchange of letters between myself and the author of the American declaration, the distinguished scholar Simon Safarti, objecting to my description of the document, and my response.

As for the lies told to justify invasion of Iraq, one had no need to wait for Paul Wolfowitz to tell *Vanity Fair* magazine that the proclaimed threat of Iraqi weapons of mass destruction — deployable within 45 minutes, as the president's ally, Tony Blair, helpfully added — was simply the theme of bureaucratic choice. True or not, it was plausible, and could be sold.

In the lead-up to the war it was painful for an American to watch Secretary of State Colin Powell present to the UN Security Council the flimsy texts, equivocal photos, and tissues of supposition that he clearly did not himself believe provided serious evidence of the Iraqi menace.

It was still more embarrassing to see Prime Minister Tony Blair try to make the same case, because Blair really does believe in the cause. Now the credulous prime minister is the man in danger, not his friend in Washington. Parliament takes a graver view of governmental lies than the sitting United States Senate. A House of Commons select committee is taking evidence on the matter.

While this is of consequence to establish guilt, as an investigation to establish truth it too is wasted time. Outraged MI6 insiders, unwilling to take the rap for Downing Street, and senior retired CIA and State Department people have for many weeks been in the corridors and on the internet to express outrage at the use by Washington and London of rigged intelligence on Iraq — reaching even into President Bush's State of the Union message in January.

That these were lies was made obvious when the U.S. proved unable to give valid or even interesting leads on Iraqi WMD to the UN inspectors, when they went back into Iraq. The Bush people disliked Hans Blix and the UN, but no one can seriously think that if they had been able to direct UN inspectors to concealed Iraqi weapons or weapons facilities they would not have done so. They could have gone to war with Iraq the morning after, with France and Germany on board.

A good deal has already been written about the institutional consequences of corrupting the intelligence services to serve ideological interests. Not so much has been said about plain lies, which travel a long way in an electorate as uninterested in international affairs and as ill-served by press and television as today's American electorate.

President Bush convinced the majority of Americans that Saddam Hussein not only had WMD but was about to use them against America.

He convinced the public majority that Saddam Hussein and Osama bin Laden were linked, and that Iraq collaborated in the September 11 attacks. He has now convinced the public that Iran is a nuclear threat, and that an American intervention in that country may become justified.

Presidential lies to Congress, strictly speaking, are constitutional ground for impeachment. They really are something more serious. They rupture the relationship of responsibility that is supposed to exist between president and public.

Partisan or personal interest and equivocation are one thing. Lies about matters of state, and about war, are another. To lie to the citizenry is to reject the confidence freely given a president. It destroys the moral bond that holds a democratic society together.

New York, July 1, 2003 — Ezra Suleiman of Princeton, who also teaches in Paris and has written distinguished works on French society, suggested in a recent newspaper article that the French position on Iraq was the capricious creation of President Jacques Chirac and his foreign minister.

He said that France had gone terribly astray in "opposing its principal ally," an "inadmissible" act in Washington's view. He said nothing to suggest that issues of principle or value were involved.

France finds few defenders in the United States. The common assumption is that Paris invariably acts from discreditable motives, while the United States tries to do good.

As Suleiman shows, even in serious circles there seems little acknowledgement that the Iraq war dispute was caused by differences of political principle and different visions of the world, and that the French and German governments were overwhelmingly supported by public opinion in nearly all of Europe.

Thus while there is considerable domestic U.S. debate over unilateralist foreign policy, Bush administration hostility to existing international institutions and repudiation of previously accepted treaty obligations, and the legitimacy of the hegemonic ambitions increasingly expressed in Washington, few have seemed willing to recognize that this is what the transatlantic conflict has also been about.

It is the subject at the center of the expansion debate now going on across the EU. There already have been independent European Union, or EU-led, crisis management operations in Bosnia, Macedonia, and the Congo. Is there to be an independent European security policy, outside NATO?

Most of Europe's policy leadership recognizes that American policy opposes that, and is now meant to "disaggregate" or divide the EU. Their concern is what to do about it. It was the theme cautiously circled about at a recent transatlantic meeting in Paris on security issues.

Those Americans who still think that current transatlantic differences are a relatively harmless disagreement with Europeans "from Venus," possessing virtuous illusions about international legality and multilateral institutions, are today being told that they are badly mistaken.

A prominent current theme of neo-conservative writing and television talk now is that a Franco-German dominated European Union, rebuilt according to the new Giscardian constitution now under debate, threatens to become "Superpower Europe" and a mortal danger to the United States.

The influential Washington weekly, *The New Republic*, has just announced that "America must wake up!" to the danger from an expanded and united Europe and the newly strengthened European currency, the euro.

It may even be too late, one author claims. Britain, Spain, Italy and others who supported Washington in the Iraq war may next time be dragged into the Franco-German orbit by economic integration and dependence, and the other constraints of EU membership.

Another writer warns that Europe's low growth and productivity statistics conceal the great advantage a stable Europe possesses over an unstable and erratic U.S. economy, undermined by corruption and excess.

France is systematically denigrated, as to a lesser extent is Germany — Germany is thought salvageable, or open to intimidation, once Chancellor Schroeder is gone. France is portrayed as suffering from "a profound pathology," and as America's enemy.

In Washington power corridor leaks to the press, in neo-conservative magazines and on the Internet, France is described as driven by hatred, national vanity and the personal vanity of Jacques Chirac, and as allied with the radical Arab world out of fear of France's unassimilated Muslim population.

It is described as incorrigibly and dangerously anti-Semitic. The French, like the Germans (the Daniel Goldhagen argument) are described as instinctively anti-Semitic and culturally disposed to totalitarianism.

France even is "not a western country anymore" since in "many cities" [undoubtedly a confused reference to the heavily immigrant suburban "cités" or public housing developments] "no teenage girl can go out in the evening, at least without a full burqa." (These quotations are from a neo-conservative American website whose contributors include quite well known figures, including some from the political right in France itself).

This kind of nonsense sets the tone. Few Americans acknowledge any intellectual or moral weight or merit on the "old" European side, and certainly not on that of France.

Only one person in the Bush administration has acknowledged a European intellectual challenge, the National Security Adviser, Condoleezza Rice. Speaking in London last week, at the International Institute for Strategic Studies, she made a reasoned condemnation of an international system of multipolarity, and implicitly of the "efficacious multilateralism" (the EU's term) that Europe defends.

She said multipolarity is outmoded, in the past "a necessary evil that sustained the absence of war but did not promote the triumph of peace." Something different, under American leadership, must take its place.

However the argument is not only a European-American one. It is an American-American debate, worth talking about in a second column.

Paris, July 3, 2003 — From the 1920s to the 1960s, America's students were taught a simple and cautionary story about international relations.

This story said that the United States had until the early twentieth century wisely heeded George Washington's advice that the new American republic avoid "entangling alliances" with the old nations of Europe. The latter practiced ignoble "power politics," inspired by imperial rivalries and dynastic quarrels.

The United States had launched a "new order of the ages," to replace the old European order. Novus ordo seclorum was inscribed on the reverse of the Great Seal of the United States, as testament to the historical significance attributed to the new republic's creation.

The story went on to say that the United States was forced to re-engage with Europe in 1917-1918, but brought with it Woodrow Wilson's plan for universal peace, based on national self-determination and a new parliament of nations.

When the League of Nations failed (for reasons including Congressional conflict with Wilson), Europe was left in disorder. The second world war followed.

After that, the story continued, a new American plan to bring universal peace to the world, the United Nations — inspired by Franklin Roosevelt, and again designed in Washington — was blocked from functioning by the Soviet Union, which launched the cold war.

This was a simplistic, sentimental, and fundamentally misconceived story. Its essential elements nonetheless reappear in the policy of the George W. Bush administration.

The Bush version might be called a muscular and well-armed version of the conceived American mission to bring universal peace to the world, this time identified as victory in the war on terror.

Among the obstacles to this victory is the notion, defended even by some American critics of the administration, that a multipolar and balanced international system, composed of several centers of power, is more conducive to the national interests of all, than a system where there is a single national leader, and centralized or hegemonic power. The latter is inherently unwieldy and oppressive, generating resistance and disorder.

Condoleezza Rice, the president's national security adviser, offered her version of the traditional American story about international affairs at the end of June, speaking to the International Institute for Strategic Studies in London.

She said that the time has come "to break the destructive pattern of great power rivalry that has bedeviled the world since the rise of the nation state in the seventeenth century."

Europe must repudiate the "multipolarity" that in the past "was a necessary evil that sustained the absence of war but did not promote the triumph of peace. Multipolarity is a theory of rivalry; of competing powers — and at its worst, competing values. We have tried this before. It led to the Great War...."

There must be a new mechanism for enforcing peace. The national security adviser asked "why should we seek to divide our capacities for good, when they can be much more effective united? Only the enemies of freedom would cheer this division."

Extrapolating from what she said, instead of an allegedly discredited multipolar international system, making use of the United Nations (now declared irrelevant), there should be a new system which goes beyond the limitations of NATO today.

The existing NATO alliance no longer is satisfactory because it actually incorporates an internal multipolarity. Some NATO allies have policy visions rival to that of the U.S., and competing values — as in the case of invading Iraq. Since NATO is an alliance of equals, these allies are obstacles to united action.

This judgment would be consistent with the idea widely heard in Washington that a new NATO is needed, transferred eastwards and incorporating the new Europeans. To judge from the current Washington debate, this should take the form of an enlargement of the present Iraq war coalition. Coalitions are not composed of equals.

The merits of such a change may be disputed, and will be. Dr. Rice's version of history, and of the workings of international systems, must be challenged.

The first world war did not happen because there was a balance of power. It happened because Germany attempted before 1914 to overturn the balance, thereby turning Britain against Germany.

The pre-1914 convention of European great power relations had ceded naval primacy to Britain in exchange for German predominance in land power. Germany set out to have naval power too.

War did not break out in the Balkans because multipolar power existed there, but because of resistance to hegemonic power. The war was ignited by the efforts of radical nationalists to break free from the Austro-Hungarian Empire.

The second world war was not caused by a multipolar power system but by the failure of the Versailles settlement to reestablish balance — either among the major powers, or in the Balkans, where the Versailles treaty created disputes rather than ending them.

Unmistakable in Dr. Rice's argument about multipolarity is that Washington is no longer willing to deal with its allies, in NATO or elsewhere, as equals.

July 15, 2003 — The Bush administration's extraordinary capacity for undermining American national interests while attempting to advance them is on prominent display this week as British Prime Minister Tony Blair, until now President Bush's closest ally, arrives in Washington to address a joint session of Congress, the first British prime minister to do so since Winston Churchill.

The prime minister's visit coincides with the decision taken by his friends in the White House and Pentagon — one perhaps should now say his former friends — to make him take the fall for President Bush in the matter of the false information used in the president's State of the Union address to justify invading Iraq.

The White House had first tried to lay the blame on George Tenant, head of the CIA, who obediently put his head on the block last week, saying that indeed it was he and his agency that did it.

However the CIA is under the president's responsibility, so it was thought better that Tenant add that the CIA got its information from Britain.

A distraught Downing Street in turn said that Britain got it from still another source — which the British government has conveniently sworn never to reveal.

The White House spokesman, Ari Fleischer, declared on Monday that "the bottom has been gotten to." The buck has stopped. Unknowable unknowns did it.

The president is guilty only of taking seriously what faithful friends told him. One is expected to assume that his friend the vice president, Richard Cheney, neglected to tell him that his office had ordered the uranium from Niger story checked out in February 2002 and had found there was nothing to it.

One must wonder why these people expect the public to take seriously such bamboozlement, producing, along the way, the disgraceful victimization of one of the few true friends the Bush administration has had in the whole Iraq adventure.

Does anyone really doubt that before the war Washington was sweeping absolutely everything remotely useful into packaging for public opinion an Iraq invasion already decided upon for ideological and strategic reasons?

The White House, Congress and the press, under a variety of political interests and headline and television pressures, have collaborated in turning the issue of whether the public was lied to about the reason for the "preemptive" invasion of Iraq into an argument over who was responsible for saying that Iraq attempted to buy a form of processed uranium from Niger.

This successfully trivialized the matter, as the administration wishes. The American public, normally disposed to support the president, is naturally inclined to say that if that's all the controversy is about, it's a minor matter compared with the big issues of Iraq's liberation and what now is happening to American troops occupying Iraq — 140,000 Americans surrounded by 23 million Iraqis (with the deployment of the poor 3rd Infantry Division, which fought most of the war, extended indefinitely; what happened to that American army that was going to fight three wars at once?).

The British press and public are not taking this betrayal of Tony Blair calmly, least of all at a moment when the U.S. refuses to yield up to Britain the two British citizens about to be put on military trial at what we must, alas, describe as the U.S. political prison at Guantanamo Bay — outside the reach of

American constitutional guarantees and the formal legal jurisdiction of the U.S., or of anyone else.

The prime minister seems too badly hounded and confused by critics of his own government's handling of the Iraq affair to think straight about these betrayals by Washington. He might have salvaged some dignity by canceling the Washington trip and making it plain that London's terrorism policy is not totally dictated by Washington.

The Bush administration has distinguished itself by its inability or unwillingness to deal with allies as equals, with legitimate interests, and views of their own to be respected.

This is the issue Washington obfuscates and London has refused to raise. Prime Minister Blair's support for the U.S. has been exploited to lend legitimacy to a war entirely conceived and controlled by Washington.

The United States has a new kind of government, which takes a new view of what allies are worth, and how they are expected to behave. This has been an underlying issue throughout the U.S.-European drama of the past ten months. It will determine the future of the western alliance, as well as the character of the new European Union now being ushered into existence by an EU constitution, EU expansion, and an independent EU security policy.

PART SIX

July to December 2003: From Victory to Defeat

July 17, 2003 — George Robertson says NATO will provide no further help to the U.S. in Iraq — meaning that NATO's principal European members refuse to let the alliance do so.

This is a reluctant choice by the Europeans, but their perception of the U.S. has in the last two years changed dramatically. The U.S. now is seen in Europe as a threat to Europe's independence. The American side does not understand this.

The Europeans simply no longer agree with the United States. They don't agree about the terrorist threat. They don't think Osama bin Laden is a global menace. They don't take Washington's view of rogue states. They don't agree about preemptive war, clash of civilizations, the demonization of Islam, or Pentagon domination of U.S. foreign policy.

Such views are interpreted in the United States as "anti-Americanism." The truth is, as the (conservative) leader of one ex-Communist state said to me recently, the Bush administration has turned America's friends into anti-Americans.

He said that throughout his political life he had been an admirer and defender of the United States against left-wing European critics, but now he has become what he calls a "new anti-American."

He defined new anti-Americans as "former anti-anti-Americans, now forced to become anti-American themselves."

He said that in his own country, the American ambassador behaves in the way the Soviet Union's ambassador did before 1989. This simply is unacceptable.

Washington and the U.S. policy community seem to have completely misunderstood what has happened. They blame the French, Germans and Belgians, and think they have explained the problem. They like to tell Europeans that Europe doesn't understand that 9/11 "changed everything" for the U.S. They fail to realize that 9/11's aftermath has changed everything for Western Europe.

Neo-conservative officials from Washington continue to celebrate American power and victory in Iraq, and demand apologies from the Europeans for having failed to support the U.S. They go on saying that if you didn't agree, you are "irrelevant."

Analysts from American universities and policy centers are often condescending to their European interlocutors, saying that Europe needs to "grow up" and face the terrorism threat (seemingly indifferent to or ignorant of the history of IRA, German and Italian Red Brigades, Basque ETA, PLO, and Algerian terrorist operations in Europe).

They talk about Venus and Mars — the fashionable Washington theory about passive, peace-obsessed Europeans, in need of realistic leadership from tough-minded Americans.

The Europeans by now have heard it all before. They now laugh, but take the implications seriously. The so-called European common security and foreign policy has until now been a subject of lackadaisical debate. Now, even the people from the most Atlanticist allied states, closest to the U.S., shrug and say, "there's no choice."...

July 22, 2003 — Tony Blair's current crisis, with a Law Lord inquiring into Ministry of Defense advisor David Kelly's death, surely derives in part from the prime minister's intense but puzzling commitment to George W. Bush's leadership in the Iraq war. If he or his entourage cut corners to justify Iraq's invasion, it was to serve the common cause.

The Blair government has turned the 61-year old Anglo-American security alliance into an unprecedented subordination to the United States of Britain's security and foreign policy.

This was the unspoken message of Tony Blair's emotional address to a joint session of Congress last week.

Defense Secretary Geoff Hoon had already, in late June, announced that British military forces are to be reconfigured so as to function henceforth as Pentagon auxiliaries.

This is because from now on "it is highly unlikely that the U.K. would engage in large-scale combat operations without the United States."

By depriving itself of the ability to operate independently, Britain will abandon one of its most important assets, its present possession of balanced and autonomous multi-arm military forces, capable of operating nationally, serving distinct British interests.

These operations might be small, such as the recent intervention in Sierra Leone that rescued that country from the catastrophe now overtaking next-door Liberia (the latter effectively a colony of the United States, or of the Firestone Tire and Rubber Company, between 1822 and the end of the second world war, currently abandoned to its fate.)

The British operation in Iraq was composed of an autonomous force integrating infantry, armor, artillery, and air and naval support under independent national command.

However an independent British operation can also be large and audacious, as in dispatching an expeditionary force to seize the Falkland Islands from Argentine aggression in 1982, a feat of arms and military improvisation without parallel since World War II.

(Its incidental and serendipitous result was to overturn Argentina's military junta, end the blight of "disappearances" in that country, reinstall democracy, and terminate the modern era of South American military dictatorships.)

In Europe, only France now will have the capacity for sizable independent military operations. All other non-neutral West European forces have been turned into specialized units of an American-commanded NATO army.

As David Leich and Richard Norton-Taylor reported in *The Guardian* last week, Britain has begun reequipping its nuclear missile submarines with U.S.-made and maintained Tomahawk cruise missiles, usable only with U.S. acquiescence.

Washington no longer fully shares intelligence with Britain. London accords Washington "full transparency" with respect to intelligence gathered by MI6 and British communications interception at GHQ Cheltenham, but according to former Labour foreign secretary Robin Cook does not get transparency in return.

Britain, under Tony Blair, has allowed its principal aerospace manufacturer, BAe Systems, to be sold to U.S. investors. Hoon announced earlier this year that the company is no longer British. It now has majority U.S. control, and its high-technology military research and manufacturing are being segregated into U.S.-controlled corporate entities to which, for security reasons, British personnel no longer have full access.

The Blair government has just agreed to extradite British subjects to the U.S. on demand, without need for prima facie evidence. The U.S. refuses to reciprocate, citing U.S., constitutional protections under the Fourth Amendment (a insolent claim, one would think, when Washington holds British nationals at Guantanamo Bay, outside American constitutional jurisdiction).

The Bush-Blair marriage scarcely seems made in heaven. British Labour governments are supposed to be socially responsible, accountable to an electorate of the left. The Bush government considers itself accountable to corporate interests, and as unbound by normal considerations of habeas corpus and judicial due process.

Tony Blair, after taking office in 1997, pledged his government to a "moral" foreign policy. The George Bush government claims a moral result from its liberation of the Iraqis, but also claims, when it wishes, a sovereign exemption from the constraints of international law and treaty obligation. It asserts a sovereign right to military domination of the planet (and of nearby space).

Why does Tony Blair wish this slow suicide of one of Europe's greatest nations, whose independent legacy to modern western civilization, and certainly to the United States, is so immense? Where is his electoral mandate for so enormous a decision?

There is no evident trade-off. Britain gets nothing from the United States in return (other than Congressional cheers and a gold medal for the prime minister). If George Bush remains in office beyond next year, Britain might find itself implicated in what could become an American national tragedy.

Neither does the United States gain anything valuable, merely the ignoble satisfactions of possessing a complaisant satellite.

Far better for it to have an independent friend, who speaks its language, has independent weight in world affairs, possesses a major voice in the European Union, is capable on occasion of telling Washington home truths, and by using its independent influence, to force Washington to pay attention.

A British tragedy is in the making. For many of us who grew up under the decisive influence of Britain's history and literature, it implies an American tragedy as well.

July 29, 2003 — The word that best describes the American situation in Iraq today is irrelevance. The United States was highly relevant while bombing and attacking Iraq, creating the conditions that underlie the present semi-anarchy.

The failure to restore infrastructure and order, to secure public institutions and the streets, to secure even American forces and convoys — to convince the Iraqis that the occupation authority knows what it is doing — has rendered the United States more irrelevant with every passing day. The Iraqis now understand that they will ultimately settle what happens to their country.

The United States was supposed to be delivering peace and security, a new constitution, a new government, a new political consciousness, a new market economy and stock exchange open to foreign investment, a new alliance with Israel as well as with the United States: a whole new national life. The Iraqis in turn were supposed to deliver to the United States a new Middle East.

Paul Wolfowitz of the Defense Department returned to Washington last week, after his tour of Iraq, to claim that despite the Arab media's inflaming Iraqi opinion against the U.S., the deaths of the sons of Saddam Hussein has lifted "a blanket of fear."

President George W. Bush added that Paul Bremer, head of the occupation authority, has devised "a comprehensive strategy to move Iraq towards a future that is secure and prosperous."

But that is what the president and his men are expected to say. It is what they have to say, since their careers, including that of the president, may be over in 15 months, if things continue to go badly....

The administration's critics are drawing parallels with Vietnam, talking about Iraq as a quagmire.

There actually is little resemblance to the American intervention in Vietnam. There, the United States set out to defeat a highly-motivated national revolutionary movement, armed from outside.

In Iraq the United States is harassed by guerillas about whom it knows little, not even their true motivations, other than to drive the United States out of their country. The claim that Ba'ath party survivors control the attacks on Americans is unsupported inference. The Shi'ite religious majority remains generally silent, observing what is happening, but insisting that the Americans must eventually leave, and Iraq become an Islamic state.

The occupation, for the present, will go on doing what it is doing: rehiring policemen, recruiting a militia to work for the U.S., raiding neighborhoods by night to search homes for arms (but everybody has at least a small arm), and rebuilding schools by day to win hearts and minds.

It consists of a few hundred officials uncomfortably encamped behind razor-wire, and 147,000 fed-up American soldiers similarly sealed off from the 23 million Iraqis — about whom they admittedly know next to nothing. The subtlety of its approach was evident in massively destroying the refuge of Saddam's two sons, rather than starving them out, so they could be politically useful.

Most Iraqis, when asked, have been saying: "Thank you for having overturned Saddam. Now please fix the electricity and water plants you bombed. Then go home."

The wish U.S. troops express is the same: to go home. At the enlisted man or woman's eye-level, straightening out Iraq seems as hopeless as it must seem to the more intelligent people in Paul Bremer's office, as they lie sleepless, at 3 AM.

So what can the administration do? Hand over to the UN? The UN knows a good deal about nation-reconstruction. Its authority is legitimate. Its takeover would eliminate the tensions connected with military occupation and affronted nationalism. The UN would bring in France and Germany, and other big states with troops and reconstruction money.

However to invite in the UN would be a humiliating defeat for the Bush presidency.

It is difficult to imagine terms to which it would agree. The United States wants help but will not renounce control. The UN is not willing to be an instrument of U.S. military occupation.

Washington would also have to go on paying. No one else is going to pay for the consequences of Mr. Bush's war. This seems where UN corridor conversations currently stand.

On Monday the U.S. said that 30 governments have agreed to help the United States in Iraq by contributing to military or police operations. The list begins with Albania and ends with Ukraine. It does not inspire confidence.

The administration is trapped between the unthinkable humiliation of asking for UN help, and failure of the occupation. The trap, as George Bush is certainly aware, snaps closed in November 2004.

July 31, 2003 — The newly-nominated chief of staff of the United States Army, General Peter Schoomaker, has told Congress that the army is probably too small for what it is expected to do.

Certainly this is true if the present troop commitment to Iraq cannot be cut sharply. The administration's claimed confidence in contributions to the coalition force from 30 other countries is open to doubt.

Unless the security situation in Iraq greatly improves, not all of those troops will arrive. The Japanese contribution, for example, composed of non-combatant units, is conditioned on assured security.

The question Congress might have asked General Schoomaker is whether the army, and its sister-services, ought really be doing all the things currently demanded.

A vastly extended deployment of American forces is proposed by the Rumsfeld Defense Department. Troops would be moved from West European NATO bases to ones in Poland, Bulgaria and Romania (the current assumption), and also to "lily-pad" bases along what Washington calls the "arc of instability."

These militarized lily-pads would have minimal permanent facilities and limited permanent detachments, and would serve mobile forces dispatched from the U.S., as required.

The U.S. earlier this year identified four possible new bases in Iraq, others in Afghanistan and Pakistan, in addition to the bases in ex-Soviet Central Asia already acquired, and suggested the possibility of others elsewhere.

But what assurance is there that these new bases actually will improve the security of the United States? Might they not also constitute eventual political provocations, targets and potential hostages?

For every foreign intrusion into a country, particularly one so dramatic as establishing a military base, a nationalist reaction can be expected. There are exceptions, but that is a reasonable general rule, particularly when vast and conspicuous cultural differences are involved. Actions provoke reactions....

The American government's worldwide military deployments have already encouraged U.S. intervention in conflicts, such as the ancient autonomy struggle of the "Moros" in the southern Philippines, which have only fanciful relationship to any terrorists dangerous to the United States.

A professional characteristic both of military hierarchy and any bureaucracy is to ferociously defend every acquired expansion of its influence or numbers. There is also a neo-conservative enthusiasm for more U.S. bases, since our alleged manifest destiny is benevolent global hegemony. All find agreement in the idea that we should bestraddle the world — just in case.

Yet what is the point of possessing ultra-high-technology, "long-legged" American forces, if they can't function from bases in the U.S.?

Obviously it is easier to operate from abroad. But bases make trouble. U.S. bases in Okinawa have been a political liability for years. A growing part of South Korean opinion wants American bases out of Korea.

Any American base maintained in Iraq after this occupation is going to be a political liability, there and elsewhere in the Arab world.

Are bases in Central Asia and East Africa really necessary to pounce on terrorist bands? Surely the CIA, working when possible with local police, provides a low-key, equally efficient solution in many or most cases?

Expanding the base system encourages Washington's intellectually lazy tendency to apply irrelevant military remedies to terrorism as well as to political problems.

The main terrorist attacks on the United States, in 2001, were organized in Britain and Germany, by westernized and educated young Moslem men, radicalized by preachers in immigrant mosques. They developed their plans and established their bases in Europe and in the United States with money mainly from Saudi Arabians.

The most successful operations against these terrorists, and against al Qaeda networks generally, have been by German, French and British police and intelligence agencies, working with the U.S.

No attempt of which I know has been made either by the administration or the Pentagon to demonstrate to the public why expanding an already huge American military base system has anything serious to do with terrorist attacks of the kind that have been made against the United States, and that might be made again.

These attacks are carried out by small bands of self-motivated, and often self-supporting, sophisticated, politicized, and radicalized young men, living and operating mainly in urban societies and urban settings. They are not vulnerable to military attack from bases in Kyrgyzstan, Uzbekistan, Djibouti, or even Iraq.

Paris, August 12, 2003 — American foreign policy operates on short-term reasoning and long-term optimism. America is a nation of optimists. It took for granted that whatever followed a military intervention in Iraq would automatically be an improvement.

Plans said the country would be liberated essentially intact, with need for only modest American help in reconstituting itself, this time as a democracy and market economy.

Iraq would pay for its own reconstruction through oil exports, and would benefit the American economy through privatization of its oil sector, where American companies would be the main investors.

Most — but not all — of the blame for what went wrong belongs to the neo-conservatives making Bush administration policy. They are ideologues. Their thinking is heavily influenced by their intellectual and ideological inheritance from the American Trotskyism of the 1920s and 1930s, out of which neo-conservative thinking evolved, as a reaction against mainstream American liberalism.

Trotskyism held it "scientific" fact that revolutionary struggle to destroy historically obsolete regimes would produce progressive results. The neo-conservatives have the same belief.

The neo-conservatives also have been influenced by the economist Joseph Schumpeter, who said that capitalism progresses through a process of "creative destruction," in which more efficient competitors destroy the less efficient in a process leading perpetually upward, towards greater efficiency and enlarged material happiness. The neo-conservatives thus are, in their way, an American development of Marxism. They have an ideology of progress and happy endings that completely belies the notion that they are "conservatives." Conservatives cautiously defend proven human institutions, and oppose capricious destruction of established social, political and economic structures in the cause of some unproven, and unprovable, theory about a better future.

However an American does not have to be an ideologue to be an optimist. Optimism comes with the territory, so to speak. The religious origins of New England were, of course, millenarian. The Pilgrims were establishing God's own kingdom, successor to "old Europe" (Donald Rumsfeld spoke from a long tradition).

Immigration was fueled by optimism. Forty acres and a mule, and any man could make his future. The railroads gave the immigrant land that the federal government had given them (without consultation with the so-called Indians who had been the first to occupy the land, and not unreasonably had thought it belonged to them).

American optimism may have turned out to be a myth for many that it disappointed, but it was the necessary American myth, powering American society. It remains all but universally asserted today.

Possibly it will fade; the polls, and anecdotal as well as literary evidence, suggests a growing segment of the American population that asks where, or when, did we go wrong? But no such subversive word is heard in American professional politics.

America's optimism sustains American belief in a destiny and mission setting us apart from all the others. The idea of history as an epochal struggle between Americans and the rest, over the nature of society, is renewed in each generation.

During the cold war George Ball, a distinguished and liberal-minded American statesman, with nothing in common with today's neo-conservatives, claimed that the world had "divided like an amoeba into two opposing systems of ideology and power, one based on free choice, the other on the subservience of the individual to rigid dogma." He might as well have been George W. Bush talking about the axis of evil.

An important practical consequence of the national optimism is to make Americans, and certainly American policymakers, think that military intervention against a proclaimed enemy is a progressive act.

In Iraq, a regime without Saddam Hussein is in narrow terms an obvious improvement. But will the long-term consequences of this intervention into the Arab world really be better for the Iraqis, the Arabs, Islamic society as a whole — or for the American people, and the place of the United States in the world? And at what costs yet to be paid?

One cannot know....Is Communist Vietnam worse off today than if the United States had never intervened in an effort to save it from Communism? A million and a quarter Vietnamese and 50,000 Americans would not have been killed, and even more maimed. American society would not have been thrown into bitter divisions not yet entirely played out. All this was foreseeable, even foreseen. Washington, then as now, was populated by optimists.

Optimists don't look back. That is why they don't learn from history.

August 21, 2003 — The intensification of violence in Iraq is logical outcome of the Bush administration choice in 2001 to treat terrorism as a military problem with a military remedy — a catastrophic oversimplification.

Choosing to invade two Islamic states, neither of them responsible for the September 11 attacks, inflated the crisis, in eyes of millions of Moslems, into a clash between the United States and Islamic society.

The two wars did not destroy al Qaeda. They won it new supporters. The United States is no more secure than it was before.

The wars opened killing fields in two countries which no one knows how to shut down, with American forces themselves increasingly the victims. This was not supposed to happen.

The killing was one-way in 2001. Al Qaeda killed Americans and others in New York and Washington.

In 2002 the killing was overwhelmingly in the other direction. Taliban soldiers, al Qaeda members, and Afghan bystanders were the victims, in uncounted numbers.

This year, 2003, began in that way.

Now things have changed. Americans are no longer attacking Iraq from the unreachable sanctuaries provided by technological superiority and command of the air.

They are on the ground, amidst 23 million Iraqis, the objects of elusive and unidentifiable attacks. This is what the United States Army has sought to avoid ever since Vietnam.

There is no victory in sight. Victory has no definition. Capture or kill Saddam Hussein? The administration would claim a victory, but it is not a victory over terrorism.

A functioning democracy in Iraq with a reconstructed economy would be a form of victory. The achievement is remote, even if the country can be pacified....

The neo-conservatives believe that destruction produces creation. They believe — and this is their great illusion — that such destruction will free natural forces of freedom and democracy.

They resemble Alan Greenspan, who in 1997 expressed astonishment at the gangster capitalism that had emerged in the former Soviet Union, and still exists. He said he had assumed that dismantling Communism would "automatically establish a free-market entrepreneurial system."

Paul Wolfowitz, Richard Perle and their colleagues assumed that destroying Saddam Hussein's regime would automatically establish a liberal democracy in Iraq.

Wrecking a society's structure produces wreckage, not utopian change. To believe otherwise leads you to conduct a foreign policy of global destabilization and disruption.

You create in a succession of places anarchical political disorder, human suffering, and new foyers of violence and terrorism capable of overtaking Americans as well as those people America intends to benefit.

How is Iraq to be put together again? Washington doesn't want the UN. The prevailing insecurity deters other governments and international institutions from supporting the reconstruction effort.

What is the exit strategy? There never was one. For the philosophers of chaos in Washington, who created this situation, there is an instinctual reaction to their failure: Escalation. To pursue the elusive victory with new attacks elsewhere.

For Washington politicians, there is another possibility: find and kill Saddam Hussein, and simply leave Iraq — whose turbulent and ungrateful people, George Bush might announce, had shown themselves unworthy of America's efforts.

Does this today seem unthinkable? In 2004, when the president is looking for reelection, if Iraq is still going badly, it will be thought about.

Paris, September 2, 2003 — The reactions of the Bush administration and its supporters to the deteriorating situation in Iraq continue to be shock and denial. Denial is to be expected from the intellectual authors of the war, such as Richard Perle, Paul Wolfowitz and Donald Rumsfeld (leaving aside our phantom vice president, Richard Cheney).

It is less easily understood from those in the opposition, who like the administration are taking refuge in remedies that have little chance of being adopted, such as placing the occupation under nominal UN authority with the United States still in charge.

U.S. Deputy Secretary of State Richard Armitage says the Bush administration is "considering" a U.S.-commanded multinational force endorsed by the UN.

The idea is that India, Turkey, Germany, and even France would send troops to Iraq for a UN-approved but American commanded occupation, allowing part of the American force to be rotated out.

It seems also to be thought that with such an arrangement the governments convoked to a donors' conference in October would make financial pledges to reconstruction, which L. Paul Bremer, head of the occupation authority, says will cost "several tens of billions" of dollars.

International agreement to a force under Security Council political control is imaginable but currently irrelevant, since the Bush administration has no intention of yielding authority over Iraq's occupation and reconstruction, or over the nature of such political institutions as may eventually emerge.

It may, of course, find these ambitions turn to dust, as did its illusions about how cheap and easy it would be to take over Iraq (an undertaking initially promoted as self-financing or even profitable, because of Iraq's oil).

The question about any UN solution is why countries that were opposed to the war should assume responsibility for its painful consequences? Washington may be misreading the support the French, Germans and other Europeans have given to the notion that UN can solve the Iraq problem. The Europeans do not have in mind the same solution as Richard Armitage....

However the politically incorrect question must be asked as to why an occupation and reconstruction sponsored by the UN — with or without the United States in military command — should be expected to work any better than the present unhappy arrangement.

A UN-endorsed multinational force might be politically more acceptable in Iraq, and would certainly be more acceptable to other countries, but the primary problem today is not political acceptability but restoration of security and order.

There is no particular reason to think that a multinational or UN force could restore order and rebuild political and economic infrastructure any better (or any less worse) than Americans are doing.

The UN may not even be more acceptable politically, given that a great many in Iraq have over the last decade learned to see the United Nations as the agent of a policy of sanctions and penalties demanded by the U.S.

France's President Chirac and other European leaders are concerned for the plight of the Iraqi people. This is a worthy sentiment but draws a curtain over the responsibility the Iraqis themselves bear for their present condition.

Saddam Hussein was an Iraqi leader, not some dictator imposed from the outside. Once installed, he obviously became hard to unseat. But Iraqi elites and the Iraqi people permitted him to take power, and many collaborated with him.

Any society not under massive foreign occupation has a revolutionary option. The Iraqis exercised it against their king in 1958 (as the Iranians did against their shah in 1979). The Iraqis did not exercise it against Saddam Hussein.

Iraqis themselves were also responsible for the looting and destruction that followed the war, with ruinous consequences for the country's hospitals, civil infrastructure, and cultural institutions.

The United States invaded Iraq because it chose to describe it as a threat to the United States and to the region. It turned out to be neither. The Bush administration, like the Iraqis, now confronts the consequences of what it has done. It does not like them. Neither does anyone else.

September 11, 2003 — ...[One lesson of events since the September 11 attacks two years ago is that] the ability to overrun a country, rout a peasant army and paralyze infrastructure with "intelligent" bombing and minimal collateral damage is essentially irrelevant to solving the real problems of what George W. Bush calls the war against terror — as if "terror" were another country.

It is an obstacle to the solution, since it offers a seductive illusion of solution. The utility of military power in circumstances short of formal war is narrow. It is often more effective when not used than when it is. Threat can be more intimidating than execution — even in cases when military action succeeds.

Power of most kinds tends to be degraded when actually used because reality reveals power's actual flaws and limits, often evoking unexpected and effective forms of resistance.

The United States was a much more intimidating military power before the occupation of Iraq revealed the confusion of its regular troops when confronted with civil disorder, guerrilla resistance or popular non-cooperation, the political dilemmas, inhibitions and costs imposed on an occupying force, and — once again — the vulnerability of regular forces to irregular attack.

It also revealed the logistical and manpower limits of the U.S. professional army, now said to be incapable of sustaining its present scale of overseas deployment beyond March of next year. Iraq duty tours have already been extended to a full year, even for reserve and National Guard units (state militias), meant to be limited-service civilian auxiliaries to the regular army, other than during major wars.

There are forms of power and influence — "soft power" — that the United States conspicuously lacks, or ignores, or has been squandering through the bullying and arrogant behavior of the Bush government. This is why the Iraq affair

222

has left the United States in an unexpectedly weakened international position, overall.

The overestimation, as well as the overextension, of American military power began under Bill Clinton. An unprecedented Pentagon system of international military commands was launched (with no congressional debate), now covering the entire world, each commander responsible for monitoring developments in his region, establishing or intensifying bilateral military relations with every government that will accept them, preparing plans for regional interventions under a wide variety of scenarios involving possible challenges not only to U.S. interests but to the American perception of world order.

This reflects the hegemonic or "imperialist" conception of America's world role popular in Washington policy circles, and has produced an immense shift in power over American foreign policy from the chronically under-funded Department of State and the civilian CIA to the wealthy Defense Department, which already possessed its own political and intelligence services.

The American Constitution's prohibition of "standing armies" as a threat to democracy once more was ignored, as it consistently has been since the second world war. Congress, the Executive, and the American electorate seem all to have concluded that the Constitution's prescient restriction on the militarization of U.S. society has been outmoded by history — which is not true at all....

The U.S. tendency to treat its relations with other countries as exercises in power turns others into antagonists rather than negotiating partners with potentially shared interests. As a result they turn to power as well. How can they do otherwise?

Those rival governments that are militarily vulnerable do their best to acquire a deterrent to American military pressures. North Korea's is a paranoid government, but its wish to have nuclear weapons is not irrational, nor is Iran's. Obtaining them may actually worsen their situations, but the impulse is logical....

September 23, 2003 — Despite Panglossian optimism at the Pentagon about Iraqi operations, Tuesday's speeches at the UN General Assembly may actually prove a step towards an American retreat from Baghdad, possibly before the end of this year.

The speeches failed to advance the Iraq problem beyond where it was before the General Assembly met. If in the Security Council, the Bush administration refuses even a symbolic transfer of sovereignty to the Iraqis (as demanded by Old Europe), and refuses to cede any political authority over the occupation to the UN, Washington will continue to enjoy exclusive ownership of this problem — with all of its risks, and its (current) $87 billion-plus cost to the American taxpayer.

It's curious that Washington seems never to have considered welcoming the UN and the Europeans into Iraq to take responsibility for nation-building, claimed glorious military victory for itself, and pulled its troops out as rapidly as possible.

Baghdad military circles are now planning how to get out of the present mess. What's being discussed is a military retreat into several well-defended bases well away from Baghdad and Iraq's other cities. These undoubtedly are mostly the same bases Washington had in mind before the war as permanent U.S. installations.

The idea is to hand over Iraq's security to newly-recruited Iraqi police and militias, as well as to such semblance of a multinational force as the U.S. can put together.

While the plan looks interesting on paper, the practicalities suggest that if it worked at all, it would end by handing control of Iraq to forces incompatible with that shining new Middle Eastern democracy the Bush administration has for the last year been promising the Iraqi people and the world community.

It might look a lot like an old-fashioned authoritarian Arab state, run by generals, tribal leaders, and policemen. (The downside alternative is that it might look like Lebanon in the 1980s; but that is another, terrifying, subject.)

There is serious reason to ask whether restoring Iraqi sovereignty under UN control, as the French ask, could work — even if it were politically imaginable for George Bush in an election year. The two attacks already made on the UN are the work of people investing in exploitable chaos, not reconstruction.

Nonetheless, the Bush administration's unwillingness to spread around responsibility for the crisis and for reconstruction is curious. Something makes the President want to stay.

The cynical might say that the U.S. has to control the Governing Council and the Iraqi political process until a government emerges with sufficient international legitimacy to privatize Iraq's oil industry, to the benefit of U.S. investors. Paul Wolfowitz reminds us that the point of the war was that Iraq floats in oil.

In Dubai last Saturday, Kamel Kilani, the Governing Council's newly appointed finance minister, declared Iraq's economy — all except the oil industry — open to 100% control by foreign investors. Radical as the proposal is, there was not much enthusiasm. The legal status of any transaction under provisional authority "laws" might in the long run prove hard to defend.

As things stand, who wants to take over Iraq? The UN is not likely to resume major operations without security guarantees that the U.S. Occupation simply cannot currently provide.

The Red Cross, the development agencies and the NGOs have the same problem. Bremer might give them the same razor-wired and air-conditioned fortresses his staff occupy, but that would only confirm that the civilian agencies are not neutral, merely appendages of the Occupation.

Potential contributors to a multinational force know that it's one thing to send peacekeepers, and quite another to send soldiers to fight guerrillas and terrorism under U.S. command. To have a multilateral army, Bremer and Donald Rumsfeld have to guarantee its security; but the reason they need the army is to create the security.

Washington now plans to put Iraqis in charge of security as fast as this can be done. They want Iraqi police and Iraqi military. The Occupation Authority has been recruiting police and militia, and hiring private security forces....

Saddam's foreign intelligence service people are already being signed up. Bremer's people have already gone to the tribes to renew their traditional arrangement of subsidy in exchange for oil pipeline security.

All this may be the practical course. But it's not what was promised, either to Iraqis, or to the Americans who are paying for it all.

September 25, 2003 — Arthur Koestler, the author of *Darkness at Noon*, has written that "homicide committed for selfish motives is a statistical rarity in all cultures. Homicide for unselfish motives is the dominant phenomenon of man's history. His tragedy is not an excess of aggression, but an excess of devotion....It is loyalty and devotion which makes the fanatic."

This is one reason why the Bush administration misconceives its "War against Terror."

There is a history to cite. In the nineteenth century there was an important revival of interest in anarchism, which says society is natural and people are spontaneously good, but are corrupted by the artificial institutions of government.

The people drawn to the idea that the state is the enemy of goodness seem nearly all to have come from social and economic groups undermined by the industrial and political changes of the period. The resemblance to contemporary Islamic terrorism's recruits is obvious. The latter typically are technologically educated, and combine computer and communications sophistication, with a rigid moral and political commitment to medieval Islamic law.

The anarchists tended to be intelligent but isolated people who were convinced by books and pamphlets then in circulation that society could be liberated if the men and institutions of power and privilege were destroyed. A great popular insurrection would follow. A new society would come into existence, free of oppression, exploitation, or authority.

In Chicago in 1886, a demonstration at Haymarket Square in Chicago, demanding the 8-hour day for workers, degenerated into a riot in which a bomb was thrown. Eight were killed and 100 injured.

The police arrested eight professed anarchists. Four were hanged, one committed suicide, and three were jailed. (Seven years later the three imprisoned were freed by a reform governor of Illinois who said their trials had been unfair.)

In 1901, an anarchist killed U.S. President William McKinley, giving the presidency to the great reformer, Theodore Roosevelt.

In Europe, in the years between 1890 and 1901, believers in this version of social utopianism murdered the Empress Elizabeth of Austria, President Carnot of France, King Umberto I of Italy, and Spain's prime minister.

They bombed theatres and cafés in Lyons, Paris and Barcelona; the Stock Exchange and the Chamber of Deputies in Paris; police stations and courts, and officials' homes. There was no attack that managed to kill three thousand at one go, but it was not for want of trying. Skyscrapers were lacking, and the technology of mass destruction was not what it is today.

Police and prosecutors relentlessly pursued the perpetrators of the crimes. Governments traded intelligence on them. Eventually most were arrested. The movement lost momentum. By early in the twentieth century the affair was largely over.

The only war that followed had to wait until 1914, and it was started not by an anarchist but by a Serbian nationalist. The world war was a success for Serbian nationalism: it produced an independent Serbia.

Successful terrorists have to be distinguished from fantasy ones. A society of "no more wars, no more quarrels, no more jealousy, no more theft, no more assassination, no more police, no more judges, no more administration" is what the anarchist known as Ravachol sought to bring about by bombings in Paris.

That was fantasy. But it was not fantasy to have been a Serbian terrorist, or a member of the Zionist Stern Gang, or of the I.R.A. It is not fantasy to be a Palestinian terrorist today. What such people want, or wanted, is plainly identified, and given the right circumstances could, or did, come about.

Violence drove Britain from what now is the Irish Republic. More recently it convinced London to make drastic political reforms in Northern Ireland. Israel was established by violence after Britain was driven to renounce its Palestine Mandate.

Al Qaeda is a mixed affair. It shares the "visionary terrorism" of the anarchists, arguing that final defeat of "the Crusaders and Zionists" will cause the truth of the Prophet to prevail and a heaven on earth created.

In another respect it is highly practical. It destroyed the Trade Towers. U.S. troops have already been pulled out of Saudi Arabia, where their proximity to the Moslem Holy Places launched Osama bin Laden on his career of terrorism.

It is imaginable that more terrorism could cause U.S. forces to be pulled out of Iraq — as they were pulled out of Lebanon and Somalia in the past.

Washington thinks that it is dealing with evil men "set against all humanity," as president Bush said at the UN last week. What the leaders of the Bush administration are intellectually unprepared to acknowledge is that they are at war with the dominant phenomenon of man's history, as identified by Koestler: the pitiless violence that come from an excess of devotion.

Seoul, October 7, 2003 — It is one thing to be imprisoned in a fantasy of your own. It is much worse to be imprisoned in the fantasy of someone else. The latter is South Korea's situation today.

It is a victim of the Washington world-view, a bureaucratized form of fantasy. Long before the arrival in office of George W. Bush and the neo-conservatives, Washington was a company town, and a small company town at that. The neo-conservatives thought they would make it an imperial capital, but it stayed just a company town.

The company is government, and the product is money and power, the two intimately related, and in the Bush administration all but indistinguishable.

The town's sources of information have steadily diminished over the years. Serious newspapers have disappeared, broadcast news became entertainment, and magazines now are vehicles of ideology more than information. Virtually no attention is paid to information generated from non-U.S. sources — which are "irrelevant" (or hostile).

The result, so far as international affairs are concerned, is that nobody knows much of anything about what really is going on. Those who do, who have worked in the field — professional diplomats and intelligence people, experienced journalists — have increasingly been cut out of the policymaking chain.

(It incidentally is significant that Condoleezza Rice, a university administrator whose specialty is the defunct Soviet Union, now seems the emergency replacement for Donald Rumsfeld in running Iraq and Afghanistan. One must feel sorry for her. Why not appoint a hardened bureaucratic operator with wide personal knowledge of the Islamic world?)

Washington people think they know, but they actually deal in a limited number of ideologically constructed "stories" about the world that rely heavily on stereotype and prejudice, and are infrequently submitted to serious pragmatic challenge (dangerous inside an increasingly politicized bureaucracy).

Iraq's phantom weapons of mass destruction, and the fantasy of a quasi-spontaneous democratization of Iraq, are the two most recent examples. Both derived from the dominant "story" of this administration, that of omnipresent terrorist threats, the axis of evil, and rogue nations. On this basis are policies constructed — or reversed.

South Korea has been in a tough geopolitical situation for 50 years. It understands its problem better than anyone else. North Korea is a paranoid totalitarian state on the brink of economic implosion. It plausibly claims to be able to produce nuclear weapons and has already demonstrated that it manufactures ballistic missiles.

The South Koreans consider nuclear attack a remote possibility since its sole rationality would be as retaliation for an attack on North Korea.

The government in Pyongyang is ideologically isolated, extremely frightened of the United States, and poorly informed about the realities of the world abroad. On the other hand there is no reason to think that it is suicidal. Its entire national effort goes into survival for the ruling group.

South Korea's fear is that the North Korean regime may collapse. Both China and Japan share this fear.

They see the prospect of millions of desperate and starving refugees, with anarchy taking over inside the country. The prospect of Korea's "unification" in such conditions is genuinely terrifying, and threatens stability and continuity in South Korea and elsewhere in the region.

South Korea wants North Korea's regime and economy liberalized, but expects this to come gradually, in response to moderating and accommodating economic and political influences from its neighbors, and in an international context that reduces pressure on the regime while providing incentives for reform.

However neither Seoul nor its Asian neighbors is in control of the situation. Washington is ultimately in control, not only because it wants to be, deploys more than 30,000 troops in Korea, but because North Korea is part of the rogue nations "story."

Under the Clinton administration, the U.S. generally allowed the South Koreans, together with the Japanese and Chinese, to judge the appropriate mixture of carrot (otherwise known as "sunshine policy") and stick in dealing with Kim Jong Il.

The results were slender. North Korea prevaricated and was evasive about such agreements as were reached, but the situation was no worse than in the past and perceptibly getting better.

Then George W. Bush came to office and kicked over the negotiating table. He said the U.S. wasn't going to be blackmailed, and moreover that he didn't like the looks of Kim Jong Il.

He named North Korea to the axis of evil, and implied that he was coming to get Kim Jong Il, once Iraq was taken care of.

The U.S. began planning the withdrawal of U.S. forces away from the North Korean border, where they served as a tripwire and thus protected Seoul.

Then the U.S. asked South Korea please to send a division to Iraq to help out the U.S. The South Koreans wish that somehow they could wake up from this nightmare.

Paris, October 21, 2003 — The NATO meeting Monday in Brussels was urgently called by the U.S. ambassador to NATO, Nicholas Burns, to demand that the Europeans explain themselves with respect to plans to create a European Union military headquarters.

It was another shadow-skirmish in European-American relations. Everyone said something reassuring. No one told the whole truth. Anodyne statements were made afterwards. Nothing was solved....

The meeting was provoked because Tony Blair's Britain has rejoined the European project to create an EU military structure (and headquarters), capable of operating independently of NATO in matters in which the NATO alliance itself (meaning the United States) does not want to become involved.

That might seem harmless enough, but to Washington it is a European declaration of independence, and a major crisis.

Britain, with France, was responsible for the original plan to create an autonomous EU "rapid reaction" force, adopted officially by the European Union in November 2000. Autonomous operations under nominal EU control have already successfully taken place in the Balkans and in the Ituri Forest region of the Congo.

Worse, from Washington's viewpoint, is that Blair has reaffirmed the principle that an EU planning headquarters should develop "structured cooperation" on military matters among other EU countries who wish to join the effort. Structured cooperation means staff and planning.

The key concern of the United States, as *The International Herald Tribune* reported after the meeting, is that no European military headquarters exist that "could conduct planning and operations outside NATO supervision and control."

That means outside U.S. supervision and control. It is a political statement of considerable significance for the Europeans.

NATO legitimately exercised that supervision and control by mutual consent of its members, so long as NATO served its original military purpose: defense against the Soviet threat.

Today, when the Soviet Union and the Warsaw Pact have ceased to exist, NATO has no war to fight. President Bush's "war against terror" is not a war relevant to NATO as an organization.

Washington did not ask NATO to go to war with it in Afghanistan. It would not have dreamed of placing the Iraq war under NATO command, even if the majority of Europeans had supported that war — which of course they opposed. Some NATO nations' troops are in Iraq under U.S. command, but by national decision....

No threat to Western Europe exists that justifies the continuation of an alliance of this nature, under U.S. command. In ex-Communist Europe there is a perceived possible future threat, inspired by historical experience, from Russia. The Central and East Europeans and the Baltic states are reasonable to want security alliance with the United States, with or without NATO as the intermediary.

However when making decisions it is useful to know a little history. Poles justify their current commitment to the U.S.-led Iraq coalition because the "old Europeans" — France and Britain — failed to save them in September 1939.

In fact, they did save the Poles. They declared war on Germany. They were blocked from reaching Poland, but by declaring war they made it possible for Poles to hope for an eventual victory over Germany: and that became possible only because Britain fought on all alone for a year and a half after France's defeat, until Hitler attacked Russia in June 1941.

The United States did not go to war for Poland. It did not go to war at all until December 1941, more than two years after the fall of Poland. American troops did not land in continental Europe, in Italy, until a full four years after Poland was overrun.

Poland was "liberated" from the Nazis by the Soviet Union. (Eventually it was liberated from the Soviet Union by John Paul II, with cooperation from Mikhail Gorbachev).

The purpose of military force is to assure the sovereignty of a nation. The old NATO did that. It was an alliance against a real threat. The new NATO is not.

Now NATO has become an instrument of American influence in Europe. It provides a legitimate framework for U.S. military bases, useful to unilateral U.S. operations in other theaters.

Fair enough; but NATO bases exist in Europe by consent and not by right. People in the U.S. Congress and the administration talk about them as if they are an American favor to Europe. They are today a European favor to the United States....

October 23, 2003 — The power of the weak lies in a people's acceptance of suffering. The weakness of the strong is that disproportionate use of force against the weak eventually corrupts their own society.

The new air attacks launched last week against the Palestinians in Gaza (5 on Monday alone), using helicopter gun-ships and F-16 fighter aircraft, producing inevitable "collateral damage," have actually been a demonstration of Israeli weakness.

They led nowhere that the majority of Israel's society wants to go. The daily newspaper *Maariv* describes the message they delivered as that "Israel has gone mad."

Prime Minister Ariel Sharon claims to see blindingly bright light at the end of the tunnel. "Victory" over the terrorist infrastructure is only weeks away. Israel is about to be liberated from fear.

The new Geneva draft peace settlement (arrived at by former official Israeli and Palestinian negotiators) is, he says, mere political plotting by disloyal Israelis, "encouraging terrorism."

Yet few even in the military command can believe that aerial bombing will stop Palestinian suicide bombings. The latest, in Haifa on October 9th, justification for the new Israeli offensive, killed 21.

It was committed by a 27-year old student lawyer, a young woman with no known connection to Islamic Jihad (which claimed responsibility). Her brother and cousin had recently been shot dead by Israeli soldiers.

Prime Minister Ariel Sharon has always publicly professed two convictions: the first is that Israel must expand into the occupied territories. He sponsored the colonization movement after the 1967 war. On Thursday his government confirmed its decision to build 300 new West Bank housing units, despite its "Road Map" commitment to halt colonization.

The second is that military force in the end prevails. He seems unshaken by the destructive failure of his invasion of Lebanon in 1982, and by the failure, to date, of military repression of the two intifadas.

On Tuesday he told an Israeli audience that "Today, as yesterday, there has never been room in the Middle East for pity or mercy;...every sign of weakness only invites new aggression...."

A commentator in Israel's biggest-circulation daily, *Yediot Aharonot*, asked, "Is it conceivable that some among us now consider the entire Palestinian population our target? Then there is no longer any limit...."

The mission of civilian repression has deeply affected the Israeli military. Martin Van Creveld of the Hebrew University of Jerusalem, a military sociologist, writes that "the morale of the army has never been so low." Tsahal is in crisis, he said in an interview.

There was a well-publicized incident early this month when a group of air force pilots declared that for ethical reasons they would no longer take part in assassination attacks on civilian targets. "In the past the air force was not used to repress the intifada. Today it is regularly used. But each time there is internal debate over whether or not to accept implication [in such an attack]."

Reservists are no longer responding to mobilization orders. In some units, as many as 70% of those called up fail to respond. This, overall, is still a marginal phenomenon, "but the attention [it has] provoked in Israeli society is enormous....The impression has been created that this could end in the collapse of military morale. Look at what happened to the French army in Algeria at the start of the 1960s."

The military command has no strategic vision, Creveld says. "Nothing it has done to defeat the intifada has worked."

There is a grave lesson in this for an American Army in Iraq that now teeters on the wall separating liberation from repression.

The official claim is that it is fighting attacks from remnants of a defeated regime and other enemies of democratic reform. Yet Lt Gen. Ricardo Sanchez said last week that "We've seen a spike [in daily attacks on U.S. forces] up to 35 in last three weeks" from a previous average of 20 to 25 a day.

Liberation has turned into a security problem. Force protection is sought by tracking down attackers, with penalties for the communities or tribal groups from which the "terrorists" come. Collective punishments have begun — one hopes only on local command initiative, not high policy. Punitive destruction of crops and orchards of peasant communities has been carried out to force delivery of the names of relatives or fellow-tribesmen thought members of resistance groups.

The American presence is attacked by many for blocking the Iraqis from taking control of their own affairs — whatever the obvious risks of civil disorder and conflict.

However one undeniable reason the occupation is prolonged is to maintain U.S. control over Iraqi oil production and the economy. This may serve the interests of corporations notoriously well connected in the Bush administration. It is not an American national interest.

Least of all is it a national interest for the American occupation to go down the Israeli road. Surely that must be obvious.

Porto, Portugal, October 30, 2003 — More than nine months into the Iraq crisis, meetings between West Europeans and Americans of good will remain strained non-dialogues in which most of the American participants find it hard to admit that the catastrophic loss of American reputation abroad has anything to do with them.

Americans cite scandalous incidents of foreign anti-Americanism. The German Marshall Fund statistics are circulated that show only 8 percent of Germans today wanting the U.S. to remain the sole superpower (it was 22 percent a year ago), while 70 percent of Germans want Europe to become a superpower.

The Americans' response to such information is nearly always that there must have been some failure in communications. Perhaps the U.S. should "consult" more. But basically it's up to the European governments to take steps to correct this anti-Americanism. If not, Americans are going to become seriously upset with the Europeans. "It's as if they can't hear," is the European response.

Let me offer a metaphor. Every nation has a "story" it tells to explain its place in the flow of history and to give meaning to its actions.

The American story since 1942 (and before) is well known, and is considered by Americans and others a story reflecting responsibility and high-mindedness, whatever its inevitable component of national interest....

Because of the powerful Calvinist influence — predestinarian and theocratic — on American Protestantism, the American story has always described a confrontation between the Elect and the Evil.

When the Soviet Union no longer fulfilled the latter role, Washington tried out several possible successors, finally settling on the "rogue nations": those professing radically un-American ideas, and giving evidence of wanting to possess nuclear deterrents to protect themselves from foreign intervention.

Their feebleness, however, tended to diminish their credibility in the role of global Evil.

Then came 9/11. The problem was solved. The rogue nations now became the Axis of Evil. They were integral to a vast international threat, capable of striking the United States itself. Moreover, this threat more or less resembled (less, actually, than more) the clash between civilizations that Professor Samuel Huntington had warned would be the "next world war."

President Bush announced that the nation was "at war" with Terror.

Terror expressed itself through al Qaeda, Talibans, Palestinian suicide-bombers, South American Narco-terrorists, Chechen separatists in Russia, and Moro separatists in the southern Philippines. Terror was a ubiquitous force that could ultimately manifest itself in mass destruction weapons, supplied by the rogue states, falling on American and European cities.

Hence preventive wars were necessary; Afghanistan and Iraq had to be invaded to seize Terror's leaders and their nuclear and biological weapons. International legality must stand aside, etc.

But what actually has happened during the past nine months is something Americans have yet to grasp, and that others have yet to say out loud. People outside the United States have stopped believing the American story.

They don't think Terror is an evil force the United States is going to defeat. They say terrorism is a way people wage war when they don't have F-16s or armored divisions.

They say that Chechens, Moros, Talibans, Colombian insurgents, Palestinian bombers, and Iraqi enemies of the U.S. occupation do not really make up a single global phenomenon that the world must mobilize to defeat. They say all this looks more or less like what history has always been like, at least in troubled times.

They say that, actually, they had never really believed this story in the first place. They had listened to it because Washington said it, and they respected Washington. Now they don't....

Paris, November 4, 2003 — The Bush administration is still side-stepping the question of restoring Iraq's sovereignty, now provisionally held by the coalition occupation authority.[3]

It is under pressure even from some Iraqi members of the U.S.-appointed Iraq governing council. They and others argue that the security problem can't be solved so long as ultimate political power is held by a foreign, non-Moslem government.

Some members of L. Paul Bremer III's own coalition authority appear to agree. In recent discussions in Europe, the highest Polish official in the authority has described the sovereignty issue as crucial.

Members of the Governing Council say they are crippled by their present status as nominees of the U.S. government, and that no other Iraqi authority, local or national, can make a serious claim to functional authority in the country so long as the United States does not address the sovereignty issue.

The question is urgent because despite White House and Defense Department assurances that the security problem in Iraq is due to "a few desperate people," it is getting worse in simple statistical terms, quite apart from what common-sense political judgment says.

The number of killed and of reported "incidents" has steadily risen since summer. The Pentagon has offered no satisfactory accounting with respect to

---

3. An inexact statement, I am assured by a friend who is an international lawyer. The United States possesses no sovereignty in Iraq to restore. Sovereignty still lies with the people of Iraq, even though they have no political agency with which to exercise it. The United States only has UN-acknowledged power of military occupation, with the numerous responsibilities that go along with that status in international law.

non-fatal casualties and deaths in hospital. The administration cannot "spin" this until November 2004.

Washington argues that new Iraqi police and paramilitary forces under U.S. command will secure the country. The plan is for them to be in control a year from now (in time for the U.S. election), with Americans on their way home. The president's political advisers would be unwise to count on this.

The plan, meant to reassure Americans, conveys an unintended second message to Iraqis: that the United States expects still to be running Iraq in November 2004.

What makes the administration think that things are going to get better during the next year? Continued military occupation means fighting the hostile forces responsible for the current chaotic situation and also continued frustration of the clearly expressed wish of the Shi'ite religious majority.

The Shi'ites have been generally tolerant of the occupation until now, but their leaders have given unmistakable notice that they expect the U.S. to leave long before November 2004.

Washington is offering the Iraqis a lengthy process of consultations, under American guidance, leading up to a new constitution, with transfer of sovereignty to follow that.

This is not serious. The security and sovereignty issues are integrally connected. You can't have the first without addressing the second. Common sense and the president's own political interests would seem to recommend as fast and orderly a disengagement from a sovereign Iraq as can be managed. Why stay?

Three motives suggest themselves. The first is ideological. Having defied international institutions and international opinion by invading Iraq, the administration sees humiliation in handing over to a provisional international authority or to the UN. This would be a "defeat," and the Bush administration no longer would be "credible." (The national credibility being earned in the present situation is hard to discern.)

Second, early power transfer would defeat the announced political goal of Iraq's invasion. Iraq was supposed to provide the first in a series of "regime changes" remodeling the entire eastern Mediterranean into a system of governments possessing democratic institutions but for practical purposes dominated by the United States and Israel.

Third, there are material interests at stake. According to the Center for Public Integrity, 71 companies and individuals who contributed to the Bush presidential campaign now have contracts in Iraq (or Afghanistan). Of the $84 billion the president wants from Congress, most of the money meant for Iraq and Afghanistan reconstruction actually goes to American companies.

The Bremer authority has already approved a plan to sell at least half of Iraq's state-controlled economy to private interests before the end of this year (a distress sale, if ever there was one), as well to sell the domestic banking system to foreign banks.

The oil sector, excluded from this sale, is eventually to be privatized as well, but no major international company will bid until there is a recognized Iraqi government actually prepared to sell exploitation of the country's energy resources to a foreign company. Who is going to oversee the creation of such a government? It won't be the United Nations.

It is by no means sure that this occupation can be turned into a real liberation of Iraq. It is imaginable that U.S. withdrawal — whenever it comes — may be followed by civil war with foreign intervention. Every sensible person in the region fears that.

Rapid creation of a sovereign Iraq under disinterested international sponsorship offers a better prospect than what is going on now. Otherwise the choices are likely to get steadily worse — for the United States as well as for Iraq and the region.

November 11, 2003 — A year ago the United States was all but universally seen as wielding unsurpassed — unsurpassable — military power, such as no nation had ever held.

What a difference a year has made. The initial consequence the Iraq adventure has had for the United States has been to gravely diminish its international position.

Today nearly the entire deployable American ground force — all except units in rotation and retraining, or committed in South Korea or Afghanistan, including most of its deployable reserve force — is quite literally besieged in Iraq.

In Baghdad, American soldiers leave their fortified redoubt in the city center, surrounded by razor wire and concrete roadblocks, and by acres of dead ground to distance them from rockets and mortars, only in convoy. They must do this to protect themselves from attacks by enemies they still cannot clearly identify.

The same is true in the so-called Sunni triangle. A westernized Iraqi professional man, formerly well-disposed towards Americans, now watches armored convoys of tense and anxious young Americans go whirling by, and says to a visitor, "they are from Mars. They see nothing. They understand nothing. They know nothing about what is going on."

A correspondent visiting soldiers of the 1st Infantry Division in Al-Ramadi, the main city in the region, is told that they hardly leave the ex-Iraqi army base they occupy except at night, to run security patrols around the base, or to descend in force on some neighborhood where "terrorists" are reported. It is dangerous to go out.

A 1st Division civil affairs officer admits that "we try to limit going outside the base, and stagger the times, because even though we know the areas where people are most hostile, every route is dangerous."

The Iraqis have the initiative. Iraq is not going to be pacified and reconstructed so long as American soldiers are unable to move freely in its principal cities.

The United States has ceased to be seen internationally as a victorious superpower and is perceived, rather, as despite all its instruments of military power, incapable of fulfilling the claims it made concerning political reform in the Middle East — not to speak of cultural revolution.

The French naturally are pleased that *The National Journal* in Washington announces on its current issue's cover that the French, after all, were right. They warned the United States not to invade Iraq. The French said that the consequences would drastically destabilize the region, and implied that the Bush administration's view of the Middle East was a profound illusion.

(The magazine attributes this French prudence in part to President Jacques Chirac's service in Algeria, where the French were confronted with a nationalist uprising they could defeat in limited military terms but do nothing to solve politically. One would think the United States was taught the same lesson in Vietnam. But George W. Bush and the other current leaders of the American government assiduously and successfully avoided experiencing war in Vietnam.)

Few in France ever doubted that France was right in opposing the U.S. But what good is it to have been right when it is too late? That is why the government in Paris has scrupulously avoided saying anything that could be interpreted as taking pleasure in Washington's discomfiture. Matters are too serious, for everyone, for that.

Conceivably it is not too late, if Washington can be made to grasp the importance of a rapid transfer of power....A national assembly of notables might be called, on the model of the Afghan "Loya Jirga," to name a provisional president and government to which the U.S., with United Nations help, would pass sovereign authority....Some Democrats in Congress have proposed handing over to NATO — a terrible idea, even if NATO's European members would accept. NATO occupation would be no better than U.S. occupation....

Rome, November 18, 2003 — ...The new transatlantic drift coincides with what we know from history about sovereign national interests and the contradictions generated by the phenomenon of hegemony. It is reasonable to presume that it is not ephemeral but represents a force of long-term significance....

On Monday the European Union's defense ministers formally decided to establish an armaments agency charged to analyze the military situation and needs of the EU, and coordinate military research and the arms purchases of EU members.

The U.S. government considers this decision obliquely protectionist, meant to influence the new countries joining the EU to buy European rather than American weaponry. Those governments already are pressed to buy American arms and aircraft for the sake of NATO "interoperability" and because American equipment is held to be far in advance of what European manufacturers offer.

The latter has never been more than a half-truth. In current military technology the Europeans are very advanced in cruise missiles (the jointly produced Storm Shadow) military sensors, satellite-based global positioning systems (Galileo) and unmanned reconnaissance and combat aircraft (UAV/UCAVS), among other sectors. They also have advanced military aircraft operational, while what the U.S. promises remains in the future....

The U.S. says that European high-technology military projects are duplicated effort. It also objects because they escape Pentagon control. U.S. military sales — the Joint Strike Fighter, the advanced fighter still in development, for example — never allow even close allies full access to their base systems and technology.

U.S. technological protectionism requires "Chinese walls" that shut foreign contractors or collaborators out of the highest-technology work.

European arms coordination and protectionism thus is motivated by Europe's perceived need to be sovereign in defense. The collapse of the Soviet threat, motivating the common western defense, and since 2001, the Bush administration's choice of unilateralism and preemption as basic elements in the new American security strategy, are responsible for this European move towards strategic self-sufficiency.

On the same day as the EU defense ministers' decision, American and European experts were in Rome to talk about transatlantic security cooperation. This was a working meeting with its American participants from the Rand Corporation, Johns Hopkins, MIT and other serious institutions, so the European members were mercifully spared the neo-conservative harangue by U.S. officials that has marked most such recent meetings.

The sponsors were the EU security studies group and Italian strategic military studies and international affairs institutes. Not much optimism was expressed about transatlantic cooperation so long as the United States continues to enjoy its Unilateral Moment.

Great concern, however, was also expressed as to how to rescue the United States from its Middle Eastern imbroglio. It was also on Monday that the highest Italian government official in the Iraq Provisional Governing Authority, Marco Calamai, resigned in "profound disagreement" with coalition policy, declaring the authority non-functional and "gravely compromised."

Calamai proposed internationalization under UN control with increased European participation. As this idea is a non-starter, already rejected by the Bush administration, the meeting in Rome was left with the sentiment expressed by an American participant that the U.S. "can't be allowed" to fail. This seemed to find general agreement, but in the circumstances, no one proposed how it could be accomplished.

Paris, November 20, 2003 — The first act of the war in Iraq closed in April, with the fall of Baghdad. The second act opened when chaos rather than order followed the victory.

That second act ended with Ambassador L. Paul Bremer's sudden visit to Washington a week ago, and subsequent announcement of an accelerated but limited transfer of sovereign authority to the Iraqis by next June, implicitly acknowledging the collapse of the original plan by which the United States intended to remake Iraq.

The original plan was discarded because American forces in Baghdad and the so-called Sunni triangle to the west are effectively besieged by attacks on their patrols, supply convoys, installations, and helicopters.

These attacks have prevented them from establishing the legitimacy of either Occupation Authority or the appointed Iraqi Governing Council. Washington hopes that the promise of early limited self-government will cut support for the insurrection and lend authority to the Governing Council.

The new plan would draft "basic law" and form a nominated legislative assembly that by June would establish a new provisional government. The United States promises to hand over control of political, security and financial affairs, in advance of national elections.

The U.S. would on the other hand supervise the transition and assure that it accommodates American interests, which are economic and military as well as political. Thus it would not be a true transfer of sovereign power in Iraq, which is why the prospects for this plan are bleak....

The Defense Department, meanwhile, has brought General John Abizaid and much of his Central Command headquarters back to the Gulf from Tampa, its base. Once again the military are trying "shock and awe," with heavy missile and bomber attacks, plus infantry sweeps, against what are described as terrorist training grounds and headquarters, some inside Baghdad itself.

British officers in Iraq, as well as American critics of the administration's policies, say this a disastrous way (and dangerous, because of the collateral casualty risk) to deal with a politically directed insurrection that clearly enjoys a considerable measure of popular acquiescence, if not support.

It is, however, what the Pentagon does when it is at a loss to know what else to do. It is committed to high-technology warfare and "zero casualties," and when in trouble escalates the technological level of the war even if this is irrelevant.

It fights its kind of war whatever the war the other side is fighting. It is what it did in Vietnam, and is one reason it failed. It is what it did in Afghanistan, with limited success, now slipping away because of another U.S. Army doctrine, that it does not do nation-building.

Unable to discover the individuals or organization responsible for the resistance to the Iraq occupation, the U.S. command is "sending a message" with bombings and missiles. The message, unfortunately, resembles an avowal of impuissance.

No one can say how this now is going to develop. The current resistance clearly includes groups with separate and potentially rival agenda. Alertly observing what happens are Kurdish separatists and the governments of Iran,

Turkey, Syria and Israel, all of them capable of intervention in one or another manner.

The Iraq majority — of Shi'ite Muslims — still bides its time, but is determined to have a government acceptable to its principles.

An explosive situation exists, which is why so many Iraqis prefer the U.S. occupation to the destructive sectarian forces that could be unleashed. However the dynamics created by the invasion cannot be turned off now, and the United States cannot control them.

The possibilities include perpetuated guerrilla war against the occupation, or against whatever provisional government emerges; Lebanon-like civil war in Iraq, enlarged‘ foreign intervention, a deliberate expansion of war in the region (against the "axis of evil") — or even a devastating U.S. retreat. U.S. success logically has to be included among the possibilities, but it is a long shot.

November 25, 2003 — Washington has a new policy for Iraq, to establish a new Iraqi provisional government in June. Question one is do we have until June?...

Currently, the situation is worsening, as the monthly casualty figures demonstrate. The insurgents have been successfully using missiles against aircraft, prompting a major review of helicopter combat doctrine, and damaging a civil Airbus last weekend.

[A CIA report sent to Washington on November 10, endorsed by Ambassador Bremen and subsequently acquired by the press, said that "the situation in Iraq is approaching a crucial turning point, with ordinary Iraqis losing faith in American occupation forces and in the U.S.-appointed Iraq Governing Council."]

U.S. forces have conducted air and missile attacks against supposed guerrilla locations, and inflicted collective punishments with destruction of homes and crops. Such measures, when used by Israelis against the Palestinians, have not been a great success in winning hearts and minds.

Defenders of current policy argue that the rise in enemy activity is temporary and misleading, and will fall as a result of the successes claimed in recent attacks on alleged enemy centers....They believe that before June the resistance will have been defeated, or if it has not been defeated, it will be contained at a level that will not prevent a political transition. That is the plan....

If June is reached, will the new government be accepted as legitimate? It will have been formed on terms set by a provisional basic law drafted under American supervision.

The Coalition Occupation Authority will be dissolved. Newly recruited Iraqi forces are supposed to provide security, but Americans will oversee and support them.

Part of the existing U.S. troop deployment will be withdrawn to the U.S. before the presidential election. However the Defense Department is planning to keep 100,000 U.S. troops in Iraq for the next six years, "invited" by the new Iraq government. The State Department has announced that the coalition headquarters will be renamed the U.S. Embassy — with 3000 personnel assigned to it, the largest U.S. embassy in the world.

The economy will function under American supervision, and privatization of the state economy (and energy resources) will, if the U.S. has its way, be the new government's policy (at least at the start; the assembly might prove rebellious).

A positive response to the question of legitimacy argues, or assumes, that the majority of Iraqis will welcome any government that belongs even partly to them, and will tolerate the continued presence of Americans for the sake of reconstruction and to deter sectarian difficulties.

The negative response is that Iraqi nationalism will not be appeased with thousands of American troops remaining in the country, and with the U.S. still exercising dominant influence over the government and economy.

Major figures in the religious communities, among tribal leaders, and from the old business, administrative and intellectual classes recognize the risk of civil war — of an Iraq driven into sectarian war like that in Lebanon between 1983 and 1991.

Would the situation be different if French and other European advice was followed, and there were an immediate handover of power, with the UN called in to sponsor a new provisional government?

To the extent that the resistance is nationalist and anti-American, yes. The other political, ideological and sectarian conflicts would not be solved. Radical fundamentalists with an interest in chaos, and Ba'ath party activists, would not automatically be deterred, although both might choose to bide their time.

Tragedy is not inevitable. However the intention of the American plan is to retain economic and military influence in the guise of leaving politically. This is disingenuous. The planned new government would have only limited sovereignty, and the country would be expected to become a quasi-protectorate of the U.S.

The risks are too big for Washington to try to have it both ways. That is what the new policy is essentially meant to achieve. For that reason it will fail.

December 16, 2003 — ... Saddam Hussein's capture is a negative omen for George W. Bush's reelection, and a bad sign concerning continuing disorder and resistance in Iraq.

The ignominious circumstances in which he surrendered, hiding in a hole in the ground, otherwise living in a shed heaped with dirty clothes, eggshells, and unwashed pans, made it clear to all that the resistance to the American occupation was not being commanded from there.

Hence it is wishful thinking to expect his capture alone to slow or end the violence. It may spur the resistance. So long as the Shi'ite majority thought there was a remote possibility that he could return to power, and with him the Ba'ath party apparatus whose remnants survive throughout the country, they had reason to stay on good relations with the American Occupation Authority hunting him down.

With Saddam arrested, the Shi'ite authorities are free to express their real ambition: power in a new Iraq proportionate to their majority in the population.

Until now the most important Shi'ite leaders have remained, objectively, allies, or at least neutrals, in Washington's effort to control the country.

They now will become active players in the emerging political power struggle. Since they can bring millions into the streets, as demonstrators or as fighters, practicing a version of Islam with a powerful emotional component of suicidal self-sacrifice, they are potentially a more important force than Saddam could ever have mobilized as underground leader or as martyr.

The minority Sunni community, dominating Iraq since the time of the Ottoman Empire, ousted from power by the American intervention, has more urgent reason than ever to fight to regain power and privilege.

A new government might be a federation in which the communities (Sunni, Shi'ite, and Kurdish, to take the main ones, but there are also Turkmen, Christians of several denominations, and others) coexist on representative and more or less democratic terms.

The United States prefers the federal solution, at least in principle, but would also expect (or be needed) to remain in Iraq in order to maintain the balance. That runs into the obstacle of Iraqi nationalism, which this war has inflamed, and also robs the Shi'ites of the dominant political role.

A second possibility is restored centralized and probably authoritarian government, quite possibly with

the better-educated Sunni community back on top. Americans are accustomed to dealing with this kind of government in the Arab world. Nationalism and sectarian interests again are the obstacles.

Shi'ite majority rule would incorporate a powerful bias towards theocratic government of the Iranian kind, which is what Washington does not want.

On the other hand there is a limit on what the United States can do, short of continued direct rule. The June handover is supposed to put Iraq on its way to democracy and sovereignty....

A French political scientist, Zaki Laïdi, sums it up by saying that "the Shi'ites, who in the majority seem to have at least implicitly backed the American intervention, cannot find durable political legitimacy other than by opposing the United States, while the Sunnis, who lost most in the American intervention, would be Washington's best allies against the Shi'ites' taking power."

As for George W. Bush, Saddam's capture symbolically changes the president from war leader to the builder of a new Iraq. Electorally, he is likely to regret this change.

If questioning Saddam Hussein doesn't produce the famous weapons of mass destruction that were threatening Jerusalem, and British and American bases in the region, (not to speak of New York and Washington), the question of what the war was all about is reopened....

December 23, 2003 —...Moslem fundamentalism in Europe is a statement of political defiance of European social and employment discrimination, just as it is in the United States. For young men it is an affirmation of identity, difference and defiance, sometimes carried to self-immolation.

The forms of militant Moslem fundamentalism — al Qaeda recruitment, fighting the jihad in Iraq or Afghanistan or Palestine — are protests against the power and seeming omnipotence of the western world, and particularly the United States.

They are reactions to the successive humiliations of post-Ottoman Arab nationalist failure, first in the colonialism of the 1920s-1940s (the first militant integrist movement, the Moslem Brotherhood, was founded in 1928).

Saudi Arabia was enriched by oil but unreformed by it, remaining an opulent and dysfunctional medieval monarchy, neutered by its dependence on the U.S. In 1948 the Arabs were unable to prevent Israel's installation in what had been Arab Palestine.

Then Nasserism and "Arab Socialism" failed. The Ba'ath movement (founded by Arab Christian intellectuals, and meant to be secular, socialist and pan-Arab) degenerated into the corrupt and despotic Saddam Hussein regime in Iraq and into hereditary dictatorship in Syria. Now the Arabs perceive the United States trying to establish political and economic suzerainty over the region.

Against this, the only Moslem revolution that has succeeded is the Iranian revolution. It resulted from religious mobilization in the then most rapidly modernizing and secularizing society in the Moslem world. It gave people ideas.

Nationalism, identity affirmation, and religious fundamentalism are all intimately connected in this affair, whether in the Middle East itself or among Moslems who have emigrated to the western countries.

There is indeed a war of civilization going on, but it is taking place inside Moslem society. The West is a crude interloper in all of this. Indifferent to its own religious history and historical culture, it has substituted a shallow and commercial secularism that Moslem fundamentalism furiously rejects, but is unlikely to defeat.

In all of this, the United States is a detonator of explosions primed by cultural and political frustration. It imagines that it brings progress, but all it has brought so far is deepened chaos.

Conclusion

American foreign policy changed three years ago not only because the Republicans took power, but because the neo-conservatives became the dominant policy influence on the new Republican administration.

They brought something new to American government. They shared what Stanley Hoffman of Harvard describes as "a cult of power [that recalls ideas of] the Italian theoreticians of fascism." They had an elitist and manipulative view of how power rightly is used.

They had no taste for persuasion or diplomacy. They had a philosophical commitment to that absolutism of "with us or against us" that George Bush more naively expressed, in quasi-religious terms, in his speeches.

Their influence, combined with that of a certain traditional Republican isolationism, had dramatic results on national policy, especially after the 9/11 attacks.

By now it has become clear that the Iraq intervention and the war on terror, waged as the neo-conservatives wanted it waged, have actually undermined America's international position. They have demonstrated that in crucial respects American military power is irrelevant to the objectives it seeks. What is destruction that has no constructive political outcome?

No matter how the Iraq occupation ends, American power and authority will have diminished. The regime overturned, U.S. forces remained in Iraq as nation-builders. Their good intentions and positive accomplishments have failed to spare them the dangerous, alienating, but predictable consequences of prolonged military occupation, and of political dissimulation on the question of

Iraq's full sovereignty. Their inability to impose order on a conquered society, where many were disposed to welcome liberation, has inevitably made observers elsewhere reassess America's real power.

After the Soviet Union's collapse, conventional wisdom said that other nations had to choose between accommodation to American supremacy, becoming Washington's lieutenants in a coalition meant to order the world's affairs, or to attempt to form a coalition to counterbalance American power. The latter is the crime France is accused of committing, and to an extent, Russia and China.

However political reality itself may be removing that dilemma by demonstrating that American power, real as it is in some dimensions, is in others incompetent to produce results that respond to international reality, or even to its own proclaimed objectives. By the very manner in which this administration exercises American power, the United States has undermined its own dominant position and revealed unperceived weakness. This encourages the return of a multipolar system by default.

Such surely is an outcome Vladimir Putin would welcome. In Asia, Chinese political as well as economic influence has mounted as the American government's attention has been on terrorism, preventive wars and homeland defense. American reliance on China, Japan and other Asian countries to finance the country's uncontrolled commercial deficit has inspired a sense that the U.S. is the dependent power in the relationship. Trade and political tensions with Europe reflect an impression that Washington now is unwilling to face political facts, as well as that the war against terrorism has become an American obsession detached from reasoned analysis.

Such developments in international opinion are incapable, alone, of changing the international balance, but they greatly undermine the American position, suggesting that the American superpower is not what it has seemed.

This does not inspire much pleasure or relief abroad. It provokes concern. A destabilized international system is dangerous. On the edges, admittedly, it provokes a certain contempt, but even that is mixed with fear of the consequences of an American decline.

It is possible that the American presidential election in November 2004 will bring an abrupt end to this new course in global policy, and relegate the accompanying militaristic and unilateralist attitudes to the political opposition.

Mr. Bush and his neo-conservatives could prove no more than an eccentric but cautionary episode, ending badly, in the history of contemporary American foreign policy.

However even if the election inflicts on George W. Bush the same second-term defeat as on his father in 1992, after another war against Iraq, the younger Bush's term in office will have realized an important and significant American transition. His policy of aggressive and unilateralist employment of power to remake world affairs was justified by the neo-conservatives in terms of the old American conviction of national exception, and by the belief that the American model of society is destined to dominate the world, by one means or another, since it is held to be the culmination of human development — the world's "sole progressive power," as one neo-conservative has said.

This conviction is commonly found on both left and right. It was during the Clinton Administration that the secretary of state, Madeleine Albright, proclaimed that Americans see farther than anyone else because they "stand taller." "Globalization" was a product of the same administration, a program for opening deregulated markets worldwide to U.S. investment that was articulated by the administration as part of world society's march towards unification in democracy and market capitalism (and history's end).

It was also under President Clinton that the unprecedented Pentagon system of regional commands was established that now covers the entire world, responsible for monitoring developments in each region and preparing for possible U.S. interventions under a wide variety of scenarios involving challenges not only to U.S. interests but, as it is said, to world order.

Militarized or otherwise, American policy remains under the influence of an unacknowledged and unjustified utopianism. This is the unanalyzed background to the work of all Washington's foreign policy agencies. It permeates the rhetoric and thinking of Republicans and Democrats alike. It is the reason Americans can think that history has an ultimate solution, and that the United States is meant to provide it.

The distinguished theologian and political thinker Reinhold Niebuhr, "father" (as George Kennan once put it) of the "realist" intellectual tradition in American foreign policy, made the following prophetic statement to a world gathering of Protestant and Orthodox churchmen at Oxford in 1937.

The civilization and culture in which we [exist]...is devotee of a very old religion dressed in a new form. It is the old religion of self-glorification. This is a very old religion because it involves the quintessence of human sin as defined by Saint Paul..."they became vain in their imaginations, and their foolish heart was darkened. Professing themselves to be wise, they became fools, and changed the glory of the incorruptible God into an image made to corrupt man, and to birds, and four-footed beasts, and creeping things."

International society now is confronted with a paradox. Its most powerful member, the United States, conceiving of itself as the model of civilization, responsible for international order and progress, is committed to policies that are inherently or even deliberately destructive of central elements in the existing system of international law and existing norms of international cooperation and order, which it condemns as outmoded, if not hostile to American national interests. It does so with emphasis on military methods and diminished attention to international opinion and precedent. Even among its allies, this has provoked uneasiness, even fear of the unpredictability of American actions, and of their new ruthlessness.

The paradox is unlikely to be resolved without an eventual crisis in America's relationship with international society. That will necessarily throw into question the nation's own understanding of the meaning of the American national experiment. That will have unforeseeable consequences. The implications of what has happened since September 2001, and of present events in the Middle East, are very considerable, and will weigh heavily on the decades to come.

December 29, 2003

Appendix

May 14, 2003

JOINT DECLARATION ON RENEWING THE TRANSATLANTIC PARTNERSHIP

> The Declaration below, written by Simon Safarti, Director of the European Program of the Center for Strategic and International Studies in Washington, has been endorsed by Madeleine K. Albright, Harold Brown, Zbigniew Brzezinski, Frank C. Carlucci, Warren Christopher, William S. Cohen, Robert Dole, Lawrence S. Eagleburger, Stuart E. Eizenstat, Alexander M. Haig, Jr., Lee H. Hamilton, John J. Hamre, Carla A. Hills, Sam Nunn, Paul H. O'Neill, Charles S. Robb, William V. Roth, Jr., and James R. Schlesinger.

ONCE AGAIN WE HAVE ENTERED A DEFINING MOMENT in the history of America's relations with Europe. Once again we are engaged in a major debate that is said to be separating us from each other, Americans and Europeans. Once again we are debating the relevance of our alliance and the significance of our ties. There have been many other such debates in the past. But with the Cold War a full decade behind, and with many dangerous years of an unpredictable war against terrorism looming ahead, the transatlantic connection has rarely seemed to be at the same time so uncertain and so important.

Postwar visions emerge slowly and are never followed gracefully. After 1945, neither Americans nor Europeans easily agreed, among themselves or with each other, on the agenda that confronted them. The bold ideas that shaped

251

America'sleadership for the rehabilitation and reconstruction of post-conflict Europe were dismissed as naïve, and even dangerous: Rebuild and rearm Germany? Stay in and unite Europe? More than five decades later, even as other bold ideas are being debated for the management of a wide range of new security threats, the vision that shaped the development of transatlantic and intra-European relations must still be completed.

Our concerns are stated with some urgency. For now, there seems to be a view among many in the United States and in a number of countries in Europe that "maybe" we no longer need the partnership after all. The conditions that have allowed this sentiment to emerge and grow must be addressed and overcome. Inshort, whatever ground there may be for exasperation on both sides of the Atlantic, no disagreement should be allowed to disrupt our relations with our European allies.

Even as the fighting in Iraq winds down in the absence of the allies' full consensus, serious efforts should be made by all parties to renew, rehabilitate, and rebuild our alliance with the countries of Europe and their union. Such efforts will be facilitated by using a more moderate tone when addressing some of our like-minded, even if difficult, allies and friends.

THE INFAMOUS EVENTS OF SEPTEMBER 11, 2001, have created many new realities and alerted us to many pressing dangers. But they have not changed our central aspiration in Europe. A whole and free Europe-more united, larger, and stronger-was a central U.S. objective after the Cold War, and so it remains after September 11. Now as before, the United States and the countries of Europe are bound together in an expanding community of compatible interests and consistent values. Now more than before, our common challenge is to form a community of action whenever these interests and values are deemed to be at risk.

The U.S. interest in a united Europe has been a corollary of U.S. interests in Europe. A whole Europe can gain enough weight to form a strategic partnership whereby each side of the Atlantic can be the counterpart of the other in addressing interests-whether security, economic, or political in nature-that are shared even when they are not identical. Especially when pursuing the crucial nonmilitary dimensions of the global war against terrorism, or when attempting to defuse its sources and end its practice, there is little that cannot be done more effectively and more expeditiously when both the United States and its European allies are in agreement and act in harmony. A central dimension of the transatlantic partnership is a stable Europe in a cohesive and dynamic European

Union (EU). Nothing the United States does or says should be misunderstood or misinterpreted as a reappraisal of the continued U.S. commitment to a uniting and stronger Europe. The Europe that had been the center of two world wars during the first half of the century changed after 1945 when U.S. policymakers made the creation of a whole Europe central to U.S. policy for the balance of the century. There is also an urgent need for Europeans to do more to reassure Americans that the union they are completing will continue to make the United States feel welcome in Europe. Too much of what is achieved in the EU context is presented by some Europeans as Europe's new ability to challenge the United States. Rather, more should be done to reinforce the perception that the "finality" of Europe is being developed in cooperation with the United States. At the ongoing European Convention and at the upcoming Intergovernmental Conference, for appropriate issues and at appropriate levels, U.S. representatives should have the opportunity to observe proceedings and debates-not to participate and to influence, but to hear and to be influenced by their peers' debates. In turn, the United States should continue to elevate its political relations with the EU to a level comparable to that achieved in its bilateral relations with individual EU countries. To that end, for example, both houses of the U.S. Congress should increase their contacts with the European Parliament at all levels, including members and their relevant staffs.

The issue is not one of U.S. membership in the European Union or any of its distinctive institutional bodies, but one of association, dialogue, and cooperation before decisions are reached. At some point over the next five years, a mechanism should be adopted that allows more direct consultation between the United States and the institutional bodies of the EU. The current format of U.S.-EU summit meetings does not satisfy that need. Europe should leave no doubt about its intention to build with its partner across the Atlantic the same intimacy that the United States built with the states of Europe within NATO.

THE CENTRAL PILLAR OF OUR PARTNERSHIP with Europe — its countries and their union — remains an Atlantic Alliance that is firmly centered on a strong and cohesive North Atlantic Treaty Organization (NATO). Now as before, NATO members remain America's allies of choice, even when the organization itself cannot or need not be the primary institution for attending to the initial phases of the security missions that have grown out of the events of September 11. In the Balkans and now in Afghanistan, NATO has already proven its value in operations beyond the traditional "NATO area." Reconfiguring its structure and capabilities so that it can better serve in that role when its members see the need is a major task. In this context, we applaud the far-ranging transformations that were adopted at the recent NATO Prague summit as part of a U.S.-driven agenda readily endorsed by all other NATO members and applicants.

These transformations will give an enlarged organization the new capabilities and flexible structures needed to gain the global reach it needs, past the Cold War and into a new post-9/11 world. The broad timetable developed for their implementation should be respected.

The issue of capabilities is especially significant. Growing gaps between U.S. and European military capabilities are making transatlantic defense cooperation and interoperability more difficult. Admittedly, how much the European allies spend on defense, and how, is not an issue that can be decided by the United States, however concerned the U.S. government may be with current levels of EU defense spending. Yet, it should be recognized that continuation of the prevailing trends will have adverse political consequences within the alliance. To that end, cooperation within the EU, and between all EU members, can help achieve better value for the funding. So can, too, additional transatlantic cooperation aimed at strengthening the ability to share technologies, including reform of export control systems on all sides. But added cooperation alone will not suffice without added money. European members of NATO and the member states of the EU should agree on minimum levels of real annual growth in defense spending they themselves deem necessary and realistic.

While consideration of a "realignment" of U.S. forces stationed in Europe is in order, as part of a global reconfiguration of forward-deployed units and related military installations, such a decision must not be misunderstood either as a punitive measure or as a loss of commitment. Indeed, it should follow only after thorough consultation with all NATO countries and in the context of a postwar U.S. commitment to a larger, more cohesive, and more relevant NATO with a strategic vision that is shared by all its members.

Divisions resulting from the war in Iraq should not be allowed to stand in the way of this agenda. In coming years, NATO's role during and beyond the war against terrorism needs to increase further. In a sense, that was a mission envisioned for the Alliance and its organization at the time of their creation-aimed not only at overcoming an emerging Soviet military and political threat, but also at preventing the resurgence of the many conflicts that had previously conditioned the rise of instabilities throughout the continent.

THE TRANSFORMATION OF NATO and advances within the EU, as well as the processes that are shaping both of these institutions for the twenty-first century, are naturally complementary. Suspicions that one might stand in the way of the other as an adversarial counterweight, and complaints that one lags behind the other as an economic or military free rider, should be put to rest. Neither NATO nor the EU is a full-service institution; neither is sufficient because both are necessary-to win a war, end a war, and deal with the aftermath. For the latter, the EU can provide stability tools that complement well the NATO security toolbox. In short, while it may not be possible for us to take on everything together, it is imperative to make sure that taken together we do everything.

In the context of soft security issues, whose resolution would help avoid the rise of further hard security dilemmas, we urge that the Doha Round of trade negotiations, which was launched in October 2001, be pursued with the utmost sense of urgency so that it can be successfully completed at the earliest possible time. Failure of these negotiations would seriously threaten the global trade system at a delicate time for many of the national and regional economies that comprise it. It would also significantly hamper our ability to wage successfully the ongoing wars against terrorism and its core roots. Admittedly, it may prove difficult to conclude these negotiations by January 1, 2005, however desirable such a timetable might be. But, at the very least, on the way to completing the Doha round, other existing divisive trade issues between the United States and the EU should be resolved by that time.

THE PROCESS OF TRANSATLANTIC POLICY cooperation we are envisioning should become more feasible after the European Convention on the Future of Europe determines how best to allocate authority between a high authority responsible to the European Council and a commissioner or series of commissioners responsible to the European Commission. Meanwhile in this and other relevant areas, members of the U.S. executive branch could be associated on appropriate issues with the work of separate European Councils. The goal of such coordination would be to produce a first draft of allied policies for impending crises, including allocation of responsibilities before a crisis has actually exploded. Plans for a postwar reconstruction of Afghanistan and Iraq should be pursued in consultation and cooperation with Europe.

The Arab-Israeli conflict is a major security issue that we share on both sides of the Atlantic. With the end of major combat operations in Iraq, the quartet made up of the United States and the EU, as well as Russia and the UN, should relaunch the peace process outlined by President Bush in June 2002. Key to the success of the president's vision, reasserted on February 27, 2003, are those measures that will not only assure Israel's security but also define the kind of state Palestinians can look toward at the close of the timetable already defined by the president.

The case for complementarity begins with a better sense of what each ally can accomplish, and a better appreciation of the reasons that prompt its actions. There will be instances when a good American (or European) idea, especially about security, will not seem equally good for those in Europe (or in the United States) who will be asked to live with its consequences irrespective of their preferences. Nevertheless, across the Atlantic no less than within Europe, the logic of unity transcends the logic of cleavage.

In this context, the rise of anti-American sentiments in Europe is legitimate cause for concern. Unfortunately, the use of such sentiments as a political tactic, at home or within the EU, has been reciprocated in the United States with an occasional use of comparable anti-European and anti-EU rhetoric. Those temptations should be resisted by political leaders on both sides, even in the face of popular sentiments, inflamed by media that are often more negative toward the transatlantic partner than are the policymakers. In short, Europe's anti-Americanism hurts because those who share it undermine, or at the very least complicate, the U.S. ability to spread and defend the very values and interests that are now shared, however unevenly, by most Americans and Europeans alike. In turn, anti-Europeanism in the United States raises additional obstacles to European leaders who are struggling to pursue a demanding EU agenda in the transatlantic context within which Europe's unification should take place.

As has often been the case before, for both sides of the Atlantic there is a need for a less personal and more cooperative rhetoric. But following the war in Iraq, more than ever before, such moderation will be imperative during a get-reacquainted period when Americans should hear Europe's lingering criticism of pre-war debates and decisions with some indulgence, while Europeans should appraise U.S. military and diplomatic actions with some tolerance-more, at any rate, than has been shown on either side of the Atlantic of late.

WE HAVE ESTABLISHED THIS GROUP because of our concerns that current trends on both sides of the Atlantic may jeopardize the achievements to which all of us, and many more, committed much of our public lives. Divisions between the United States and the states of Europe, as well as among them, are serious because the issues that are being addressed are serious, indeed existential. These divisions are placing our solidarity in jeopardy at a time when unity is essential. Most of the main issues in the twenty-first century will be global in nature, and U.S. leadership in addressing them will not suffice if there is not adequate understanding and support from our European allies. In short, because neither the United States nor Europe is omnipotent, both will need help in ensuring their own physical and economic security, let alone threats beyond their respective borders. That help is most logically sought from the nations with which we have most in common. Accordingly, whatever the merits of our respective positions, it is incumbent upon us all to make of the renewal of the transatlantic partnership an urgent priority.

RENEWING THE TRANSATLANTIC PARTNERSHIP, A EUROPEAN REPLY TO THE JOINT AMERICAN DECLARATION

Signed by Susanna Agnelli, Giuliano Amato, Raymond Barre, Carl Bildt, Emilio Colombo, Jean-Luc Dehaene, Bronislaw Geremek, Hans Dietrich Genscher, Valéry Giscard d'Estaing, Felipe Gonzales, Douglas Hurd, Helmut Kohl, Giorgio Napolitano, Helmut Schmidt, Carlo Scognamiglio, Eduardo Serra, Hans Van Mierlo

[Published in *Corriere della Sera* and *Le Monde*]

We have read with appreciation a joint declaration endorsed by a bipartisan group of prominent American figures which underscored the importance of the transatlantic link. We share the view that, even after the end of the cold war, the renewed Transatlantic Alliance remains the main pillar of the Euro-American partnership, as well as the belief that the basic premise of a strong transatlantic partnership is a stable Europe, a cohesive and dynamic European Union.

In particular, we agree with the conclusion of the joint declaration that *neither the United States nor Europe is omnipotent, both will need help in ensuring their own physical and economic security, let alone threats beyond their respective borders. That help is most logically sought from the nations with which we have most in common. Accordingly, whatever the merits of our respective positions, it is incumbent upon us all to make of the renewal of the transatlantic partnership an urgent priority.*

The existence of a united Europe would not have been possible without the decisive role played by the United States in helping us to defeat totalitarianism: Europeans will never forget this and they appreciate American support to the Union, especially in this defining moment of their history. Thus, Americans will always be welcome in Europe.

In the late 1940s the Founding Fathers of Europe envisaged the creation of a long term union among Europeans; this project drew its inspiration from the lessons of history and from the determination that war between European countries should never again be possible.

Now that Europeans have joined their forces in the European Union and have established a single market and a single currency, there is a widespread consensus that this process of integration should progress further. Although each European country is proudly unique, EU members share interests, values and a way of life.

The European Convention is the expression of our determination to move even further along this path: it has the task of defining Europe's role in the twenty-first century and of creating a genuine political community. It is a major effort and we are confident that it will succeed — in particular in defining the international role of Europe, aiming at a just and fair world order. We are equally confident that the U.S. will support this project, as it is in the best interests of the West as a whole.

The process of European integration is based on democracy, freedom, market economy and social solidarity, on the universal application of human rights, on a deep awareness of the many problems that can destabilize the international community: the North-South divide, the environment, the spread of weapons of mass destruction, the scourge of terrorism as a threat to all of us, international crime and drug trafficking. Europeans believe that such problems can only be dealt with in the multilateral framework as provided by the United

Nations. To this end, U.S.-European cooperation and sustained engagement are necessary conditions.

The European Union is now a reality. It was not founded in opposition to America, and it will work closely with the United States.

Our main partner across the Atlantic has been faced with a twofold reality for several years: it deals with a plurality of friendly States on the one hand, with the European institutions on the other. With the latter it negotiates a range of issues, from international trade to competition.

This reality is still incomplete, but a full-fledged European player will soon be the main reference in transatlantic relations. The role of the individual European states in foreign policy will remain strong, but the European Union, as depository of common interests and a shared vision, will increase its profile and weight.

We are convinced that the development of an effective European defense does not endanger NATO; on the contrary, it may make NATO stronger if so the two sides of the Atlantic firmly want.

Our values and basic political aims are shared with the United States. No major problem in the world can be solved without a joint U.S.-European commitment; no problem is unsolvable when we tackle it together. Such awareness can strengthen the policy of transatlantic cooperation. The next E.U.-U.S. summit should be the occasion to concentrate on an ambitious common agenda of tasks to be carried out on the basis of strong complementarity.

We believe that, especially with the advent of a new generation of political leaders in Europe and the United States, we should draw strength and inspiration from the past but look to the future: we should thus focus on the challenges and threats of the twenty-first century, which require a full joint commitment. North America and Europe are depositories of democracy and freedom. Together we will be able to share these values with the rest of the world. By joining forces we will further stabilize the international community and give dignity to all human beings.

It would be a mistake for the very countries who forged close bonds fifty years ago, when interdependence was hardly existent, to relinquish these precious bonds in the age of globalization.

Although it is not the first time that the transatlantic partnership has raised questions on both sides of the Atlantic, short term divisions have never prevailed over the core of common values and interests which still define the Western world.

In connection with the war in Iraq and because of disagreements which have come to the fore in the aftermath of September 11th, the unity of the western world is now being openly questioned.

The debate has become harsh. Some observers and sectors of public opinion have over-simplified it into the assumption that Americans are from Mars and Europeans from Venus.

We have been involved in transatlantic cooperation for many years and we refuse to believe that the Atlantic is getting wider. Americans and Europeans have disagreed in the past and may disagree in the future. The question is whether the disagreements will touch upon essential concerns or be limited to specific and manageable issues.

Our firm answer is that the American and European democracies are united by their values. They cannot succeed in isolation from one another, let alone in opposition. Working in partnership on the basis of their common roots and shared objectives, and o mutual respect, they will never antagonize each other on vital issues.

United, we are seen by the rest of the world as interpreters of a great vision and of great wisdom; divided, we shall be losers. It is up to us to make the best of this great asset.

Message from Simon Safarti to William Pfaff, July 14, 2003

William,

I was pleased to note your interest in the Joint Declaration I wrote for a bipartisan group of eminent Americans calling for a renewal of the transatlantic partnership. But, frankly, I was dismayed by your characterization of this Declaration. My concern, and that of the personalities who signed the Declaration, was over the "urgent" need "to make of the renewal of the transat-lantic partnership an urgent priority." My intent was to help avoid further clashes during the then-upcoming G8 summit in Evian. For me therefore to read your assessment that "in short" the statement "asked for the European Union to be subordinated to the United States" is extraordinary. Hopefully, you read the Declaration. Having read it, there was no need to distort the text and the spirit of what was written, with such claims, for example, that the Declaration "asked that U.S. government officials have a role in European Council meetings" or that it "warned against European defense spending and military measures that might seem a challenge to U.S. military predominance."

There was much more in this statement that deserved your (constructive) attention, an you should [re]read it more carefully, and without some of the blinders that seemed to stand in the way the first time around. Then, you might share the consensus view in Europe — namely, that this statement was in fact quite helpful, as confirmed by the more serious responses it received — responses which you seemingly found "useful" notwithstanding your dismissive presentation of the Declaration that prompted them in the first place.

All the best.

Simon

Response by William Pfaff

Dear Simon,

I'm sorry that my comment on your text has upset you. I don't know in what paper you saw my column but I attach its original version, as syndicated. The version of your text that I know was the one published in French in *Le Monde* on the 15th of May, responded to in mid-June, in *Le Monde* and *Corriere della Sera*, by a group of prominent European political figures. I should add that I did not know at the time that you were the author of the text, although I understood that it came from CSIS and saw that you were one of the signers....

You say that I distorted the CSIS statement by characterizing it as asking that the EU be subordinated to the United States. Its appeal to the Europeans, in constructing their institutions, to allow no doubt to exist that their intention is to establish between the EU and the United States the same close relationship that already exists in NATO, seems to me scarcely open to any other interpretation.

NATO has always been commanded by an American officer and dominated by the United States, which in recent months has even taken steps to "punish" dissident European members (France & Germany; cutting off money for a new headquarters, etc).

I would have thought the EU has never permitted any doubt that its aim was other than to form a union of sovereign nations that does not include the

United States, and that this was understood in Washington. That most (not all) EU members may be in military alliance with the U.S. is a separate matter.

You proposed that representatives of the United States take part in the European constitutional convention (I recognize that this was "not to partic- ipate or to influence it" but "to hear and be influenced by their peers' debates"), asked that the U.S. Congress be given increased contact with the European Par- liament, and that it and the executive branch have "more direct consultation" with emerging European institutional bodies. You suggest that American offi- cials be included in deliberations of the European Council, the highest decision- making body of the EU, when dealing with certain dossiers.

I do not see how these proposals, however well-intentioned they are, and courteously expressed, can be seen as anything other than a demand for ultimate U.S. oversight of the EU. They have so been taken in Brussels. There are no pro- posals in your text for reciprocal participation by European officials in the work of the National Security Council or the Treasury, or for an institutionalized European role in the work of State or Defense Departments, or for some kind of formal European participation in the proceedings of Congress — and we both know what the reaction of American popular opinion, press and the Congress would be to any such suggestions.

I think you (and others in the U.S. policy community) really have not grasped how the situation here has changed. I am sure that many European Atlanticists have told you that the statement was constructive and helpful. My own feeling is that, admirably meant as it was, it was irrelevant, and that they themselves know it. As Americans say about America, but have failed to grasp about Europe, "everything" has changed since 9/11.

With cordial regards...

INDEX OF NAMES

C

Calamai, Marco, 240

Carnot, Marie FranÁois Sadi, 226

Charlemagne, 26

Cheney, Dick, 14, 54, 68, 76, 84, 106, 141, 207, 220

Chirac, Jacques, 32–33, 163, 165, 168, 181, 184, 191, 202–203, 221, 238

Christopher, Warren, 199, 251

Churchill, Winston, 66, 141, 206

Clinton, Bill, 30, 35, 90–92, 107, 117, 131, 223, 229

Cohen, Eliot, 133–134, 251

Cook, Robin, 196, 211

Cyrus the Great, 31

D

De Gaulle, Charles, 111

de Vigny, Alfred, 170

Diamond, Larry, 196

E

Eagleburger, Lawrence, 105, 251

Eban, Abba, 67

Elizabeth, Empress of Austria, 226

Erasmus, 103

Erdogan, Recep Tayyip, 188

Etzioni, Amitai, 184

F

Feith, Douglas J., 37

Fleischer, Ari, 207

Fortuyn, Pim, 79, 81

Fukuyama, Francis, 44

G

Garner, Jay, 176

Geremek, Bronislaw, 199, 257

Gibbon, Edward, 25

Giscard dEstaing, Valery, 199, 257

Gnesotto, Nicole, 87

Goldhagen, Daniel, 203

Gonzales, Felipe, 199, 257

Gorbachev, Mikhail, 231

Grasset, Philippe, 78–79, 172

Greenspan, Alan, 219

H

Hagel, Chuck, 143

Harries, Owen, 67

Hertzberg, Hendrik, 184

Hitler, Adolf, 22, 40, 73, 100, 180, 231

Hoon, Geoff, 211–212

Howard, Michael, 48, 108

Huntington, Samuel, 20, 133, 196, 234

Hurd, Douglas, 199, 257

Hussein, Saddam, 24, 27, 42, 61, 64–65, 73–74, 84, 86, 95, 99, 103–104, 106–110, 118, 121, 127, 129–130, 137–139, 142, 144–145, 149, 154, 159, 163, 167, 171, 177, 180, 185–186, 194, 201, 213, 218–222

J

John Paul II, 231

Juan Carlos, King of Spain, 84

Judt, Tony, 185

K

Kagan, Robert, 97–99, 117, 124, 189

Kant, Immanuel, 97

Kelly, David, 210

Kennan, George F., 119, 148

Keynes, John Maynard, 66

Khomeini, Ruhollah, Ayatollah, 31

Kilani, Kamel, 224

Kim Jong Il, 229

Kissinger, Henry, 100